SOUTHERN GROUND

RECLAIMING FLAVOR THROUGH STONE-MILLED FLOUR

JENNIFER LAPIDUS

PHOTOGRAPHS BY RINNE ALLEN

TEN SPEED PRESS
California | New York

Contents

Soft Red Winter Wheat 207

Blends and Outlier Grains 237

PART ONE

The Community

The Story

If the fire went out, my eyes would open at exactly 2 a.m. From my bedroom within my little shotgun house adjacent to the bakery, even from a deep sleep, my body always knew 2 a.m. I'd be pulled from sleep because my wood was green or because it was raining, or both—moisture from the wood and the air threatened to smother the flames.

The evening before each bake, I'd carefully choose the wood that would burn in my oven—ideally, seasoned hardwood—aiming to get the right amount of heat built up within the time it took for my bulk doughs to ferment, get divided and shaped, and perform their final rise or proof. For twelve hours the fire would burn within the chamber that would eventually bake the bread. The fire burned to coals, the coals to ash. The ash was swept out and the hearth mopped clean before well-proofed loaves were loaded into the chamber and baked within the heat radiating from the oven's mass. My normal baker's hour was 4 a.m. For over a decade, this was my life. Rising before the sun, tending to fire, flour, water, and salt. With my Natural Bridge Bakery, located in the mountains outside of Asheville, North Carolina, I produced naturally leavened breads baked in a wood-fired brick oven. And then, after fourteen years, my focus shifted and my lens widened. I stepped away from baking and became a miller.

What started as a concept—to revive a regional grains economy centered on a community mill—became Carolina Ground, placing me, as miller, between the farmer and baker, bridging these worlds—from farm-grade to food-grade, from crop to ingredient. Cold stone-ground flour of predominantly Southern grains, this flour is the conduit between Southern, independent, often conservative farmers and innovative, mostly urban, Instagram-savvy bakers. Although I can never quite remove the baker from my core self, it was the flour that pulled me in this deep. How I arrived in the position of miller is one unbroken narrative—from baking for my community to harnessing a community of bakers. It is a narrative that seeks to reclaim elements of our past that I believe should never have been sacrificed in the service of progress.

◆ ◆ ◆

I first attempted to bake bread in 1990, my junior year of college. Flour, water, salt, honey, oil, commercial baking yeast, and sometimes eggs and milk went into those loaves. I had my mother's copy of *Beard on Bread* to guide me, and I stumbled through some pretty awful bakes before I finally began to find my way. With each bake, I understood a little bit more. Baking pulled me in. I was drawn to something at the core—a history, a story of a different time, and a different way of life. After graduation, I continued to bake weekly. I was studying for the LSATs, with plans to go to law school, and had started a little baking business out of my apartment. Friends and friends of friends picked up bread from me once a week. And with each weekly bake, my interest grew, and not just to baking, but to a deeper understanding of bread. I felt a familiarity with bread baking. It was a visceral attraction not grounded in my own experience of time and place. I began to wonder about the RapidRise yeast I was using. The claim *rapid* implied that there had been an improvement on a slower method, that something had come before in bread's story. With each bake my gut kept telling me I was just skimming the surface. There was no World Wide Web to search yet, and very few publications addressed natural leavening at the time, as there were very few bakers producing naturally leavened breads. But I had this gut sense that the bread I was baking was not living up to the potential of what bread could be, so I began looking for the information, trying to find some crumb of evidence that revealed bread's past. And then during a weekend work-stay on an organic farm in Blairsville, Georgia, at the end of a long day of weeding, I was flipping through a copy of *Biodynamics Journal* and came to an article entitled "Berkshire Mountain Bakery—The Art of Natural Baking." The article was an interview with Berkshire Mountain's baker, Richard Bourdon, and it began: "Before the art of baking joined forces with the brewing industry, the baker would assemble his commonplace ingredients on the stage—simple things the peasants knew quite well, like flour, water, and salt—mix them together, and then pull out something entirely different, something that could never have been predicted with those three humble ingredients." Reading those first few words, I knew I had landed on something: I'd found a glimpse into bread's past. The article's author, Joel Morrow, affirmed, "The taste had nothing to do with the floury, yeasty, grainy, adulterated products that are passed off as bread today, even in the organic health food industry, even among dedicated small organic bakers." Here was the evidence: just *three humble ingredients.*

A few weeks later, at a local bookstore in Athens, Georgia, I picked up a copy of *The Laurel's Kitchen Bread Book* and opened directly to a section titled "Flemish Desem Bread." Laurel describes this naturally leavened old-world bread as "Composed of just a few ingredients— wheat, water, salt—the loaves are light and delicious without sweetener, milk, fat, or yeast... To us, this is the perfect Staff of Life." Laurel counsels the home baker that "it can be done, it is not all that difficult, and once you get set up, making the bread is simplicity itself." One begins by making the desem (pronounced *day-zum*) culture or starter, what Laurel calls "the spirit or soul... that gives life to the dough." The process sounded simple: just form a stiff dough ball out of flour and water, bury the dough ball in a sack of flour, and every day for two weeks, pull out the dough ball, discard half of it, dissolve the other half in water, add flour until another stiff dough ball is formed, and then bury it again in the sack of flour. But fresh stone-ground whole-wheat flour was listed as the first ingredient needed to make this bread. Although I could get whole-wheat flour in the bulk section of my local food co-op, I had no idea how the flour was milled or how fresh it was. I attempted to follow Laurel's instructions, but my inability to find the key ingredient was disorienting. Developing the desem culture required temperatures ranging from 50° to 65°F. It was summertime in Georgia. I was to rely on my senses to guide the process—the smell of the dough ball each day—but nothing seemed right, and I wasn't even sure if I would recognize *right.*

I was supposed to be studying for the LSATs, but I was determined to find my way with this bread, which morphed into finding bakers baking this bread. I wanted to see the bread being made, feel the dough, and smell the culture. In search of bakers, I scanned my bookshelf for the few baking books I owned and pulled down *Uprisings,* a compilation of recipes by cooperative and collective bakeries from around the country put together by the Cooperative Whole Grain Educational Association. On the inside cover I found a phone number and called. A friendly voice on the other end of the line informed me that bakers would be gathering for the association's annual meeting in two weeks in Fayetteville, Arkansas, at a bakery that was producing desem bread.

Propelled by this single focus, I traveled to Arkansas. And I met bakers. Which was what led me in the opposite direction from law school to the hills of Marin County, California, and an apprenticeship with Alan Scott, a mythic figure who was baking naturally leavened whole-grain breads for his community in a wood-fired brick oven he'd built in his backyard.

◆ ◆ ◆

Alan Scott was a creative. And he was a dear friend of Laurel Robertson, author of *The Laurel's Kitchen Bread Book.* When Laurel was testing the Flemish desem bread for her book, she was baking it in her gas oven. She brought a loaf to Alan, who felt this old-world bread would be well served by the similarly old-world technology of baking in a wood-fired brick oven. And so

Alan designed and built his first wood-fired brick oven for Laurel's desem bread. The radiant heat of the masonry oven provided the bread with added oven spring and produced a deep golden bronze crust. Alan was so excited by the results that he learned to bake desem bread himself, built his own oven, and began baking.

At Alan's, we made only that whole-grain Flemish desem bread. We mixed and kneaded the dough by hand. He welcomed visitors readily, and I suspected it was to get more help with kneading the huge mounds of dough. The only machinery employed was the small stone-burr gristmill we used to grind our flour freshly for each bake. He believed in fresh flour. This was key, and so, too, was the stone mill used to create the quality of flour he deemed essential. There is simply no mistaking fresh, stone-ground flour, especially when working with whole grains. It is the difference between an original piece of artwork and a print. Since there was no local mill from which to purchase freshly stone-ground flour, milling grain was the first step in our bread-baking process. We milled whole-grain flour to feed the desem culture, which would eventually leaven our bread, made with only the culture, whole-grain flour, water, and sea salt. The oven was fueled with wood we collected on the property.

Alan's kitchen was hardly legal for a baking business—we kneaded dough on the same table upon which we had eaten supper only a few hours earlier. The mill where we ground our flour was kept under the stairwell in the foyer of his house. There was no name for this baking endeavor—it was just Alan's bread. His customers kept standing orders and we delivered warm bread directly to their doors, sans packaging.

Because of this old-world bread, so well paired with the ancient technology of a wood-fired brick oven, Alan turned designing and building wood-fired brick ovens into a business. His ovens could be found all over the Bay Area and beyond, in both residential and commercial settings. He drew a constant stream of visitors ranging from backwoods hippies to chefs from highly acclaimed culinary circles. It was the early '90s. A renaissance of artisan baking was unfolding, and Alan was at its forefront.

Eventually it was time for me to leave and begin my own bakery. I returned to the South because of a boyfriend. He was farming vegetables on his great-grandparents' land in Tennessee. I taught him to bake desem bread, and with Alan's help, we built an oven and launched a bakery. We named it Natural Bridge Bakery because in its first location, in Sewanee, Tennessee, there was a natural bridge at the end of our road, and because the desem culture we used to leaven our breads provided a natural bridge between grain and loaf, Old World and New. I modeled the bakery after Alan's, though it was housed in a health department–sanctioned kitchen next door to our home kitchen. I ordered a small stone-burr mill from a tiny company called Jansen Grist Mills. The Jansens, of course friends of Alan's, were building wooden-hulled mills in a shop behind their house in North Carolina's Brushy Mountains.

I married the boyfriend and our daughter was born. The marriage didn't last, but the bakery did, and after four years of baking in Sewanee, we relocated to Western North Carolina, where I became the only wood-fired-brick-oven baker of naturally leavened breads in the Asheville area.

By the early 2000s, the renaissance in artisan baking begun in the '90s had taken hold nationwide, and I soon found myself part of a vibrant baking community in Western North Carolina. I was no longer the sole wood-fired-brick-oven baker—Flat Rock Village Bakery in Flat Rock, North Carolina, and Wake Robin Farm Breads in Marshall, North Carolina, had joined the ranks. In 2004, the Asheville Bread Festival was born, bringing together all of us bakers from Asheville and the surrounding communities of Brevard, Sylva, Saluda, Flat Rock, Marshall, and Boone. A common thread connected us: we were bakers, rising before the sun, working long hours, passionate and committed.

◆ ◆ ◆

When I set up my bakery, I assembled what I considered the crucial pieces: the culture or natural leavening, the stone-burr gristmill, and the wood-fired oven. The farmer was not yet a part of my equation. I bought my grain from a miller in Middle River, Minnesota, and he bought his grain from the growers that lived in the vicinity of his mill—a thousand miles from where my bread was baked. For the other bakers in my community, their situation was not that much different—although many bought their flour from North Carolina mills, most of that grain was grown a thousand miles from where it was milled, in Kansas and beyond, and blended into functional, homogenous, commodity flour. In the spring of 2008 our lack of connection to the farmers who grew our grain became painfully apparent. The price of wheat rose to a historic high. At its worst, the price would rise as much as 130 percent, far beyond what we bakers could pass along to our customers in the cost of a loaf of bread. The cause of the price hike was unclear, though the effect it had on our businesses was profound. This was not the normal highs and lows of commodity pricing influenced by crop conditions. There was something else at play that had affected the price and availability of wheat, some entity far removed from the interplay between soil, sun, and rain, or wheat, water, and sea salt. We had no direct relationship with growers and we were left in the dark.

What occurred in 2008 could be traced back to 1991, with the establishment of the Commodity Index fund established by Goldman Sachs. This was followed by changes in US monetary fund policy that enabled futures contracts on funds one step (or many steps) removed from the actual commodity. And then in 2007, a decline in the value of the dollar and an increase in the price of oil spurred the Federal Reserve to lower interest rates, which resulted in a rush by investors globally to trade dollars for commodities—including wheat—thus causing volatile price increases. And yet because a loaf of bread must remain affordable, the baker took the hit. Our daily bread—sustenance and symbol—was at the mercy of Wall Street.

◆ ◆ ◆

In 2001, public wheat breeder and pathologist Dr. David Marshall arrived as the new research leader of the USDA Agricultural Research Service (ARS) in Raleigh, North Carolina. He'd moved from Texas A&M University, where he'd been breeding bread wheats since 1985. Shortly after he arrived, he was presented with a question, *did he think bread wheats could ever grow well in this part of the country?* Hard wheat is the type of wheat used for bread. Most hard wheat is grown west of the Mississippi, a lower rainfall area than the East Coast and a well-suited environment for this type of wheat. But David Marshall was up for the challenge and he began to breed and trial hard wheat varieties that could withstand the rainfall and humidity of the southeastern United States. In 2008, the first of these bread wheat varieties was released to the public. What this meant was that farmers in the South, who had traditionally grown soft wheats, suitable for biscuits and pie crusts (though a good bit of it sold for animal feed), could now plant wheat for bread.

In the spring of 2008, I made an appointment for a haircut. Although this may seem irrelevant to our narrative, it is in the most unlikely places that signposts appear. Sitting in the waiting area at the salon, I picked up the March 2008 issue of *Gourmet* from the table in front of me and opened randomly to an image of an ancient brick-and-stone building, with the words SMALL WORLD in large print at the top of the page, followed by, "Is it possible to both resist globalization and profit from it? In Normandy, a handful of local heroes think so—and are proving it with an ancient tradition and a great baguette." The piece, written by Bill McKibben, was about the revival of a community mill. Within the region of Perche, the town of Nogent-le-Rotrou, population 11,000, supported thirteen bread bakeries, yet all the wheat grown in the surrounding hills was sold as feed for animals. Two Frenchmen, Philippe Gallioz and Jean Larrivière, connected the dots and took over a four-hundred-year-old mill near the town of Mortagne-au-Perche, forty minutes away from Nogent-le-Rotrou. The flour they produced they called *la farine du Perche*—a flour milled within the region of Perche from grain grown by local organic farmers. Gallioz explains, "Right from the beginning...our idea was to link the farmer, the miller, and the baker. For centuries that link existed, but in modern times it didn't. The baker bought his flour from some distant warehouse; the farmer sold his wheat for animal feed; the mill stood idle." To ensure a market for their flour, they centered their endeavor on the concept of *terroir*, a French term with no exact English translation, but whose meaning is something to the effect of that the conditions in the place where something is grown—the soil, the air, the climate—are contained within the flavor and essence of that which is grown. In other words, place matters.

Reading this article, I was struck by its relevance to our current circumstances. A couple months later, our bakers' community converged at a field day in Waynesville, North Carolina, where Dr. Marshall gave a talk and a tour of his trial plots of wheat. Dr. Chris Reberg-Horton from North Carolina State University's Organic Grains Project spoke about organic grain production. The timing was ideal. Before this point, none of us bakers had dared to change our key ingredient—baking was challenging enough, even with midwestern commodity flour, but the events of 2008 created a ripe moment. The idea of forming direct relationships with North Carolina growers seemed within reach. Our bakers' community came together again for the first of many meetings to discuss the idea. We envisioned a mill centered upon the idea that place matters: a community mill connecting farmer, miller, and baker, one that was environmentally and economically sustainable, decreasing food miles, and stabilizing pricing. Excitement grew around this idea. I wrote a grant proposal and shared it with our Cooperative Extension Agent who share it with Roland McReynolds, the director of the Carolina Farm Stewardship Association, a nonprofit organization focused on sustainable agriculture and food systems. Roland called me, introduced himself, and explained their efforts over the last few years of working alongside NCSU to promote organic small grains in the state as an economically and ecologically beneficial winter rotation crop for organic growers. He felt that having a baker on the project would help further their mission. Having the voice of the baker meant there would be a market for this crop.

◆ ◆ ◆

Alan passed away in January of 2009. His half-page editorial obituary in the *New York Times* began, "Alan Scott, whose blacksmith's skill in using radiant heat led to a revival of the ancient craft of building brick ovens, allowing bakers to turn out bread with luxuriously moist interiors and crisp crusts, died Jan. 26 in Tasmania, Australia." My mentor, a hero for so many of us bakers, was no longer with us.

Alan had called me in the spring of 2008 to tell me of his latest venture. After years of building wood-fired ovens around the world, he'd moved back to his hometown of Oatlands, Tasmania, with a diagnosis of congestive heart failure, but even with his heart pumping at 30 percent capacity, it proved difficult for Alan to actually accept a sabbatical. He'd been in Oatlands for about a year and a half and had begun organizing the bakeries in his region. He told me he'd been speaking with farmers, too. And he'd purchased a huge stone-burr gristmill. Over the months that followed, we emailed back and forth. He told me about the bakers in Tasmania and the mill he'd purchased: "I went ahead and ordered a giant mill from Austria … with 48-inch stones and a capacity of a couple of tons a day. It's handmade by an old couple and is just beautiful." Alan was still well when the mill left Austria, but it was sent to Tanzania instead of Tasmania by mistake and had made it as far as Leipzig, Germany, before the error was discovered and the mill rerouted. By the time the ship carrying the mill finally arrived at the port in Hobart, Tasmania, Alan's health had begun to deteriorate. His daughter, Lila, became the responsible party for the 5,000-pound mill, sitting in a shipping container at the port. After Alan died, she called to tell me she thought my project should use this mill. Even posthumously, Alan was pushing forward the next chapter in bread's story.

Alan's mill represented something. It carried the promise, for farmers, of a market for North Carolina–grown grain and, for bakeries, of the potential for truly local bread. It was the link between farmer and baker. After months of phone calls and emails to Australia and Austria and among agencies here in North Carolina—North Carolina State University, Carolina Farm Stewardship Association, the North Carolina Department of Agriculture, the USDA—as well as among seven bakeries in Western North Carolina that had come together through this effort—the mill departed from the port in Hobart.

From Hobart the mill traveled to Melbourne, Australia, where it was placed on a ship bound for Long Beach, California. From Long Beach, it traveled by rail to Charlotte, North Carolina. In Charlotte, it was loaded onto the flatbed roll-back truck, provided by the North Carolina Department of Agriculture, that would finally deliver it to Asheville.

◆ ◆ ◆

In the spring of 2012, through a community effort of crowdfunding, peer lending, grant awards, and empathetic investors, Carolina Ground was launched, with Alan's mill as its centerpiece. My focus shifted from concept to reality as my lens narrowed to the craft of milling. I knew, as a baker, that the quality of our flour would outrank its place of origin, and it would be my task to ensure that *local* and *quality* became synonymous with the flour we produced. I approached local organic farmers who were growing commodity grain for animal feed to persuade them to grow bread wheat for our mill. Growing this crop would require more from these farmers, and their grain would need to meet higher quality standards, but in exchange, we were slowly creating a niche market for Southern grains. Separately, I engaged the Southern bakers themselves, through group emails and bakery visits, speaking the language we bakers know, of baker's percentage, hydration, and bulk fermentation, to help them navigate the challenges that our Southern grains could present. I sought to inspire our bakers to interact with their ingredients in ways that they may not have done in the past. I encouraged bakers to share information, their successes and their challenges, so we could learn from each other. This mill would make us better bakers.

La Farm Bakery in Cary, North Carolina, and Flat Rock Village Bakery in Flat Rock, North Carolina, agreed to test-bake grains for the mill, helping us determine which crops we should purchase—assessing gluten strength and tolerance, and mix and fermentation times. Modern mills use machines to test flour and flow charts to assess quality, but we embraced our skills as bakers. Harry Peemoeller, a passionate German baker and senior bread and pastry instructor at Johnson & Wales University's Charlotte campus, insisted we send him the most challenging flour to work with, so he could engage his students and deepen their understanding of flour. When mistakes were made in the mill room, like running rye over our finest screens or accidentally filling the hopper with rye, pastry wheat, and bread wheat instead of a single type of grain, we turned these mistakes into opportunities. We ran to our kitchens and came up with solutions, making our highly sifted Light Rye flour into shortbread cookies filled with lemon curd and mascarpone cheese (see page 202 for the recipe), and a Trinity Blend flour that our student intern from Johnson & Wales made into a teacake with lemon thyme glaze (see page 251). We then added these flours to our offerings.

Like a chef-driven restaurant, Carolina Ground is a baker-driven mill. Although the mill was born out of need, what transpired in the creation of Carolina Ground was more than we had ever imagined: the mill transformed the quality and kind of baking in our region, impacting not just a handful of bakers in Western North Carolina but a huge community of bakers throughout the Southeast. By working with our flour, these bakeries are revolutionizing the kinds of baked goods they're delivering to their communities, and the number of these communities is increasing exponentially.

In Atlanta, the Little Tart Bakeshop elevates the Georgia peanut with our stone-ground whole-grain spelt flour in their Salted Peanut Butter Cookies with Cacao Nibs (page 261); in New Orleans, Levee Baking Co. pairs the flavor of Louisiana blood orange with our wholegrain pastry flour made from soft red winter wheat in their Rough Puff with Pecan Frangipane and Louisiana Blood Orange (page 212); and outside Asheville in Walnut, North Carolina, in the little wood-fired-brick-oven bakery that was once Natural Bridge Bakery and is currently Walnut Schoolhouse, baker Brennan Johnson is teaching baking with our flavor-forward, regional stone-ground flours. Throughout the southeastern United States, a significant number of bakers are engaging with regional stone-ground flours in unique and creative ways. We are inspiring them and they are inspiring us.

Carolina Ground is changing the landscape for our bakers, moving them from industrial commodity flour to cold-stone-milled flour, variety specific, of place, flavor, and character, so they can deliver to their customer extraordinary taste, texture, and story. We are moving our growers from feed-grade to food-grade grains, to richer and more diverse crop rotations, and from a commodity to an agricultural product of distinction. Carolina Ground is an integral part of a burgeoning movement of regional mills popping up nationwide and of bakers engaging on a level that has not been seen before in this country. Through these regional milling endeavors, farmer, miller, baker, and customer are together helping to rebuild a more sustainable food system.

The Mill

By the end of the nineteenth century, our country's landscape, once rich with local water-powered stone mills and regional grain growing was transformed. Stone milling, the method of milling used for thousands of years, had been practically abandoned. In its place: the roller mill, which processed grain to flour with speed and efficiency, producing a flour whiter than anyone had ever seen prior to this, with an appealing, powdery texture.

This is the flour we are all familiar with, the flour that dominates grocery store shelves and most bakeries. It is a different flour from what is produced on a stone mill. Roller milling separates the three components of the grain: the endosperm, the germ, and the bran. Steel rollers slice away the oily germ and peel off the bran, producing a white, endosperm-only flour with a long, stable shelf life. Stone milling crushes the intact grain between stones, and although the larger bran particles can be sifted out, the oily germ is spread into the starchy endosperm flour, resulting in an off-white or cream-colored flour rich in flavor and nutrients, but with a limited shelf life, as it is the oils in the germ that limit the shelf life. The roller mill's speed and efficiency and the longer shelf life of the resulting flour were the mainsprings for the centralization and vertical integration of the growing and processing of grain to flour, transforming the Great Plain states into the modern US breadbasket.

Speed, efficiency, and the assumed availability of cheap fuel superseded local fresh flour, nutrients, and flavor. But the local grains movement has reclaimed this part of our past. The reintroduction of stone milling, the oldest technology used to turn grain into flour, has appeared hand in hand with regional grain efforts. And cold stone milling, a method that ensures the temperature of the resulting flour stays well below 100°F, thus protecting the oils in the flour, has elevated the process.

For us, the choice of stone over steel to process our grain into flour was a given, as cold stone milling produces flavor-forward flours that highlight the *terroir* of our region. This is part of the story we seek to tell—flavorful flours of geographic distinction. This flour is a different product. Roller milling is incredibly efficient, but it strips flavor and nutrients from the resulting flour, and although flavor can be conjured out of any flour through the process of slow fermentation, cold-stone-milled flour offers the baker a whole new palate of flavor and tooth to engage with—whether applied to slow ferments, straight doughs, pastries, or cakes.

Milling as Craft

As millers, our task is to transform grain into flour. Although the quality of our flour is hugely affected by the quality of our grain, the miller plays a significant role in the end result. Our goal as millers is twofold: to expose the grain fully, also known as damaging the starch (in this case, the term *damaging* just means to break up the starch granules within the grain berry), and to protect the nutrients. Whether working in a small regional stone mill or a large industrial mill, the miller aims to damage or expose the starch enough, but not too much. The perfectly damaged starch results in a flour with improved water absorption and the release of enzymes that feed yeasts. Flour with overly damaged starch can absorb water in excess, but will not be able to carry the weight of that water in baking, producing a flat loaf of bread.

As stone millers, we arrive at our flour by feel. We seek to release the oils and produce a uniform grind. We listen to the cadence of our grain entering the mill and to the sound of stone against grain—avoiding the sound of stone against stone. We feel the resulting flour with our hands, then fine-tune and make adjustments, as the mill's settings affect particle size and starch damage, which in turn can affect the functionality of the flour. We keep an eye on the flour's temperature, aiming to hold it well below 100°F, as we seek to protect the wheat germ—the wheat berry's bank of nutrients, a highly concentrated package of unsaturated fats, B vitamins, folate, phosphorous, thiamin, zinc, magnesium, and vitamin E. Though our approach differs from industrial milling, where we really diverge from the milling industry is in our goal to not simply create a flour that functions well for the baker, but one whose nutrients are preserved in the milling process.

Our mill is a simple machine, belt-driven, with two stones that sit horizontal and parallel to one another. Our top stone is the runner stone, which rotates around the stationary bed stone. Grain enters the mill and becomes whole-grain flour—whole wheat or whole rye or whole spelt. This whole-grain flour has nothing removed. If it is to be sifted, it is then diverted to our bolter (or sifter), where it passes over various screens. Sifting is where the miller's craft is honed, but before delving into the art of sifting, we must first understand the grain berry in its whole form.

As a whole, the wheat berry is a perfect combination of starch, protein, fiber, vitamins, and minerals. The majority of the wheat berry is the endosperm, about 82 percent by weight, mainly consisting of carbohydrates (in the form of starch), protein, and iron. The bran is the outer sheath, the grain's shield against the elements as it grows in the field. It constitutes about 14 percent by weight and is rich in B vitamins, folic acid, fiber, and minerals. The inner-most layer of the bran/outermost layer of the endosperm—or what lies between the bran and the endosperm—is the aleurone layer, a thin layer rich in minerals, fats, proteins, and enzymes. And the germ, which is the wheat berry's embryo and the powerhouse source of nutrients, constitutes just 3 to 5 percent by weight.

When sifting flour, we are changing the ratio of these components—removing the lighter, larger granules. Sifting is achieved by gravity and velocity. We use a machine called a bolter, which consists of three chambers and strip brushes that rotate, sweeping the whole-grain flour over three sets of screens. Each screen has holes of a different size, and separate the flour by both weight and fineness to produce sifted flour, middlings, and bran. The middlings (also called farina and often found sold under the brand name Cream of Wheat) run past the first two screens because the granules are larger than the holes in the screens. The size of the holes in the screens and the pace of milling will determine the ratio of bran to starchy endosperm, the heaviest part of a whole-grain flour, in the end product. Sifting brings an exacting measure to our mill flow; the miller's skill and attention ensure we produce a consistent product.

Flour by Type or Flour by Extraction

Since the majority of minerals are found in the bran (which contains ten to twenty times more minerals than the starchy endosperm), the amount of bran in flour is assessed by a measure known as ash. Ash is measured by incinerating a sample of flour at high heat. The organic components (starch, protein, sugar, and fats) fully combust, but the inorganic material (the minerals) are left behind in the form of ash. The ash is then weighed. Whole-grain, unsifted flour produces about 2 grams of ash per 100 grams of flour; pure endosperm contains 0.35 grams ash, so it follows that the lower the ash, the whiter the flour. In Europe, the measure of ash is how flour is designated and regulated. In Italy, for example, type 00—the fine white flour used in Neapolitan pizza—has a maximum allowable ash of 0.55 grams and is the equivalent of type 55 in France, which is a close equivalent of Germany's type 550 (with a maximum allowable ash of .063 grams).

At Carolina Ground, we designate our sifted flour by extraction—the amount of flour left after sifting—instead of by ash. This is a less exact method, as mineral content can vary depending on soil and climate, but in this way, each year's particular harvest lends its own signature to the flours we will produce. Whole-wheat or whole-grain flour is not sifted and is therefore 100 percent extraction—grain in, flour out. High-extraction flour is sifted flour from which the least amount has been removed. Our high-extraction flour is also called 85 Extraction, meaning 85 percent of the flour is left after sifting (15 percent has been sifted out). Our 75-Extraction flour has about 25 percent sifted out.

A good rule of thumb when navigating one's way around the nomenclature, whether type (which refers to ash) or extraction, is that the higher the number, the more whole the product. High-extraction would be type 2 in Italy, type 110 in France, and type 1050 in Germany, and it is our 85 Extraction.

In the United States, there is an industry standard maximum allowable ash (although this is not regulated or overseen by the FDA), but this is not information readily available to us as consumers. Flour on the grocery store shelf is designated neither by ash nor extraction, but by intended use: all-purpose flour, or bread flour, or pastry flour, or cake flour. Without ash minimums or extractions, we as consumers are removed from the process. We are offered only white flour or wheat flour. When making a cake, measuring by volume works because the industry standard ensures that a cup measure of all-purpose flour or bread flour will weigh in fairly consistently at 125 grams, and a cup of cake flour at 120 grams. Our cold-stone-milled flour, produced within a less exacting framework, requires measure by weight to ensure success in recipes.

Converting Ash Value from European to US Standards

In determining ash content in the United States, flour is tested on a 14 percent moisture basis, whereas in Europe, flour is tested on a dry, or 0 percent moisture, basis. To convert the ash value, the math is simple—divide by 0.86: 0.52 percent ash at 14 percent moisture basis divided by 0.86 would be 0.60 percent ash at 0 percent moisture basis.

From Harvest to Mill

We grow winter grains in this part of the country, which in the South means seeds are planted in late fall and harvested in early summer. There are six different classes of wheat grown in the United States; these are divided by growing season (winter or spring), color (red or white), and hardness (soft or hard). Winter wheats are planted in the fall and harvested in the summer; spring wheats are planted in spring and harvested in late summer to early fall. Hard wheats are typically used for bread and pasta, whereas soft wheats are used for pastry, cakes, and biscuits. Typically, spring wheats are grown west of Kansas, in regions too cold for wheat to overwinter, and winter wheats, grown from Kansas east, require vernalization (exposure to cold) to initiate flowering. In the South, soft red winter wheat is the variety typically grown, and in North Carolina, we grow more soft red winter wheat than any other Southern state. However, the regional grains movement is redefining which wheat is grown where. Spring wheats are now being grown in western New York and Maine, and hard winter wheats are being grown in the South.

Here in the South, there is just a single grain crop per year (unlike our friends up north, who are able to grow both winter and spring wheats), and it must meet certain criteria to make it into our mill room. New crop grain undergoes lab tests and baking tests to ensure the resulting flour will have acceptable performance characteristics and is safe for human consumption.

The first thing I do when a sample of new crop grain arrives in our mill room is look at it. A visual inspection says a lot. A healthy crop has a visually detectable glow; plump, vibrant grain simply emanates strength. A healthy crop has a strong immune system, protecting it from insects and disease in the field. When I see this, I am reminded that we are working with plant life. Conversely, an unhealthy crop looks pallid; there are often broken kernels. Still, looks are not everything. A few years ago, I received a grain sample from one of my growers who warned me that the crop looked pretty bad. He said it had not rained in weeks and many of the wheat berries looked shriveled. When I received his sample, after a quick glance, I tossed a handful into my mouth. I chew on bread wheat to assess gluten strength. I'm looking for elasticity and extensibility—I want the grain to transform into the consistency of chewing gum. This crop, even with its share of shriveled berries, passed my chew test. I would come to learn that lack of rain at the right time (especially during those last ten days before harvest) contributes to increased protein. This crop would serve the baker well. For the grower, yields were low, but even after screening out the shriveled kernels at cleaning, we were able to offer him a better market for his grain than if it were sold for feed, and we landed on an especially flavorful crop with strong performance. Here is the value of a regional grains economy in action.

A visual inspection and chew test is followed by a measure of the test weight. Test weight is the actual weight of a bushel of grain. A true bushel weight should be 60 pounds for wheat and 56 pounds for rye and is typically a good measure of a quality crop. If test weight is low, this could be an indicator of disease or sprout damage, or just that it was a stressful growing year. If test weight is above 55 pounds and moisture is below 15 percent, the sample has made the cut and is sent off for lab testing.

Lab testing tells us, among other things, the grain's protein value, though it is our baking tests that really guide our understanding of the grain before us. A protein number is one-dimensional, but the proteins that determine the baking characteristics of a grain are not. More important than the quantity of protein is the quality. Gluten accounts for 80 percent of the protein in wheat and delivers the strength and structure for bread wheat; the other 20 percent are soluble proteins that have no impact on bread-baking quality but do contribute to nutritional value. Gluten itself is made up of two proteins: glutenin and gliadin. Glutenin contributes elasticity and strength to dough and is derived from extrinsic factors such as planting date, seeding rate, soil fertility, weeds, and rain. We were able to transform crop of partially shriveled grain into viable bread flour in part due to those last ten days before harvest, which were especially hot and dry, just the right conditions for increased glutenin. Gliadin, on the other hand, provides extensibility or the ability to stretch the dough and contributes to dough's volume. It is derived from intrinsic factors—the genetics of the seed variety. The gliadin is coded into the DNA of the variety of wheat—it is a set amount, while glutenin increases or decreases depending on growing conditions. The ratio of the gliadin to the glutenin is what defines the quality of the protein. Within an industrial system where bread is mass-produced and an average-size flour mill in the United States produces one million pounds of flour a day (according to the North American Millers' Association), the ability to quantify the quality of protein becomes essential. Various lab tests are employed to measure mix time, water absorption, elasticity, and extensibility. At our small mill, producing between 1,500 and 2,500 pounds of flour a day, the baking test provides us with the information we need to know: Does the dough have sufficient strength to contain the gases produced by fermentation? Is it especially active? Is it thirsty? Can we make bread out of this crop?

Phenotypic Plasticity in Heritage Wheats

Glenn Roberts, owner of Anson Mills in Columbia, South Carolina, tells me one of his favorite terms is *phenotypic plasticity*. For the baker driven by the nuanced flavors of heritage grains, this is a term worth knowing. It refers to the adaptability of heritage wheats not only to extrinsic factors, but to intrinsic ones as well. While in modern wheats, the glutenin will vary depending on growing conditions, it is the change in the ratio of gliadin to glutenin that will have the biggest impact on the quality of the wheat for baking performance. Older varieties seem to have a tendency to adapt to their gliadin availability, so growing conditions that may have a more dramatic effect on modern varieties are more mitigated in heritage varieties.

The Seed

In early summer of 2008, a package arrived at my bakery containing samples of wheat. The package was from the United State Department of Agriculture, Agricultural Research Service (USDA-ARS) and the wheat was from Dr. David Marshall's Uniform Bread Wheat Trials. I was curious, and also amazed. My little bakery, tucked away in the mountains of Western North Carolina, seemed an unlikely candidate to provide any feedback of value to this federal agency. I had assumed their work catered solely to agribusiness and industrial food production, with wheat breeding focused on industrial bakery applications. And yet the origin of the USDA-ARS is rooted in the idea of providing for agriculturally based trades, establishing a link between scientists and those producing our food—farmers, ranchers, and processors (bakers!). The agency was founded as part of the Hatch Act in 1887, when the agricultural landscape looked very different from how it looks today. In today's world of mega agribusinesses and industrial food production, I had not considered the possibility that a small artisan bakery could have a voice. But when I reached out to Myron Fountain of the USDA-ARS to thank him for sending the grain and share our positive results with him, his response was immediate and engaging, and he expressed a willingness to collaborate in bringing these wheat varieties to the attention of the baking community.

A few weeks later, the first bread wheat field day in the southeastern United States was hosted by the USDA-ARS and North Carolina State University in Waynesville, North Carolina. It was titled, "Bread Wheat and Organic Production." Bakers from throughout Western North Carolina showed up. We were curious. We had all received invitations. The flour we used to make our bread was ground from grain grown at least a thousand miles away, in the Great Plains states or Canada.

Trial plots of wheat forming a patchwork of varying shades of amber provided the backdrop for Dr. David Marshall, the USDA-ARS's lead researcher and wheat breeder. He introduced himself and his Uniform Bread Wheat Trials, providing a brief history of his breeding program, which began in 2002, to identify and breed wheat having hard-wheat quality (aka bread wheat) for production in the humid environments of the eastern United States. Bread wheat is traditionally grown west of the Mississippi. East of the Mississippi, North Carolina grows more soft wheat (used for pastry flour and/or feed) than any other Southern state. Dr. Marshall explained that for the identification phase of his program, he collected varieties and advanced breeding lines from breeders in Texas, Oklahoma, Kansas, Nebraska, Colorado—principally the Great Plains—and planted them in Georgia, North Carolina, Kentucky, Virginia, Maryland, and Pennsylvania. His rows of wheat contained both old and modern varieties, soft and hard. Old varieties such as Federation and Red Fife grew next to newer varieties such as Dual, Hondo, ARS03-3806, and ARS505-1234. Because there is only a single crop of winter wheat per year, he'd established a partnership with a program in New Zealand so he could get two generations of wheat per year, and since 2002, more than one thousand crosses had been made annually, breeding for disease resistance, yield, and baking quality. Even still, it would take seven to ten years for a variety to be deemed acceptable for public release. Dr. Marshall employs classical breeding practices with no modification of genes between species. All the genes he works with are within the wheat family. And all his breeds can be traced back to the Fertile Crescent, where wheat originated.

Dr. Marshall is a public breeder and his Uniform Bread Wheat Trials is a public breeding program. In 2008, I barely understood the significance of this, although the willingness of Myron Fountain, Marshall's assistant, to engage with my bakery was a tangible clue. I had worked with this agricultural product—wheat—milling my grain, grown by organic farmers who had clearly benefited from plant breeding, for over a decade before meeting Myron Fountain or Dr. Marshall and still I was challenged by the idea of science and food being so closely aligned. But as I fully immersed myself into the agricultural side of baking, I came to appreciate the vision and conviction of our forefathers who established public institutions that would bridge the science community and those growing our food. Preceding 1887's Hatch Act, the Morrill Act of 1862 (also known as the Land Grant College Act), signed by President Lincoln, established a system of higher education within this country "for the common good of the industrial classes." It democratized higher learning and established state agricultural colleges that enabled both research and access to pragmatic application for the benefit of society—*for the common good.* The Smith-Lever Act of 1914 built upon both the Morrill Act and the Hatch Act by establishing the Cooperative Extension Service, which provides liaisons between land grant universities and farmers. North Carolina State University, the USDA-ARS, and the Cooperative Extension—all these entities working in concert were fundamental to the success of Carolina Ground. Having access to seed varieties bred for resistance to disease specifically for our region—regionally adapted varieties—that produce acceptable yields has been essential to building lasting relationships with our organic growers. And for the growers to be introduced to these varieties through field days put on by these agencies, addressing production, harvest, and postharvest handling, has been foundational to our ability to rebuild a sustainable grain-based food system. And this is not to say that heritage varieties—varieties that predate modern breeding practices of the mid-twentieth century—do not also have a place at the table, because they do, and we need the diversity both on our farms and on our palates. But having a foundation of seed varieties that the farmer feels comfortable planting and that produce yields enabling a price point where bakeries can afford to make real commitments to mills like ours has been an essential piece of the equation.

A few months after that field day, I traveled down to Columbia, South Carolina, to visit Glenn Roberts, whom I met for the first time at the field day. A decade earlier, Glenn had launched Anson Mills with the sole purpose of bringing back the ingredients that defined the antebellum Southern larder: Carolina Gold rice, Red May wheat, Sea Island red peas, Sea Island benne seeds, and numerous varieties of Southern colonial mill corn. I'd assumed that because his focus was reviving ingredients from the past, he would have little interest in Dr. Marshall's work, but Glenn noted how lucky we are to have Dr. Marshall in North Carolina. He described Dr. Marshall to me as part of a dying breed (a concept propagated by a 2003 *Nature* magazine article by Johnathan Knight entitled "A Dying Breed," which explores the loss of public sector research into classical breeding). Just as I began to fully realize the significance and value of this public sector work—that Dr. Marshall is a public servant and his breeding program is for the public good—I also had to accept the reality that he is, as Glenn described, "part of a dying breed."

Over the past twenty years, the decline in funding for public sector plant-breeding programs and the decline in the number of public breeders has been profound. According to the USDA, "between 2008 and 2013, real (inflation-adjusted) public food and agricultural R&D fell by about 20 percent while real private R&D increased by 64 percent."[1] But wheat, unlike corn or soybeans or canola or cotton, is one of the few remaining field crops that is still largely in public hands because commercial seed producers have a more difficult time realizing a robust return on investment for wheat. Wheat is self-pollinating, reproducing itself to near purity, so growers can save seed to replant without losing too much of the desired characteristics of the variety, thus hindering commercial interest. Wheat is not the only one of the few remaining vestiges of a system that was put in place for the benefit of society as a whole, but projects like Dr. Marshall's Uniform Bread Wheat trials underscore the greater return on investment that public sector agricultural programs have on a community. The social return on investment is not going to equate to immediate and direct profit from, for example, the sale of seed, but is realized with each bakery that chooses to forgo their imported commodity flour and instead engage with growers in their region through their use of regionally grown and ground flour. It is through breads and pastries made with that flour that bakeries are making an economic and social impact on their communities. And it is through flavor and story that they engage their customers in reclaiming this fundamental piece of a sustainable food system.

Breeding for Flavor

At that first field day, someone in the audience asked Dr. Marshall about breeding for flavor. Traditionally, breeding programs for wheat have focused on disease and pest resistance, and yield on the farm, and baking performance in the bakery. Most flour is industrially processed, removing the most flavorful aspects of the wheat berry—the oily germ and the bran. Function is everything. Dr. Marshall's response to the question in the moment was that he did not feel this was a marker that could be identified, or captured. Within the confines of a breeder's laboratory, flavor is an intangible, but when breeders and millers and bakers come together—when the community is invested in the outcome—taste becomes an accessible component. This has been another outcome of the greater regional grains movement and, here in the South, of Dr. Marshall's work as well.

Dr. Marshall maintains a grading system where he provides a score for his numerous experimental varieties, assessing dough characteristics that range from mix time to dough strength. These are quantifiable traits that can be assessed with various pieces of lab equipment and flow charts. In order to establish qualifiable data—how do these varieties taste?—and to see how his scores are reflected in the physical baking results, Dr. Marshall has engaged millers and bakers. He's sent me numerous experimental varieties to mill and distribute to bakeries, and we then come together to taste the baked goods made from those experimental varieties. Words like *buttery*, *nutty*, and *coffee-like* have become part of the lexicon. Baker participants Lionel Vatinet of La Farm Bakery in Cary, North Carolina, and Harry Peemoeller, senior bread and pastry instructor at Johnson & Wales University's Charlotte campus, not only share in the tasting, but also can speak to the dough characteristics as they experience them.

A few states away, at the University of Kentucky, public wheat breeder Dr. David Van Sanford is also breeding for flavor in his pastry wheat varieties. He has been screening all his breeding lines for flavor and dough functionality in a 50 percent whole-wheat boule that is baked and tasted weekly on campus in the lab of Chef Bob Perry, whom Dr. Van Sanford describes as "another partner in crime." One of Dr. Van Sanford's inspirations is public breeder Dr. Stephen Jones in Washington State, who established the Bread Lab, where flavor is seen as fundamental to the success of the regional grains movement. The Bread Lab, founded in 2011 in a laboratory within Washington State University's Mount Vernon Northwest

Washington Research & Extension Center, is, according to their website, "a combination think tank and baking laboratory where scientists, bakers, chefs, farmers, maltsters, brewers, distillers and millers experiment with improved flavor, nutrition and functionality of regional and obscure wheats, barley, other small grains and beans."

Dr. Marshall, Dr. Van Sanford, and Dr. Jones know each other. They are part of a small group of public breeders, public stewards, helping us rewrite the narrative.

Dr David Marshall's Small Grains Research Area within the Lake Wheeler Road Field Laboratory, Raleigh, NC.

The Farmer

"You have chosen to get involved in one of the most difficult projects in American Agriculture."

This was the first line of an email I received from a well-respected miller in Kansas to whom I'd reached out, hoping for a bit of guidance. The rest of the email delineated the various pre- and postharvest challenges we would need to overcome, from seed availability to grain quality, storage, cleaning, and packaging. It was early on in the concept stage of what would become Carolina Ground, and in my initial email, I had mentioned the possibility of collective ownership by the bakers and/or farmers; to this, his response was that farmers are an independent lot. Fair warning. I was initially intimidated by this "independent lot." The chasm that existed between baker and farmer was not just our lost connection to the agrarian roots of our trade. There were cultural differences as well. It had been more than a hundred years since the community mill had bridged this gap. And there was justifiable mistrust from these growers. They had been burned in the past, many times, by markets over which they had no control.

I attended field days put on by the Cooperative Extension Service, hoping to learn about the production challenges these growers face. Understanding their farming culture as a whole would prove just as important as our single crop, since grain fits into a rotation. These large-scale organic Southern growers rotate wheat crops with tobacco or sweet potatoes, corn, or, more recently, hemp. The timing of harvest and planting as well as potential benefit or disease from the previous crop in the rotation can add to or detract from the quality of our grain. I wanted to know about all of this. And I also wanted to know more in the hopes of forming long-lasting relationships.

At left: Carter Farms, Eagle Springs, North Carolina.
At right: Soft wheat harvest at Barham Family Farm, Wake Forest, North Carolina.

The Baker

The bakeries are the reason Carolina Ground exists. Driven by a desire for something more than the industrial commodity white flour that is readily available, less expensive, and easier to work with, these bakeries—often small to medium-size businesses—have passionately embraced our flour with a willingness to engage deeper with their ingredients, allowing the flour to inspire their recipes.

What you will see on the following pages are the old and the new: those of us who have been baking for ten- or twenty-plus years, and a new generation of bakers that has arisen perhaps because of the regional grains movement. I am especially intrigued by this new wave. They embrace regional grains, and the flours—from whole-grain to sifted—ground from them, and they know their grain varieties as if this is the way it has always been. Perhaps because it should have always been this way.

Natural Bridge Bakery

WALNUT, NORTH CAROLINA

It was a simple operation: a masonry oven and a pile of wood, a stone-burr gristmill, grain, and salt. This bakery was witness to my marriage, the birth of my child, my divorce, and my move from Tennessee to North Carolina. I would raise my daughter in tandem with the bakery, our house located just a stone's throw from its massive brick oven. This was our world, tucked away in the mountains of Western North Carolina. It was its own universe of cultures and dough, kindling and coals, children's books and beeswax crayons and an array of stuffed animals. It was a life composed by my much younger self, lured by the ancient craft of bread baking.

More than a decade has passed since this was my world, and more than twenty years since I began piecing together that dream. The sign for Natural Bridge Bakery still hangs from the wooden beam that supports the large metal roof, covering the outdoor wood-fired oven. It is a reminder of its beginnings. The bakehouse has since morphed into an incubator space producing three more bakeries—Dave Bauer's Farm and Sparrow (see page 36), Tara Jensen's Smoke Signals (see page 39), and Brennan Johnson's Walnut Schoolhouse (see page 43). Although our ingredients and techniques have been similar, the aromas that have defined this baking space have changed with each baker.

Farm and Sparrow

MARS HILL, NORTH CAROLINA

Dave Bauer was one of the eight bakers who came to the many meetings that led to the launch of Carolina Ground. Eleven years my junior, Dave first launched his Farm and Sparrow out of my bakery space. He was the next-generation baker. What I had gleaned from Alan Scott—the concept of a microbakery, of natural leavening, wood-fired oven, and gristmill—Dave took to another level. When he eventually moved into his own space, the oven he had built for the bakery, although inspired by Alan Scott, was a wholly new design by Antoine Guerlain—a massive oven fitting sixty-three loaves at a clip with three doors, side by side, to minimize heat loss while loading. Focusing the lens even more on flavor, he sourced heritage varieties of grain for seed to be planted. And he planted seeds in his front yard with the intention of bulking up his supply to ultimately hand over to a farmer. Turkey Red was the first variety he had a farmer grow for him, in Old Fort, North Carolina. He purchased a mill with a sifter from Austria, so he could produce both whole-grain and sifted flours for his bakery. And he added laminated pastry—wood-fired croissants and puff pastry—to his offerings. He built up a team of bakers: milling, laminating pastry dough, mixing bread dough, and delivering products to the booming farmers' markets of Asheville, as well as to restaurants and grocery stores. He and a chef-friend opened a wood-fired pizza restaurant, enabling him to pair his flavor-forward flours with seasonal local ingredients.

And then after thirteen years of baking, Dave paused and reflected deeply on what he had been working toward for over a decade, and he realized it all came back to the seed. In 2018, he closed his bakery. He got married and moved into a hundred-year-old church in Mars Hill, North Carolina, reopening Farm and Sparrow in its current iteration, which he describes as an "Appalachian-based seed project, grain collection, and mill." For Dave, above and beyond his seed work, what inspired his breads and pastry and pasta, driving all if it, has always been flavor.

Tara Jensen

POUND, VIRGINIA

My first introduction to Tara Jensen was as an artist. She was working for Dave Bauer of Farm and Sparrow, bagging granola and selling at farmers' markets. I was looking for an art teacher for my daughter, and Dave suggested Tara, who had recently returned from Japan, where she'd put on two art shows of soft sculpture and taught workshops on sewing and papier-mâché. At the time, I figured baking was just a job for her and art was her real passion.

Growing up, Tara had always done art. She figured she would go to art school, but the art world felt too competitive to her, and she ended up choosing a small, more holistic liberal arts college in northern Maine. She majored in human ecology. This multidisciplinary degree is the study of people and their relationship to their environment, be it a man-made environment or a natural one. And what better environment for the study of human ecology than a bakery. Bakeries are common ground. They can alter the social landscape of a town, create place out of space. Tara got her first job in a bakery while in college. The bakery was owned by a husband-and-wife team; the wife was also a midwife, and many of the customers were pregnant women and babies. It was a social space, both for the employees and the community. Tara fell in love with the potential of what could happen within those walls.

After college, she moved to Vermont, got a job at Red Hen Baking Co., and began a crash course into the world of artisan bread. She would learn the discipline, repetition, and quiet beauty of production baking. She worked in the bakery by day and made art at night. These two worlds—art and baking—were separate. After six or seven years of production baking, she moved down to Asheville and naturally fell in with the city's artist community. At the same time, she was selling baked goods for Dave at farmers' markets and observing people's reactions to food. "Watching people eat the food you made—it was such a gratifying experience," she says. "It wasn't a composed, intellectual response, it was the body's response, which is what I ultimately became more interested in."

Tara would become increasingly jaded by the art gallery world; to her, it felt uninspired and lacking substance. At a certain point, she declared "*no more art,*" and in a dramatic gesture, she burned all her paintbrushes. She began dating a fellow farmer vendor from the farmers' market, eventually started farming with him, and then began her own little baking operation, which she named Smoke Signals. She baked out of a pizza shop in Marshall after hours and sold her breads and pastry at the farmers' market. By this point, my relationship with Tara had evolved into a friendship. She'd launched Smoke Signals just a few months after we'd begun milling, and she used our flour exclusively. When the farmers' market season started to wane, I was ready to hire an assistant to our miller and asked Tara if she wanted to join our team. She readily accepted the offer. The chance to deepen her knowledge of baking through a closer proximity to the source of her ingredients excited her. She worked in the mill room one day a week, and she farmed, and she baked. She also test-baked flours for the mill. And if we made a mistake in the mill room, she was the best candidate to run to her kitchen with some odd flour and inspire us with the incredible baked goods that resulted.

My bakery space had been sitting vacant for three years. It felt lifeless and sad. I showed Tara the space. She would transform this place, infusing it with new life and aromas and creativity that is uniquely Tara. She thought she had left the artist at the door, but one day, she started rolling out a large sheet of pie dough to cut into pie tops and bottoms. Then she just kept cutting and realized she could make various shapes and arrange them into layers. She loves surface design and texture and thought she could layer the shapes in interesting ways, which she documented on social media. At the time, nobody had ever seen a pie top like that, or at least it was yet not as prevalent in the social media landscape. It caught a lot of people's attention—including, fortunately, that of the editors at *Bon Appétit*. This ability to make art with food—with pie dough—inspired her to use baking as her canvas. Initially, this was baking art with a focus on what it would look like, but eventually, it became the art of baking for flavor and taste.

Teaching came next. She began with pie because it was something she could fit within the window of time between farming and baking for market. For her first pie workshop, she chose the least intimidating thing she could do: apple pie. Maybe eight people showed up, mostly people from Marshall, and they all had a great time. She decided to do more of these workshops, bringing in various elements from her background in art, sculpture, and human ecology, which incorporated value systems, use of resources, and lifestyle. She found that being in the position of having to explain baking to others made her a better baker herself. Having to explain the value of growing practices and fresh flour made her more passionate about fresh flour and flavor and gave her the tools to tacitly affect the positive change she believes is essential for our planet. Her workshops evolved into multiday retreats, drawing participants from all over the United States. Now many years later, Tara is an author, mother, and wife and teaching workshops and weeklong retreats using her mobile wood-fired oven.

When I ask her about her path, she tells me, "This is my lifelong craft, something I will be working on and tinkering with and exploring every day until I'm done walking on the planet." And then she adds, "When I first started working at Red Hen, we loaded everything with this huge wooden peel, and I still remember what that felt like as a young woman standing in the middle of this huge long crazy tool with all this bread on one end and this hot oven and the rhythm of moving the peel in and out, just this feeling that this is the position that I'm supposed to be in. I say this is my lifelong practice because I feel like I'm still understanding why I'm in this position or what I have of value to offer, as it is constantly changing. But that balance point, it was intoxicating finding myself in this great fit."

Ashley Capps

ASHEVILLE, NORTH CAROLINA

The first time I met pastry chef Ashley Capps, she was rolling out dough. This was when she worked at Farm and Sparrow Bakery. I was meeting with Dave, and I remember noticing how Ashley used her entire body as she rolled and folded large sheets of dough layered with butter. A few years later, shortly after I'd launched Carolina Ground, she reached out to me to ask for flour. She was working with Chef John Fleer at the time, as part of the opening team for Rhubarb, Fleer's farm-to-table restaurant in downtown Asheville. Having worked for Dave, she knew the significance of good flour. Another few years later, images of iconic Southern desserts she'd crafted for Chef Elliott Moss's Buxton Hall BBQ started appearing on my social media feed, with Carolina Ground tagged.

Since 2008, when the idea for Carolina Ground was first conceived, Asheville has evolved into a dining destination. Ashley has been an integral part of putting our small mountain city on the food map, and in doing so, she brought Carolina Ground into those kitchens. She insisted on using our flour—and other stone-ground regional flours—challenging the precept that flour is just there to carry eggs and butter and other additions.

When I ask Ashley what she loves most about baking, her first response is, "That's like asking, what's your favorite movie?" But after taking a moment, she tells me that what she loves most about baking right now is "the fact that I know that every day is the same and different. So every day is the same: you put on your favorite apron and you put your hair up and you put on your favorite playlist and you clean up your station, you weigh out your ingredients. So there are things that are the same and that ground you and anchor you, and there are things that are like, 'Oh, it's spring, now we have strawberries, now it's fall and we have local pumpkins,' so it's like there's this awesome dichotomy of everything is the same and everything is different."

Walnut Schoolhouse

WALNUT, NORTH CAROLINA

Brennan Johnson is the fourth baker to occupy the space that was once Natural Bridge Bakery, and in his hands it has become part classroom, part community gathering place, and part bakery. Brennan grew up in an environment where baking bread was closely aligned with the concepts of community and spirituality. His father was a Methodist pastor who started baking bread as an outlet after years of pastoral work and built an oven in the backyard of Brennan's childhood suburban Minnesota home.

For a summer job, his dad suggested Brennan use their backyard oven to bake bread to sell at farmers' markets. With Jeffrey Hamelman's *Bread* to guide him, he launched his first bakery the summer of his junior year of high school.

Baking followed him to the small liberal arts college where he baked between classes. When his father received a grant to study community brick ovens in Western Europe, he brought Brennan with him. "An incredibly formative trip," Brennan reflects, "To a young American boy, especially one that had grown up in the Midwest where culture always seems to take the longest to permeate, seeing that there's this wisdom in older traditions, and seeing what that can do for community and regions, and also to see that there are all of these older cultures surrounding bread; I think in America, we are lacking in terms of the wisdom of long traditions. My favorite bakers and chefs and millers are taking older ideas and traditions and putting them into context in the modern day, bringing them to life again."

I ask Brennan what he loves about baking, and in his answer, I see how intrinsic baking has been to his life: "It's always for me been sort of a refuge, a sacred space, an opportunity to remove myself from the day-to-day stress or the everyday tasks—when I was growing up, it was my social anxiety; when I was in college, it was the stress of homework and being in college; and the real world has its own set of challenges. But baking has always been this place where I can just simply let that go and work with my hands and listen to the bread. I don't have a mixer in this space, and I'm just using sourdough and I'm just sort of guiding the bread along and listening to it, in conversation with it, and it's been a chance to sort of exit from the day-to-day world and just have a conversation with a different way of being or a different way of living, the aliveness and the activeness of the dough itself—it's really beautiful. I don't always get to grasp that when I'm trying to make a living off of it, too—that's the irony of the whole thing. But that's what I love most about it."

Flat Rock Village Bakery

FLAT ROCK, NORTH CAROLINA

In mid to late June, just after harvest, samples of new-crop bread wheat arrive in the mill room. If the grain looks promising, I send part of the sample to the lab and the rest I mill into whole-grain and high-extraction flour. I then drive forty minutes south to Flat Rock Village Bakery, where the majority of our baking tests are done. Depending on the year, this can be a few bakes or numerous bakes using various iterations and/or blends in order to find our way with the year's harvest. Bakers Daniel Goodson and Jon Hartzler take the lead. Because this will be the flour they will be using for the next nine to twelve months, these bakers have a vested interest in the outcome.

Flat Rock Village Bakery co-owner Dave Workman is one of the bakers who came to Waynesville in 2008 for that first field day. He also came to the many meetings that followed to discuss the possibility of launching this mill. Eight of us bakers pulled our chairs into a circle and imagined what this could look like: the chance to lessen our food miles, to know our growers, to engage in the process. We considered the challenges, too—the few challenges we understood at the time—not the least of which was, what if the flour doesn't perform in the bakery? Baking is hard work, and to add to the mix, the possibility that one's key ingredient may not work is no small thing. But from the moment we began milling in 2012, Dave shifted all of their whole-grain flours to Carolina Ground and created a bread with our high-extraction 85 bread flour that would become their signature North Carolina Sourdough (see page 120 for the recipe). "In one sense, it was an easy decision," he explains, "as for Flat Rock Village Bakery, it has always been about the ingredients." Flat Rock was the first bakery to make such a bold commitment. I ask Dave why he stepped in with both feet—because at the time, this really was no-man's-land—and he replies, "As nervous as I was, it seemed like a good thing to stand behind, in the sense that it seemed important to what we were doing as a small business." Dave has a degree in economics, and so I'm curious what drew him to baking. He tells me he liked that "baking turned nothing into something, and it brought pleasure to people." Dave spent the first eleven years working as a baker for others, until 2005 when he partnered with Scott Unfried, the founder of Flat Rock Village Bakery.

Scott opened the bakery in 2001. His degree was in accounting, though he realized, while working as an editor of math software in the San Francisco Bay Area, that he was not suited for a desk job; in his free time, he visited bakeries. He also sought out Alan Scott and worked with him building an oven at a residential location in Sonoma County, took baking classes at the

California Culinary Academy, and staged at Wild Flour Breads, a wood-fired destination bakery and garden located in Freestone, California. Eventually, a move back east to be closer to family brought him to North Carolina.

Inspired by the concept of a destination bakery, Scott opened Flat Rock Village Bakery in the tiny historic village of Flat Rock, North Carolina, which is home to the Flat Rock Playhouse, North Carolina's state theater, and to the Carl Sandburg Home, a National Historic Site. At the time, the village of Flat Rock had no center; Flat Rock Village Bakery became its nucleus. Herein lies the transformative nature of a bakery—it can change a place.

Initially the bakery just had a walk-up window where customers could come to buy three varieties of hand-kneaded, wood-fired-oven-baked bread. Indoor seating and then outdoor seating were eventually added. And the menu grew to include pastry and pizza and more varieties of bread. Scott's vision was a place for people to gather for coffee and a scone, to meet friends for a pizza, or to pick up their weekly bread.

Scott and Dave's partnership enabled them to expand their concept into a restaurant in the adjacent town of Hendersonville, where there were very few options for quality food at the time. They eventually opened Fletcher Village Bakery in Fletcher, on the northeast end of the county, which had none of the charm of Flat Rock. It was to be their commissary bakery, enabling them to move pastry production out of the cramped Flat Rock space. But the bakery in Fletcher, like the original space, grew into more than that, with added seating and a full lunch menu, motivated by the same intentions of creating a place where very little existed—or, just as Dave had described baking, "turning nothing into something."

Choosing to create new pathways, like opening a bakery on a less traveled road, and committing to flour grown and ground regionally, instead of taking the worn path of business as usual, is a transformative act; it is taking an active role in creating the place we wish to live in.

◆ ◆ ◆

There's a little fairy-tale twist to this story. Scott and I were briefly the only two wood-fired-oven businesses in Western North Carolina. We maintained a mutual admiration and respect for each other over the years, though we rarely saw one another; we were both busy running our respective bakeries and being parents. But twelve years after meeting, we ran into each other at a cyclocross clinic. (Cyclocross is a form of bicycle racing, sort of like a steeplechase on bikes—there's something about bakers and bikes.) Neither of us knew the other was a cyclist, let alone racing cyclocross (this was a very brief stint for me). A few weeks later, we ran into each other at his bakery. I showed up to get bread from Dave for a demonstration and talk I was giving, and Scott was working at the bench, shaping loaves, something he had not done in years, but they were down a baker and he was filling in. We decided to share a ride to Winston-Salem for the next cyclocross race. And then we began dating. And now he is my husband, which has been the biggest (and most wonderful) transformation in both our lives.

OWL Bakery

Maia Surdam started baking while working on her PhD in US history. Her gravitation from the intellectual toward the tactile began with gardening and then developed into an interest in cooking, as she learned to cook the foods that grew in her garden. And from cooking came an interest in learning to bake. These activities helped her stay sane during the academic rigors of her graduate work, which focused on industrial agriculture and its effect on rural communities and on the people doing the work of farming. As she delved into the history of farming and farm workers, including that of the migrant families and women and children and older people who worked in the fields together, and explored how domestic responsibilities and manual labor intertwined in the fields, she herself experienced the visceral work of growing, cooking, eating, and sharing food. She had every intention of continuing on an academic track and becoming a professor, but as she was writing her dissertation in 2008, the economy crashed, derailing her well-laid plans.

A move to Asheville was prompted by her her partner, Dave (a historian who she'd met in her graduate program), who had friends in the area. After completing her dissertation, with a historian's craving to understand the history of Appalachia—the region in which they had chosen to reside—Maia began reading the Foxfire books. Published in the 1970s, these books tell of mountain wisdom, community, and self sufficiency. Maia learned about the tradition of making an apple stack cake, which, she says, "really appealed to me because it's such a story of people being resourceful. This is a simple cake of many layers that would be made for a celebration. Whoever was hosting the celebration would provide the filling, and the people that came to the celebration would bring the layers, so the whole community together made this cake. I thought it was such a beautiful tradition."

Soon after, Maia picked up a copy of the *Mountain Xpress*, Western North Carolina's weekly arts and entertainment newspaper; on the front cover was a picture of Susannah Gebhart, founder of OWL Bakery, holding an apple stack cake, with the headline "Preserving Appalachian Flavors." The story's focus was the Appalachian Food Storybank, which Susannah had started in 2011 as an initiative of Slow Food Asheville's Heritage Foods Committee. Susannah had studied food anthropology in college, and while living and working in Sylva, North Carolina, she'd gotten to know the old timers at the farmers' market. After moving to Asheville, she learned that many of them had passed away; regretting not having the opportunity to hear more of their stories

and record them, she began the oral history project. Maia had learned to do oral histories during graduate school; seeing the article, she thought, "Here's a baker who was interested in history and also doing oral history projects about food, which is where my interests had all come together at that point in my life." Maia reached out to Susannah, and they hit it off.

At the time, Susannah's OWL Bakery (OWL stands for Old World Levain) was just her, working out of a tiny rented kitchen, with weekly offerings and a rich and poetic newsletter. On Valentine's Day, when Susannah had more orders than she could fulfill by herself, she hired Maia to assist. Valentine's Day happens to be Maia's birthday, so it was especially significant, and the two started working together regularly after that. Maia began helping out as Susannah's business grew, and Susannah told Maia about her dream to turn OWL into a brick and mortar bakery. Maia became a partner in the business, and in the spring of 2016, they opened their newly expanded iteration of OWL.

For the first nine to twelve months the bakery was open, Maia spent most evenings mixing bread dough. She embraced the repetition of it, got to know bread, and found that she loved it, and although she learned how to make everything they offered, it was bread she ended up drawn to the most. As a historian, the act of baking bread brought in a whole new dimension for her: "It's history that's at the core of human civilization, and it's visceral and has to do with bodies and myth and labor and all of these things that I'd studied in school, but so much more expansive than that. What I've learned about industrialization in terms of the vegetable industry in the Midwest and Texas helps me understand where we are with bread and milling and growing grains and what was lost. When farming was more localized, those activities brought different people together and so the farmers were not disconnected from the people that ran the mill or sold their product. There's this social cohesion that really became part of making food in agricultural communities, and then as industrialization came, not only did it change how labor was structured and what the daily lives of workers looked like, but it also changed the social fabric. I think that's one of the things that seems really rich and rewarding—that we can look back and understand more about how people used to do things and choose which methods could be sustainable for the world we're living in today, and then think about how that can enrich our connection to each other in different areas. History is not just about getting stuck in the past; it can provide a map for us. for the present"

Asheville Bread Festival

The first Asheville Bread Festival took place in 2004. Husband and wife bakers Steve Bardwell and Gail Lunsford organized this one-day event, inviting bakers from throughout Western North Carolina. None of us bakers quite knew what this would be, but we brought bread, and customers came—an overwhelming number of hungry, very excited customers. It was clear that this was going to become something. Steve organized a dinner for all the bakers that evening, after the festival wrapped up. It was the first time many of us had ever met. The night began with polite exchanges; this was our competition. But as wineglasses were filled, conversations began to unfold. A common thread connected all of us—we were bakers, that unique slice of humans who would choose to rise before the sun and work long hours for a humble living. We shared a common respect for one another and became friends that evening. Fast-forward five years, and those same bakers would pull chairs into a circle and discuss the idea of working directly with grain growers here in the South. Three years after that, Carolina Ground was born.

Steve and Gail have since stepped down as the festival's organizers and I've taken an active role in their stead, along with my cohorts Cathy Cleary, Rich Orris, and Joe Bowie. The event has grown considerably over the years, expanding to include a bread fair, workshops for home bakers, and a day-long master class for professional bakers. We are striving to bring diversity to this festival, hoping to cultivate a space that draws more people of color and women in the roles of instructor, vendor, and/or participant, as the demographic surrounding artisan bread has historically been as white as the flour. But this is no longer the case. Just as our breads have continued to evolve—incorporating regional flour and more whole grains—so too has the fabric of the artisan bakers' community.

La Farm Bakery: Lionel Vatinet

CARY, NORTH CAROLINA

Lionel Vatinet always tells his students, "Do not blame the ingredients." This was something instilled in him during his seven years of apprenticeship in France as part of Les Compagnons du Devoir, the centuries-old French guild of artisans. From the age of seventeen, traveling throughout France, changing cities each year to learn from a different master baker, Lionel was used to having a mill supporting him as a baker within the city, town, or region where he was living and baking; there was always a relationship with the mill in the vicinity of the bakery. This was not what he found when he came to America in 1991.

Lionel would spend the next eight years traveling, teaching baking, and consulting for bakeries throughout America, a Frenchman bestowing his baking tradition on a country in need of assistance. At the time, very little had been published on artisan baking, and what was available was not in English. Lionel was a direct link to the Old World, of artisan guilds preserved through the tradition of passing knowledge from master to student. He helped open the San Francisco Baking Institute as part of its inaugural faculty in 1996, and coached Team USA in the Coupe du Monde de la Boulangerie (World Cup of Baking) in 1999, the same year the US took gold as a team for the first time. Through his consulting work, he met his wife, Missy, and they decided to plant roots in this country, opening La Farm Bakery in Cary, North Carolina, in 1999.

Those of us who had come together in early 2009 to discuss the possibility of launching this mill did so in the wake of a profound rise in the price of wheat; very real economic uncertainties motivated us to action. But when Lionel became part of the conversation, he was motivated by something different. Lionel saw the opportunity to re-create what he had experienced in France, and as a member of Les Compagnons du Devoir, he stood by his pledge to give back to his profession. I brought flour samples for him to test. He reflects, "The results were incredible! This is the beauty of knowing your farmer and your miller."

Lionel had an intrinsic understanding of the value of what we set out to build between farmer, miller, and baker here in the South, grounded in his own tradition and experience in France. La Farm would play an instrumental role during our nascent stage, pushing us forward and validating our efforts. They shifted all their whole-grain flour—whole wheat and whole rye—to our flour, creating their Piedmont Loaf (page 116), Rye Hand Pies (page 190) and Rye Chocolate Chip Sablés (page 193) to showcase these flours. Lionel and Missy insisted on meeting our grower, Billy Carter, and wheat breeder Dr. David Marshall, and they brought this story back to their customers, as education is part of the guild pledge that Lionel lives by. Lionel jumped at the opportunity to test flour for the mill and to test flour for Dr. Marshall, as we continue to explore the nuances of flavor between experimental varieties.

Having a relationship with millers and growers in the region has enabled him to continue to use his profession to impact his community. "As bakers, we deal with the weather every single day. The farmer does the same thing. And the flour may be from a crop during a dry season, or rainy season. We're the alchemists who adapt to these changing ingredients and seasons. The dough is never going to be the same, but in a skilled bakers hands, it can be transformed. This is the challenge and the beauty of the bread baker, but our biggest challenge is to continue to educate the consumer."

Boulted Bread

RALEIGH, NORTH CAROLINA

I ask Joshua Bellamy, co-owner of Boulted Bread, what he loves most about baking. There's a long pause, and I realize he's overwhelmed with emotion. He says, "I try really hard not to think about that question much at all in my life because—" (There's another long pause, and co-owner Sam Kirkpatrick interjects, "This is one of those questions where you instantly have Joshua crying.") Joshua continues: "'Attracted' is not the right word, but I'll say it because I don't know a better word. I'm attracted to the whole process of baking so intimately that if I evaluate it or try and study the whys too much, I'm afraid I'll lose it. But there are a few things: building something and growing something on a daily basis is really attractive to me. My dad builds houses. As a child, watching him turn a wooden log into a home and then a family lives there was really cool, but that took six months, and I was less patient. This takes every twenty-four hours and the cycle repeats, so I've been getting to experience that magic and adjust it every twenty-four hours. It's a distinct part of the process that I love."

Sam is not a baker, but he is like the salt in bread, enabling all the other ingredients to perform well. Sam had planned to be a high school English teacher, to give back to his community in this way, but the 2008 economic crisis (and ensuing layoffs) altered the course of his life. Yet his core intentions have remained the same, just applied in a different way—to building community through this bakery. Joshua reflects, "Sam allows us to have a macro perspective on things, on Raleigh, on the way the shop feels, the way the customers see the shop, which has been invaluable." When I ask Sam what his role is at Boulted, he says, "What comes naturally to me is helping people be their best selves, and it's really fun when you can do that behind a product that's screaming to be shown off, like 'help free me,' and I get to nudge it along to be free. I get a big kick out of that."

Chicken Bridge Bakery

PITTSBORO, NORTH CAROLINA

Milo points to the loaf of naturally leavened 100 percent whole-wheat bread sitting on the stainless-steel table and emphatically states that this is his favorite bread. He tells me he eats a slice of this bread every day, toasted, with honey and butter. Milo is six years old.

Simon is fourteen and passes on the opportunity to have his picture taken alongside his dad and brother in front of their cottage bakery. He is very much a part of this place, though. He grew up helping out around the bakery, and this past summer he worked as his dad's assistant, dividing and shaping dough, unloading bread from the oven, and packaging the loaves.

Mom (and pastry chef) is out on deliveries.

This is Chicken Bridge Bakery. Located in a residential neighborhood in Pittsboro, North Carolina, a small town on the outskirts of Raleigh-Durham, this home-based, wood-fired-brick-oven bakery owned and operated by husband-and-wife team Rob and Monica Segovia-Welsh is more than simply a profession—this bakery is their life. Rob admits there really is no clear divide between their home life with their two sons, Simon and Milo, and bakery life—"they're absolutely entwined." He says that in this way, they have more in common with their farmer friends than with other brick-and-mortar bakeries. The bakery's relationship with farmers has been part of their story since day one, when they launched as a community-supported bread (CSB) program in 2007.

◆ ◆ ◆

I ask Rob what he love most about baking, and even after thirteen years of wood-fired-oven baking, he replies, "I still think that the most exciting thing to me continues to be that every day is different, that every flour is different, every grain is different, and just as you grow as a person, you grow as a baker. There are new yardsticks or new goals always, because it seems like when you start out as a baker, you just have this picture in a book, like this is what I'm aiming for, this is what I want it to be, but as you develop as a baker and get into techniques and the science of it all and the creativity of it all, you can find yourself developing your own idea of what you want to be striving toward and I feel like that's the thing about baking that's exciting. If I make one loaf that I'm super proud of, like this is it, I can pretty much guarantee that the next ten loaves are going to be like, ah, I could have done better, but rather than feeling demoralized by this, it is kind of an everyday way of learning you can do better."

Weaver Street Market Bakery:
A Cooperative Model

HILLSBORO, NORTH CAROLINA

"What does it look like to be a baker at fifty-five if one doesn't own the building or have some stake in a business that can provide beyond a salary or an hourly wage?"

I was asked this question by a baker in his early thirties at the end of his eight-hour shift, which had begun at 2 a.m. I think the question was rhetorical. He'd been a baker for close to a decade and is talented and committed, but three years earlier, he became a father, which changed the equation for him.

A few days before that conversation, I sat down with baker Jon McDonald of the Weaver Street Market Bakery, the bakery end of Weaver Street Market, a cooperatively owned grocery and bakery in Hillsboro, North Carolina. Jon shared with me Weaver Street's mission, which seeks to address the full picture—to provide for both the community they serve as well as for those doing the serving and baking. For Jon, who is also in his early thirties, this has meant a viable and lasting livelihood as a baker.

◆ ◆ ◆

Weaver Street is differentiated from other co-ops by its particular form of cooperative structure. Most grocery store co-ops are owned only by their shoppers, but Weaver Street's equity is split equally between worker-owners and consumer-owners. Jon reflects, "That makes it a really unique place to be a worker." The workers have strong representation on the market's board, and when there is a profit, the board decides what to do with it. If they declare a dividend, it is split equally between the worker-owners and the consumer-owners. The workers' dividend is based on hours worked that year, and the money is held in an internal account at the co-op; when a worker-owner leaves, they receive all that money. Jon explains, "We have some people who have been working for twenty or thirty years who have $30,000 in the Weaver Street Bank. And so having that as a foundation, inside of the bakery, enables us to hire really good people and keep them. I feel it's unique that we are able to do artisan bread at the scale that we do it and still attract bakers that are interested in pushing the craft. They're not just grunt workers. They really care about the co-op mission, and they really care about the role the bakery plays in the co-op and take a lot of pride in what they do. And so that makes it a really fun place to work."

◆ ◆ ◆

Our flour was a natural fit for Weaver Street, guided by their mission to support local "by the community, and for the community." Jon recalls, "It seemed the simple, obvious choice was to switch our whole wheat and whole rye to stuff that's grown right around the corner"—a goodly amount of our grain is grown less than an hour from Weaver Street Market Bakery—"that's milled in the same state, and if we need to work through the process of making the breads a little different, we can handle that because we have skilled bakers. And it's made it more exciting for the bakers and the customers because you can know you're working with a product that's unique and close to home. It's totally in line with our co-op values, supporting farmers, supporting the local economy, and it has ended up being a very rewarding transition, resulting in new products, like our dark rye (page 166). That bread came about because we had this Wrens Abruzzi rye. The bread literally arose out of the grain itself; there's not that many breads that are developed in that way."

Carolina Ground began with a vision similar to Weaver Street's, which was about building something in order to create the kind of place we want to live in. Weaver Street's buying power has had a real impact on our ability to succeed, helping us reshape the food landscape by enabling us to increase our acreage with Southern growers. They recently opened their fourth location, and for the opening ceremony, the mayor of Raleigh, along with Weaver Street's founder and General Manager Ruffin Slater and other co-op owners, broke a six-foot-long baguette instead of doing a ribbon cutting. Jon reflects, "We want to be a sustainable marketplace—intentionally a marketplace—not just a market. We want to be a gathering place, sort of that third space for people to have good experiences with their families and have it all centered around food, and then we want the co-op to be the center of the community; and bread is such an emblem of that."

Beach House

BRADENTON BEACH, FLORIDA

I quickly scribble down the phrase *amplification and modulation.* This is something Ed Chiles says when we first meet at Beach House, his oceanfront restaurant. He is on fire, talking about oyster shell recycling and building new oyster habitat. He points to the restaurant's amber-glassed deck lights, which ensure that turtle hatchlings, guided by moonlight and starlight, are not thrown off course by the artificial lighting, leading to their death. And then he mentions kitchen culture and team building, and I follow him back to the kitchen. He shows me the dish pit, where food scraps from dirty dishes are scraped. The 55-gallon barrel of food waste will go to Gamble Creek Farm (owned by Ed's company, the Chiles Group) to be composted and the compost mixed back into the soil. The farm grows certified organic produce for Ed's restaurants: Beach House, Mar Vista, and Sandbar. We drive over to Gamble Creek in Ed's Tesla and he talks about Seminole pumpkins and serving acorn-finished wild boar, and about bottarga, salt-cured and sun-dried striped gray mullet roe, wild-caught and produced a few miles away.

Teddy Louloudes is his head baker at Beach House, and Teddy is the reason I am here. He sources our flour to use in his Ciabatta Sandwich Rolls (page 127), his Hemp Crisp Breads (page 128), and anywhere else he can integrate flavor-forward flour. Teddy is a native of Bradenton Beach and worked at Beach House as a teenager, returning to bake at the restaurant after college and culinary school. Ed allowed him to start the bread program for Beach House, and when they began a weekly farmers' market at Gamble Creek Farm, it was Teddy's breads that drew people. *Amplification and modulation.* It means to increase the strength of a signal while also enabling the signal to travel a longer distance.

Harry Peemoeller

CHARLOTTE, NORTH CAROLINA

Carolina Ground began with a small group—in Western North Carolina—that helped bring the idea to life. We had numerous meetings. We shared a vision. These bakeries replaced some or all of their Midwest-grown whole-grain flours with our North Carolina–grown stone-ground whole-grain flours; some created breads specifically inspired by this flour. But outside this core group, it was a slow climb with plenty of challenges to overcome, from infrastructural to cultural, both on the farms and in the bakeries. To convince another bakery that they should give up the flour they were using and use our flour instead was not that simple. To understand the value of what we were trying to do with this mill would take some time; this was a very different kind of conversation than bakers were used to having with their millers. But early on, there were a few people who helped push us forward, lending some validity to what we were doing. Harry Peemoeller was one of those people.

Harry understood this mill because he had lived the story I was trying to tell. As I was attempting to piece together the past—what this farmer-miller-baker relationship had once looked like—Harry was cheering us on, asserting the value of local grains. He was in the ideal position to do so, too, as senior pastry and bread instructor at Johnson & Wales University's Charlotte campus. To educate the next generation of bakers on the value of whole grains and local flours was a fairly new concept in the culinary world, traditionally dominated by white flour, but Harry knew that this was the direction forward.

Harry first learned of our mill not long after competing in the 2012 Coupe du Monde de la Boulangerie (World Cup of Baking), a prestigious, invitation-only competition that takes place every four years in Paris. He was part of the three-person Bread Bakers Guild Team USA, which placed second overall. During the competition, Harry's teammate Michael Zakowski pushed the envelope with his use of whole-grain flours, and this reignited something in Harry, bringing up memories from his youth of his stepfather's bakery in northern Germany, where the flour mill was located next door and all the breads were made from freshly stone-ground whole-grain flour. Harry tells me, "I thought, 'What am I doing over here! I need to go back to my roots.'"

* * *

Harry grew up in a small town outside of Hamburg, Germany, on a farm with a thatched roof home and an outhouse. His father farmed during the Green Revolution, which meant new seed varieties, heavy use of nitrogen fertilizer, and an urge to get as much yield as possible. This was a farming system that sought to end famine in India, but its impact on Harry's village

in Germany was less promising, he recalls, "When it came to spring, the whole town was smell-
ing like these chemicals."

Harry's mother grew up in a farming family and would tell him how when she was a little
girl, they had had a horse and a wagon, and her parents had harvested their grains—wheat
and rye—by hand, forming shocks in the field that they would then thresh. She remembered
she had to wear gloves because of the thistles bundled in with the wheat. And Harry vividly
remembers a conversation she had with his father: "She said to him, 'What happened to the
thistles? I don't see any of these weeds, and thistles especially, anymore. What happened to
the balance between what we want and what nature has, because they're not bad, they're
contributing something to the ground.'" She convinced his father to stop using the chemicals,
and instead, he employed rich crop rotations, growing rye and wheat and potatoes and beans;
they also raised animals. When the crops were ready, Harry's family would harvest what they
needed; afterward, the townspeople would come into the family's fields and take home the rest
of the harvest, offering what they could in compensation. He reflects, "It was the best upbringing I could have had."

When Harry was ten, his parents got a divorce. Eventually, his mother remarried a baker.
Harry explains that his mother, having grown up during wartime, felt that another war was
to be expected, so she told Harry and his four brothers, "When the next war comes, you don't
want to be a tax accountant, you need to do something with your hands—a farmer, a baker, or
a butcher—because these were people that had something to eat." And so he and his brothers
all became bakers. When he was a teenager, he began apprenticing in his stepfather's bakery,
with the stone mill next door. He recalls, "We'd get freshly milled flour, and I remember when
I opened a bag, the smell, I was transported back to my father's tractor. When he harvested rye,
that's how it smelled. It was always amazing. And then we made the bread. We made hundreds
of volkorn and michebrot; there was not so much white bread. Our bread was something that
sustains, that keeps you full. All the farms had lots of kids over there, and they needed bread
that would feed you."

Eventually Harry was drafted into the German Navy and traveled around the world for
two years as a radio operator on a destroyer. When he returned, his stepfather was ready to
give up the bakery, and he encouraged Harry to get his master's certification in bread baking, a level of study one must achieve in Germany in order to have apprentices. He became a
German Master Baker, but he had traveled and seen the world; with his master certification,
he wanted to do something different with the bakery, but his stepfather was married to tradition. Harry felt he needed to leave Germany for a time to try this on his own. It was 1989, and
he was offered a one-year position in a place he'd never heard of—Orlando, Florida. He recalls,
"I thought I'd died and gone to heaven. America! It was like [*in an affected American accent*],
'We don't care, if it ain't broken, break it and put it together new, and if people like it, you've
got something!' It was really crazy—I was like, what a country!"

In Orlando, Harry worked in a bakery that supplied the Walt Disney Company, but eventually he grew dissatisfied because, as he recalls, "The mouse was in charge; everything for the mouse." Harry had fled the rigidity of centuries-old tradition in baking only to find himself creatively stunted by Mickey Mouse. He did meet his wife in Orlando, though, and they left for a job opportunity in Miami, where he became lead baker at Biga Bakery, the first artisan bread bakery in Miami, creating high-quality European-style breads. When the bakery was sold to a consortium, Harry stayed on and was sent to Mexico City to learn about the breads of Mexico so the bakery could market to Miami's ever-growing Latin American community. Harry loved the work, loved to travel and learn and bake, but he was now also a father, and he was not able to strike a healthy balance between his roles as a baker, husband, and father. There was a job opening at Johnson & Wales University's campus in Norfolk, Virginia, and his wife encouraged him to apply. He got the job, and in 2002, the family moved to Norfolk. It was not an easy move for him, but he says, "Looking back, I see that it was the next step. I could now have more time with my family, I could enjoy baking again." And it closed a loop—when Harry was in the German Navy twenty-two years earlier, the first harbor his ship landed in in America was Norfolk.

In 2004, Johnson & Wales closed its Norfolk campus, consolidating with their Charlotte campus, which brought Harry to North Carolina. Although Harry says that when he first began teaching, he was not very good, I find that hard to believe. I have witnessed Harry in action, and he is an inspiring teacher, which is why Carolina Ground was so fortunate that he reached out to us for flour in 2012, the first year we were milling.

With such a rich and long baking history, I wonder if Harry still loves baking, but when I ask what he loves most about it, he smiles and tells me, "What I love is that it never gets old. I like the magic of fermentation. It's like a religion. When they tell you, if you're a good boy you're going to go to heaven, and if you're a good baker, you follow the rules, you are going to bread heaven. So you've got to trust the process. When I bake at home, sometimes I just want to go back in time a little bit and create something that wakes up memories, this aroma that smells like what I remember of my grandma's home and definitely remember from the bakery that I worked in, and the memories it evokes from my childhood."

Jackie Vitale

CAPTIVA ISLAND, FLORIDA

Scrolling through Instagram, I come to a photo of a naturally leavened whole-grain bread sliced open to expose the crumb, posted by Jackie Vitale (@SunshineandMicrobes). In the caption, Jackie opines, "Crumb shots on Instagram stress me out the way that a photo of an Instagram influencer lounging on a beach in a bikini might stress other people out. Just as I have no interest in scrolling through carefully staged photos of homogeneously pretty ladies, I have mostly scrubbed my feed of impossibly open-crumb white bread. What I'd love to see more of is the type of bread that I make and enjoy eating. Humble, flavorful loaves made with stone-ground whole-grain flours."

Jackie is formerly one of the owners of Ground Floor Farm, an urban farm, food establishment, and community space in Stuart, Florida (now under new ownership at Colab Farms), where she used our flour in all of their baking. She then brought our flour with her to her new position as resident chef at the Rauschenberg Residency on Captiva Island. She is co-creator of the Florida Fermentation Fest and co-author of the food blog, Sunshine + Microbes.

I ask Jackie what she loves most about baking, but also what she loves about fermentation, because this is the larger theme for her, both literally and figuratively. "It feels like a good reminder that I can do my best and I can create the right circumstances, but at the end of the day, I'm not in charge. These invisible creatures are in charge," she says, referring to microorganisms, "and they might decide to do a different thing. I can try and create the right boundaries for getting the result that I want, but there is a kind of allowing the world to take charge and to remember that I'm a small part in all of this and I can do my best but can't control everything. I grew up very anxious, and I think working with food, and lots of therapy, have helped me let go of a lot of that. And to know that there is joy in the mistakes."

Anisette

RALEIGH, NORTH CAROLINA

Unlike most of the bakeries we work with, which are bread-driven, Anisette is driven by something less tangible. Stepping into their tiny neighborhood bakeshop in Raleigh, I am met with lovely sweet buns glistening with sugar, piles of small biscotti-like cookies called cantucci (see page 154), slices of cream-filled cakes, pie, the smell of coffee, and something else that I cannot quite put my finger on until I sit down with Nicole and Jason Evans Groth, the wife-and-husband team that conceived of this enchanting bakeshop, and ask what this is all about.

Nicole sought out our flavor-forward flour to play a prominent role in her clearly delineated approach to baking. "I'm always thinking about how to best make the recipe fit the flour." She expounds, "What I think of as 'classic' recipes/flavors are often traditional Italian recipes—much of the inspiration for Anisette is from a few trips to Northern Italy and Istanbul—or totally nostalgic/traditional American recipes, like something adapted from *Joy of Cooking*. I like the idea of making something that's totally familiar to people but that often tastes like a bland sugar bomb, and giving them a version that's been made with really beautiful/delicious/healthful ingredients and actually tastes like those ingredients!"

I ask Nicole what she loves most about baking. She has to think about it, like she's sorting it out, and then she says, "Oh man, there's so many layers." Jason chimes in, "She mentions her Aunt Della a lot, how she was her touchstone for flavors and how flavors and memory are so wrapped together, and so a lot of the flavors and the foods that she shares with others evoke memories that are pleasant for her, and she wants to share that experience with others. When I'm working the counter and people say, 'this reminds me of X,' I feel like we've accomplished this goal. It's like when people connect through the music we play (Nicole and Jason are also musicians) and they tell you so, it's not because you're a star, but because you shared this thing that you can't really speak out loud and people have understood it. The same thing happens when people experience food that way." Jason turns to Nicole and says, "You talk about evoking memories or making nostalgia not just a thing that makes us feel good in the moment but actually helps us to understand the present. I think Nicole is really good at expressing feeling through her food, and it's often read by new customers as nostalgia at first, but then moves into more of a relationship, a common ground between the baker and the customer."

And then Nicole adds, "Yes, it feels like sharing feelings with people."

Joe Bowie

COLUMBIA, SOUTH CAROLINA

My initial introduction to Joe Bowie was via his Instagram moniker, @brooklynbreadnerd. He started buying flour from us through our online retail store, then tagging us in pictures of what appeared to be professionally executed breads and pastries baked in his tiny Brooklyn apartment. Instagram had launched just a year and a half before we began milling, and it became this vehicle that pushed us forward by way of the bakers, providing a platform for us and any talented bakers using our flour. I'd imagined @brooklynbreadnerd was a really serious, super-devoted, avid home baker. When he posted an image of some incredible-looking salted chocolate rye brownies, I wanted the recipe (see page 185), so I sent him a message, asking him to be the first guest blogger on a recipe blog I was trying to maintain.

My second introduction to Joe Bowie was as one of our wholesale customers, buying flour for his Cola Bread Club in Columbia, South Carolina. Joe had moved down from Brooklyn to join his husband, who had accepted a position as a professor at the University of South Carolina. I wasn't too surprised to learn that Joe was, in fact, a professionally trained baker, having studied artisan bread baking at the French Culinary Institute (now the International Culinary Center) in 2011.

Baking was Joe's second career. He'd been a professional dancer for twenty-five years, and his shift into professional baking happened by way of a grant from an organization called Career Transitions for Dancers. Joe would spend the next six years baking in various kitchens in New York. He worked at Le Pain Quotidien fresh out of school, then went on to work for world-renowned chef Daniel Boulud, Dean & DeLuca, the Brooklyn-based bakery Ovenly, and bagel maven Melissa Weller. And he began engaging with different flours from regional mills.

As a child, Joe had a lot of food allergies. "I couldn't eat bread as a kid. So watching how one's diet can change how one responded to things was really important to me. I didn't feel the draw to just bake cool things, it wasn't just about that for me. I wanted to bake things that helped people and made people feel like they were putting something good in their bodies."

About this transition from New York to launching his bread club in Columbia, South Carolina, Joe explains, "You have to find a balance between your audience and your baking. I know that when I first came down here I was thinking, well, I would like for people to eat more whole grains—of course I cannot decide what they eat, but I wanted to keep it as local as possible because in addition to the nutritional thing, it was a flavor thing. And it's always easy to

stick whole grains into pastries, especially things that people are used to, like chocolate chip cookies, just finding really good combinations. I realized that with most of my subscribers, it's not until they taste something made with beautiful whole grains or beautiful flour that's local, that they realize it can taste like that."

I ask Joe what he loves most about baking. "I love that I can take four or five ingredients that look nothing like what it's going to turn out to be. I put them in a bowl, I mix them up, and it's science of course, but also it's like alchemy. I love that I can take flour, water, salt, and culture, mix it together, let it sit, with some stretch and folds, and then the next day I can bake a beautiful loaf of bread that looks nothing like those ingredients. And there is that moment—every time—you've watched it ferment, and then you shape it and you stick it in the fridge overnight, and score it, stick it in the combo cooker, and that moment when you take off the top [of the combo cooker] to let the crust form—every time, it never gets old, I'm like, 'Oh my! How beautiful.' And sometimes there's a little more or a little less oven spring but every time, it amazes me."

Joe's tone shifts as he speaks in more technical terms: "Everyone says the bread directs things, but there are variables we can control. I like that scientific aspect of it, too, that we're controlling these variables to try and create consistency. When I would teach I would tell my students, 'Here's why you weigh things: because you'll have a better chance of having consistency, even if you're just baking cookies.' And I tell people when they're baking bread, really keep track, because the bread doesn't rule; there are ways you can control it—you can put things in the fridge. You can control fermentation, and you can control your day. I tell my students, take the time, let it be a different thing, let the bread baking be a different thing. The only way to get good at it is through practice."

[NOTE: Joe has since relocated to Chicago, where he and his husband have taken positions at Northwestern University (Joe is teaching dance), though he is still baking up a storm.]

Albemarle Baking Company

Sitting in the retail side of Albemarle Baking Company, one can see into the pastry prep kitchen through windows that divide the retail space from the production. Beyond pastry prep, another set of windows provide a clear view of their massive multideck bread oven and, just above the oven, spanning 7 feet of the 10-foot width of the oven, is a steel sign with a message stamped out of the steel: *This Machine Surrounds Hate and Forces It to Surrender.* The sign was installed on the one-year anniversary of "Unite the Right," the Charlottesville white supremacist rally that resulted in the death of Heather Heyer. The street where she was run over, a short walk from the bakery, has been renamed Heather Heyer Street. The bakery was open during that weekend, as it had cake orders to fill: weddings on Friday and Sunday, and a fortieth wedding anniversary that Saturday night. This is a role that bakeries play in civil society: baking cakes for significant life events. Bread is the centerpiece for gatherings of friends and family. The concept of breaking bread is intrinsic to a balanced and healthy society, and one could not break bread without the baker.

◆ ◆ ◆

Gerry Newman began his baking career in 1981, as an apprentice for a Swiss Master Baker. "He took me in, he had a very suspect look, like, 'Here's another American that is not going to work hard,' and truth be told, about six months in I was ready to quit. He was unrelenting in what his demands were and he wasn't always kind about it. But when I told him this just wasn't working, he asked me in this really broken English, 'Gerry, how long it take to make a baby?' And when I said nine months, certain that my answer wasn't correct, he said, 'That's right. You're not going to learn how to bake in six months. Just relax and pay attention.' He believed in me and I relaxed and it started coming to me. I stayed for four years."

When asked what he loves most about baking, after this many years, Gerry replies, "It's very rewarding. And the difference between the bread side and pastry is that the pastry is pretty scientific: you've got to cook these ingredients at this temperature for this period of time; everything has to be done with these steps to follow; and with some variances they're not usually affected by any other thing. But there's nothing about bread that's the same every day or throughout the day, and you can't approach it like that, and so that part is nice, the attentiveness that you have to have to what you are doing, the stewardship that you have to have. And then this many years into it as well, to be with a lot of people who believe the same thing, that work with us, and especially the younger people that come in and work with us with that same passion, it's really nice."

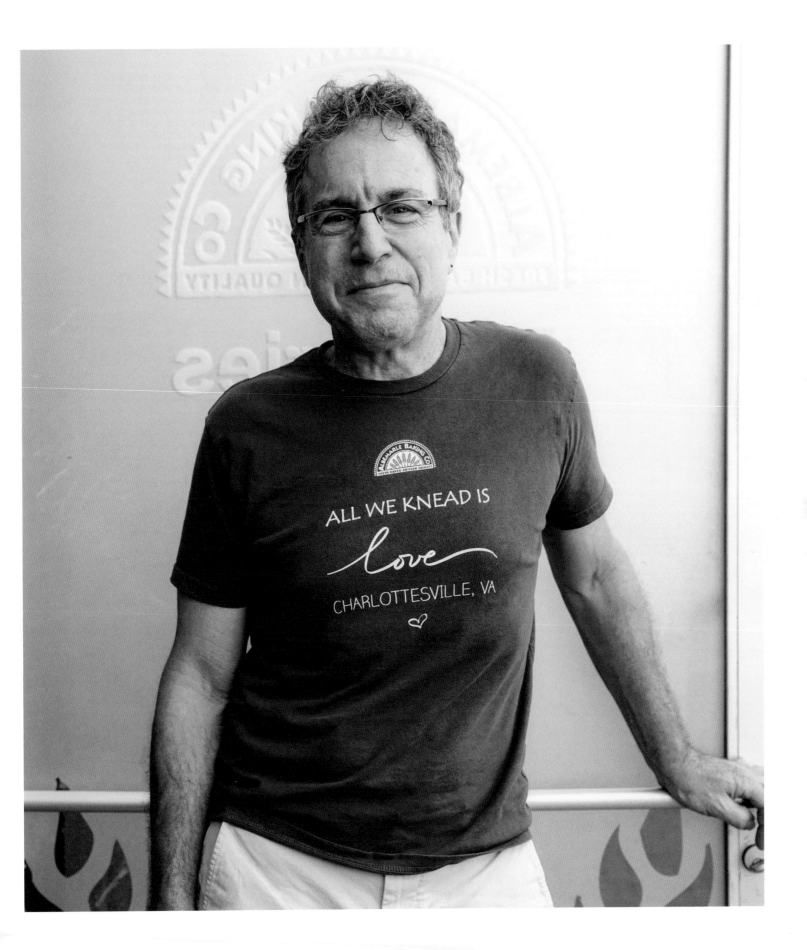

Betsy Gonzalez: Osono Bread

ATLANTA, GEORGIA

"In Latina culture, food is very much connected to family and community; you come together at the table," explains Betsy Gonzalez, Latina and first-generation American. Betsy grew up in Canton, Georgia, and was raised by a single mother. At an early age, ten or eleven, Betsy took an interest in baking. "We would go to la panadería every week and get tons of different baked goods—that is one of the first memories I have associated with bread." These trips ignited something within her: "I wanted to participate," she recalls. Her mother, who had always encouraged her to find a creative outlet, bought Betsy baking tools and books and gave her free rein to bake whatever she wanted.

Betsy baked throughout middle school and into high school, where she took all of the culinary programs available. She wanted to go to culinary school but they simply could not afford it, so she moved to Atlanta to attend Georgia State University and study journalism, though she had no clear ambitions or goals in the field. One day, she saw that there was a job opening for a front-of-house person at the Little Tart Bakeshop. She recalls, "The first time I walked into Little Tart, I was very much in awe of it, like, 'Oh wow, there's a real bakery in the city.'" Betsy applied for the job, and when she met the owner, Sarah O'Brien, she mentioned that she'd love to bake. The front-of-house position got her in the door, and eventually she made her way into the kitchen, reawakening her love of baking. Betsy worked at Little Tart for a couple of years and enjoyed the work, but a desire to learn the craft of bread baking tugged at her. She was specifically interested in working with sourdough or natural leavening and engaging with regional flours, but there were no bakeries in Atlanta at the time doing that kind of baking.

Through social media she gained access to the greater baking community, and Betsy contacted six bakers in six different countries: "The way I went about choosing the certain bakeries overseas was: Are they doing sourdough? Is bread their main thing? Are they using local flour or trying to incorporate it into their programs? That's the checklist I had."

Betsy would spend four months traveling and baking overseas, working twelve- to sixteen-hour days and learning her craft. She was exposed to rye breads for the first time at Riot Rye Bakehouse & Bread School in Cloughjordan, Ireland; she engaged with stone-ground British flours at Bread by Bike in London; and Spanish grains at Yellow Bakery in Barcelona. In Otzberg, Germany, she spent a week with Paul Lebeau at the headquarters of Mockmill, producers of countertop stone mills (see Resources, page 276). Paul gave Betsy the opportunity to engage with a variety of grains. "Paul was all about using freshly milled [flour] and using local grains, which got me excited as well," she says. "He introduced me to grains I did not even know existed." She spent a few days shadowing Maxime Bussy at Le Bricheton in Paris, a tiny operation inspired by the peasant baker movement in France, which started in the 2000s with the aim of reviving old seed varieties and baking methods. She traveled to Norway and spent a week at Ille Brød with Martin Ivar Hveem Fjeld, who uses only stone-ground organic Norwegian grain flours and mixes high-hydration doughs. "Spending time with him molded the idea for me that flour is as much of an ingredient as an apple for an apple pie. Flour is more than something that sits on a grocery store shelf, flour is more than a dry good." Her final stage was at Egt Brood in Genk, Belgium, where she worked alongside two women bakers: Tina, the owner, and Ceria. The bakery was just a short drive to the farmer and the miller who produced their flours. They baked with 100 percent rye and 100 percent spelt flours, which was a whole new experience for Betsy. She was thrown right into mixing dough, "three women just cracking it out. By the end I was not only mixing and shaping but also baking. So much more interesting than culinary school. My time with Tina really influenced what I do now because she also emphasized the need for local grain and that it's really up to us as local bakers to start that conversation. She definitely shaped a lot of my philosophies, she and Martin, because they were both 100 percent local. And then I had to go back home."

When she returned to the United States from her four months overseas, she was at a loss. "I'd been surrounded by these cultural norms of real bread, the concept of it, and local grain and local flour and things being fresh. I wanted to start a dialog with people here," she says. "Because at that time, I didn't even have any intentions of starting a business, I just wanted to bake and start a dialog with my family and my friends, that bread is more than just white flour. There's just so much more out there, and I wanted to share what I had learned overseas. But I was baking way more than I could eat, and more than my family and friends could eat, so then it was friends of friends, and delivering bread door-to-door throughout Atlanta."

She created her community supported bread (CSB) program without really knowing what it could mean: "I didn't really realize the emphasis of community behind it at the time, but I do now." She reached out to local business owners to see if they could act as drop-off locations and she found willing businesses at opposite ends of the city so both communities could have access to her bread. Word spread, and an urban farm reached out about adding her bread subscription to their existing CSA, with a pickup at their weekly urban farm stand located in a different section of Atlanta from her two CBS drop-off points. And she also started selling breads directly at the farm stand, engaging with customers who were buying their produce right where it was being grown. "All the vegetables are grown right there, and customers get to walk around this land, which furthers the idea of the importance of knowing where one's ingredients come from and knowing the people that are behind it all, and also honoring all the work that goes into it."

◆ ◆ ◆

Betsy's mother was born in Guatemala and her father in Mexico. She is a product of three countries, and Osono Bread is an amalgamation of her upbringing, her global baking community, her Atlanta community, and her relationships with farmers and millers. When I ask her what she loves most about baking, she closes the loop: "I like that baking not only provides a creative expression, but also the opportunity to be selfless in it and give to people. Being able to just provide, make a memory, whatever that may be."

Michael Matson

This mill would not exist without the bakers. But baker Michael Matson sees it the other way around: "Without Carolina Ground, I don't know what I would do, because this bakery would not be what I want it to be, it would not reflect the Southeast in grain. You allow me, aside from at certain times when things on the growing end get rough, to be a regional bakery. I get to work through all of the obstacles and experiments that come along with using flour from the region, while also getting incredible flavors and the ability to contribute to the regional economy. I get to be a part of the farmer-miller-baker chain in a way that many bakers around the country working with larger mills do not."

This was from an email Michael sent me in 2016, a few months after launching his micro-bakery in Nashville. His email continued with reflections on the current baking culture: "More and more bakers are beginning to mill in-house"—he, too, was vacillating over whether to go in that direction—"I love the process of milling. I like the work, I like the idea of working directly with growers, but based on my current experience trying to source local grain to mill myself, I'd be in the position of simply buying grain from the Midwest and Interior West to mill just for the sake of milling." He asked how I feel about the bakers who have chosen to mill in-house: "Are you thankful that more bakers are beginning to care more about this aspect of the process, or are these folks you see as potential customers that would help Carolina Ground continue to grow and thrive?"

Michael's email hits at the core of what and why we do what we do at Carolina Ground. He chose to allow us to be his miller, and his bakery to be part of the change we are trying to effect here in the South. Carolina Ground is proof that the whole is greater than the sum of its parts. And yet my answer to his question is that I think any approach to fresh flour is good. I think it further strengthens the ground beneath all of us working to rebuild regional grain economies because it's changing the conversation, transforming this once homogenous ingredient into a dynamic agricultural product. And yes, ideally one would hope that milling in-house would go hand in hand with an increased demand for regional grains, but none of this is simple, and it will not happen overnight. A mill like ours brings bakeries together, enabling them to become a formidable voice, creating a dependable market for our regional growers, but fortifying that market is diversity, so a farmer who is able to work directly with a baker milling in-house is a good thing, as it enables that farmer to fetch the highest price for his or her grain, with no middleman (or middlewoman). That single bakery, though, will likely not use as much grain as the farmer can grow, so having more than one market is ideal. To truly reshape the food landscape is going to take all of us—from small to medium bakeries milling in-house to regional mills like ours, specialty mills like Farm and Sparrow, and larger mills like Lindley Mills here in North Carolina, who include a local flour in their offerings.

Michael and I have continued to correspond over the years via text and email as he has transitioned from his own microbakery with a mobile wood-fired oven selling at farmers' markets to teaming up with Rolf and Daughters, a seasonally inspired farm-to-table Nashville restaurant that would eventually open Folk, the wood-fired pizza restaurant where Michael led the bread program, to his current iteration as Ornette Bread, located in a studio of an art gallery.

◆ ◆ ◆

I ask Michael what he loves most about baking and what drives him to bake. "I just love the act of baking most days, the tools, the honesty and physicality of it all, the tradition and history in it," he says. "It's not going anywhere, you know, and that's no small thing. And frankly, it's the only thing I've ever felt 'good' at, the intuition, the bodily memory is there. I just know it now. I know how to do it. That's not to say there isn't room to learn, it's just that I feel comfortable doing the work every day. I've learned what this labor means, and so the motivation comes in some sense, too, from the fact that I'm not certain there's anything else I can hold in that way. To me, that's special, I suppose, or at least a reason to forge ahead, regardless of the form." He tells me this through text. And then he says he needs to go put his son to bed. I tell him to enjoy these moments with his son, as children grow up faster than one can imagine, and to this he replies, "Ha, that's the only other thing I know, how fast it goes."

Christina Balzebre: Levee Baking Co.

NEW ORLEANS, LOUISIANA

As soon as Christina Balzebre graduated from Loyola University in New Orleans, she got a job at Satsuma Café, a small farm-to-table restaurant. She had decided she would get a full-time job working in a kitchen, and if she liked it, she'd keep doing it, and if she didn't like it, she'd go to graduate school. Her first position was as a juicer, and from there she progressed to line cook, and then a position for a baker opened up. She'd always loved baking and was given creative freedom. "We would get fresh stuff in and I could make whatever I wanted that was seasonal," she says. Three years later, she left the intimacy and seasonality of this little café and stepped into the corporate restaurant world in pursuit of a mentor to teach her the art of bread baking. "I went to stage (an unpaid internship) at a restaurant group in New Orleans," she recalls. "They had a commissary kitchen for all of their restaurants, and they were doing all of the bread and all of the pastry from scratch there, which is not that common for big restaurants to do." She found the mentor she was seeking and her stage turned into full-time employment, but they weren't making the kind of breads she wanted to be making, so she would go home at night after work and make the kind of bread that she wanted to be baking: 100 percent sourdough and incorporating whole grains. She eventually felt uninspired at work, so she started an Instagram account to pursue creative things and learn food photography, baking out of her tiny home kitchen and posting images of her baked goods on Instagram. Her project began to evolve into a little business doing wholesale for a small café and then making a wedding cake for a friend and pies for another wedding, and soon she was Levee Baking Co. She had an opportunity to do pop-ups every Saturday at a place called Mosquito Supper Club, owned by her former boss from Satsuma, and this offered her boundless opportunity for creativity and she incorporated what she'd learned at Satsuma, working with local and seasonal ingredients. She also sold at farmers' markets and was able to establish relationships with local growers.

For three months, Christina did pops-ups while also working full-time. But when she started making more money in a single day at the pop-ups than she was making in an entire week at work, she quit her job and Levee Baking Co. became her full-time gig.

Ten years after graduating, Christina launched Levee Baking Co.'s brick-and-mortar bakery on Magazine Street, with all of her farmer friends in attendance at the grand opening. Levee is part of a new wave of bakeries embracing seasonality and locality, inspiring employees, and educating customers.

Meghan Bourland: Meg's Bread

COOKEVILLE, TENNESSEE

"Bread dough is like how I wish clay would feel," explains Meghan Borland, the "Meg" of Meg's Bread. Meg is a ceramicist turned baker, though more accurately, she is an artist who changed her medium. On her application to become a Carolina Ground wholesale customer, she wrote, "The bakery will be a connection point between people and their food, a way to tell the story of the farmers who grow and of the baking process itself. Seasonal ingredients are the focal point to highlight a local producer; through this, a customer learns what's in season, who grew it, and why it tastes so good when it's fresh." And although she does not consider herself a farmer, farming was the catalyst for her transition from art studio to bakeshop and continues to inspire and inform her baking. Meg's husband, Luke, is the farmer.

♦ ♦ ♦

As a ceramicist making sculpture, Meg sought to engage all the senses. She experimented with using essential oils to add scent to ceramics, and she honed in on sound and feel through installations that required walking on ceramics. But when she started making pastries, she realized baking was the ideal medium: "I could put rosemary on top of something and you smell it and the texture of it and the way it looks and the way you hold it and the size, and so that was all of a sudden my aha, like, 'This is my ceramics now.'"

When I ask Meg what she loves most about baking, she responds, "I love being creative. And everything I do is in season, so I love that challenge, the restriction of what can I do with this and what accentuates that and what completes this whole circle. So for me it's kind of that creative puzzle of restrictions but then of what you can do within it. What my husband likes most is the preproduction, and I love the postproduction. There's magic in both sides. The magic of a seed to a vegetable, that's magic, and then there's another step of magic, like a sweet potato is so sweet when it's in season, you don't have to do much to it to make it the postproduction of a sweet potato galette or a sweet potato pie."

PART TWO

The Recipes

Tools and Technique

The following is intended to provide you with tools to enable you to dive into these recipes. An amazing amount has been published on bread baking in the last twenty years, so for more in-depth detail, please refer to the Resources section (see page 276), where I have listed my recommendations for further reading.

Measuring + Baking by Feel

Most of the world measures their ingredients by weight; in the United States, we still measure with cups. The problem with measuring by volume (cups) is that it is inherently imprecise, even with commodity roller-milled flour blended to specification, and an industry standard for the weight of a cup of roller-milled flour. Enter regionally stone-ground flour, whose lack of homogeneity is valued, where the weight of a cup of stone-ground flour varies from region to region and mill to mill, and the equation becomes even more challenging.

In bread baking, adjustments are made proportionately, and measuring by weight is pretty much essential. For this reason, in the following pages, all of the bread recipes require a digital kitchen scale. If you don't have a kitchen scale, please get one. They are inexpensive and a worthy addition to your kitchen.

In the following nonbread recipes, volume has been included as a secondary measure. If you are without a scale, use the Spoon and Sweep method to measure your flour (and cocoa): Pour your flour into a bowl and stir it a few times, then lightly spoon the flour into the measuring cup until the flour mounds to nearly overflowing (don't shake the cup or pack down the flour). Using a straightedge, cleanly level off the top of the flour, sweeping the straightedge over the top of the cup a few times. (Don't use this method for brown sugar. For brown sugar: firmly pack brown sugar into your measuring cup, using a straightedge to level it off. It should hold its shape when emptied into your bowl.)

All of the following recipes were written by weight, which means as long as one has a scale, flour from any regional mill can be used. If you want to use stone-ground flour in recipes written for roller-milled flour, simply use the weight measure, and if weight is not provided, follow the industry standard that 1 cup of roller-milled all purpose or bread flour weighs 125 grams per cup; and 1 cup of roller-milled pasty flour weighs 120 grams per cup.

Because the recipes were created with metrics as the primary measure, you'll find that volume equivalencies vary slightly across recipes. Sometimes ½ cup of butter will weigh a gram or two more or less in different recipes. This isn't an error. This is written so that those using the volume measures don't have to measure super precise quantities, such as ½ cup plus ¹⁄₁₆ teaspoon.

Beyond measure, even with the greatest precision, one may need to make adjustments (whether stone-ground or roller-milled). In bread applications, you may need to add or withhold some of the water (the value of becoming acquainted with Baker's Percentage, page 92) is having this easy tool at one's disposal to make adjustment to a bread formula). And in pastry applications, developing an intuitive sense for what something should look or feel like will help you engage not only with the recipe, but also with the ingredients themselves, giving you the confidence to add a splash of this or a pinch of that. Repetition will make you a better baker, and opting for freshly stone-ground flour will amplify the flavor of your resulting baked goods, whether a total success or a work in progress.

Baking Terminology

AUTOLYZE: This technique involves premixing your first two or three ingredients: flour and water, and sometimes leaven. The mixture is then covered and left to rest in the bowl for at least 20 minutes and up to 4 hours, or even longer (this longer period is without leaven). This process jump-starts fermentation by activating the amylase enzymes in the flour, which convert starch to sugar, which in turn feeds yeast. It also allows for improved absorption of water (hydration) in the dough. And it begins the process of gluten development.

COUCHE: A linen cloth used for the final proofing of shaped, unbaked loaves. The cloth is floured, and the shaped loaves are placed side by side on the cloth, with a folded crease of cloth dividing each.

HYDRATION: This simply refers to the liquid in a dough. On the ideal amount of hydration, Sharon Burns-Leader says, "Everyone and their mother has an opinion about which hydration is best. There is no 'best.' There's just bread."

LEAVEN: The substance that enables dough to develop into a risen loaf of bread is known as the leaven. This can be commercial baking yeast or a natural leavening agent such as sourdough. Although the term *sourdough* is used interchangeably to refer to natural leavening, not all natural leavening is technically sourdough, and thus not all sourdough is sour. We have provided more than one technique for making natural leavening; for simplicity's sake, *leaven* will be the term used in the following bread recipes when natural leavening is called for, as opposed to commercial baking yeast.

PRE-FERMENT: A portion of the dough that is made several hours before mixing the final dough.

PROOF: This is the final fermentation or rising of a shaped dough. This period allows the gases formed by fermentation to expand into a risen loaf. Aim for loaves to be 85 to 90 percent proofed when loading them into the oven; learning what this looks like takes some time and repetition. One approach to check if your dough is ready is with the pad of your finger, gently make an indentation, pressing down about ½-inch deep, in the center of your dough for 2 seconds. If the indentation quickly springs back, your dough is not ready. If it slowly and evenly retreats, leaving just a shadow of the indentation, then your dough is ready to load into the oven. If it does not spring back at all, the dough has overproofed, which will result in a flattened loaf, as the gluten strands have lost their strength.

SCALD: A portion of flour covered with boiling water and then allowed to soak for some number of hours is known as a scald. Scalding a portion of the flour to be used in a dough partially gelatinizes the flour's starches, contributing pliability to the dough. It also allows for increased hydration in the dough.

SCORE: The surface of proofed, shaped unbaked loaves is scored with a razor or other sharp blade before the dough goes into the oven to create an intentional pattern for expansion to occur.

SOURDOUGH DISCARD: This is what is removed from your sourdough before feeding your sourdough. It can either be composted or used in recipes such as Hemp Crisp Breads (page 128) or Mississippi Market Galettes (page 228).

WARM WATER: When warm water is called for, aim for 85°F to 90°F.

Equipment

BAKER'S LAME OR RAZOR BLADE: Used to score your proofed loaves.

BOWLS: I like stainless-steel bowls and am well served by a few small (4¾-inch) bowls and a couple medium (8-inch) and large (11-inch) ones.

DIGITAL SCALE: I prefer OXO scales, but everyone has their favorite.

DOUGH KNIFE (AKA BENCH KNIFE OR BENCH SCRAPER): This is a metal scraper with a wooden handle.

DUTCH OVEN: Made from cast iron or enameled cast iron, the heavy, tight-fitting lid of the vessel traps in the steam, contributing to both oven spring and a crisp, caramelized crust. Other forms achieving the same concept (an enclosed baking vessel that traps the steam) is a Baking Clouche and Combo Cooker.

Nearly all the hearth-style breads in this book range from 510 grams to 1,500 grams in weight. A large 5½-quart Dutch oven, about 10½ inches in diameter and 4¾ inches deep, should cover most of the bases in terms of various bread sizes (though having an extra large, 7¼-quart one, at least 13 inches in diameter, will enable you to bake the large miche from Flat Rock Bakery on page 122 and Weaver Street Market Bakery on page 137).

Another point of reference is choose a Dutch oven that is larger in diameter than the basket your loaves proof in.

LOAF PANS: Most of the following rye bread recipes call for a Pullman loaf pan (either a 9 x 4-inch or a 13 x 4-inch). These straight-sided pans are ideal for rye-heavy breads, providing the characteristic square bottom and assisting in more even baking.

PARCHMENT PAPER

PASTRY BRUSH: A silicone brush is easy to clean, though I prefer a 1½ to 2-inch natural bristle brush.

PLASTIC DOUGH SCRAPER(S): I religiously use two different plastic dough scrapers—a flexible one that is also known as a bowl scraper, and a hard plastic (less flexible) one, that professional bakers know as "the orange scraper," though they're not all orange.

PROOFING BASKET (AKA BANNETON OR BROTFORMS): These breathable baskets used for final proofing of shaped loaves come in various sizes and shapes—oblong, round, or even triangular. They can be lined with linen or unlined (which results in a lovely impression of the basket on the finished loaf). The size of the basket depends on the size of your loaf. The breads in this book range from 510 grams to 2,000 grams. Other than the miche that require a round proofing basket, I use oval baskets left over from my bakery—oval wicker-style baskets I obtained from a restaurant supply store (sold as "bread baskets," for serving, not proofing bread). They measure 9 inches long x 7 inches wide x 3 inches tall and are made of a poly material, so they can be washed. With these, I forgo the linen cloth and just flour the baskets well.

OVAL BASKETS:

8-INCH BASKET—small loaf (500 to 600 grams)

9-INCH BASKET—medium loaf (up to 850 grams)

10-INCH BASKET—large loaf (up to 1,200 grams)

13-INCH BASKET—extra large loaf (2,000 grams)

ROUND BASKETS:

10-INCH BASKET—large loaf (1,500 grams)

11½-INCH BASKET—extra large loaf (2,000 grams)

SILICONE BAKING MAT: A great option in place of parchment paper on a baking sheet.

THERMOMETER: I like to have more than one type, both instant-read digital and dial for safe measure, as batteries die and I have found dial thermometers can lose their accuracy over time.

Ingredients

MALT FLOUR: In the following recipes, when malt flour is called for, this is a diastatic malt. We mill Riverbend Malt House's floor-malted barley that bakers use in bread application to assist in fermentation, or in pastry as a flavor-forward sweetener.

NUTS AND SEEDS: Opt for raw, and organic if possible. Because of the high oil content, nuts and seeds should be stored in a cool, dark place. I store all of mine in air-tight containers in the freezer.

SALT: The function of salt, especially in bread, is no small thing. In bread applications, the autolyze period, during which the flour and water have time to integrate without the obstruction of salt; jump-starts fermentation. Salt slows down the fermentation process to a pace that results in a balanced flavor. It also tightens the gluten structure of the dough, providing strength. With just three or four ingredients, the choice of salt used matters to me. In all the recipes in this book, fine sea salt is called for. In my own bakery, I used Celtic Sea Salt, which is mineral-rich and unrefined.

SWEETENERS: When granulated sgar is called for, opt for an unrefined organic cane sugar, ideally. Where sorghum syrup is called for, one can use cane molasses (though not blackstrap) as a substitute, but adjustments may need to be made, as sorghum is sweeter than molasses, so one may want to increase the amount of sugar called for, up to one-third of the amount specified.

WATER: I highly recommend using filtered water in general, and specifically in bread making. Chlorinated water straight from the tap can interfere with microbial activity, and so narrowing the scope of one's conditions can lead to greater success.

Baker's Percentage

For all of the following bread recipes, baker's percentage can be found listed in the Baker's Percentage Index (page 271). If you're not familiar with baker's percentage, it is the percentage by weight of the ingredients in relation to the flour in the recipe. For example, if water is shown with a baker's percentage of 75, this is 75 percent of the weight of the flour. Why provide this information? Baker's percentage is an incredibly useful tool for understanding a recipe or formula (bakers don't actually follow recipes, we follow formulas).

The basic architecture of a bread formula is flour, water, leaven, and salt. Understanding these components in relation to each other reveals a lot—whether a dough will be wet or stiff, or when considering fermentation time; for example, in many rye breads, one will see a much higher percentage of leaven than in most wheat bread formulas. Baker's percentage is also a tool for the baker who wants to alter a formula, for example, by increasing the water (the hydration) in a dough. Learning how to use baker's percentage enables you to make changes to a formula while adjusting the ratio of ingredients proportionately. As a baker running my Natural Bridge Bakery, having this tool at my disposal allowed me to methodically take risks, going beyond the established limits of a bread formula. You can use the following bread recipes/formulas without engaging with baker's percentage, but don't let it intimidate you. The value of having this in your baking toolbox cannot be understated. It becomes especially relevant when working with stone-ground and regional flours, as these flours have not been blended to a specified industry standard (although even an industrial roller-milled flour blended to spec will have variation, as it is an agricultural product).

Because baker's percentage expresses the proportion of ingredients by weight as it relates to the flour in a recipe, the baker's percentage of flour always equals 100. The most basic way to understand this is to consider a dough made with 1,000 grams of flour (I credit the French for this approach, and baker and author Chad Robertson for writing it down and sharing it with the rest of us):

INGREDIENTS	QUANTITY	BAKER'S PERCENTAGE
Flour	1,000 grams	100
Water	800 grams	80
Leaven	200 grams	20
Salt	20 grams	2

In the above bread formula, the water, or hydration, of the dough is 80 percent, the leaven is 20 percent, and the salt is 2 percent; 800 grams, 200 grams, and 20 grams respectively. If one wanted to pull back on hydration (decrease the water) to, say, 75 percent, then the quantity of water would be 750 grams.

To take this a step further, said formula makes 2,020 grams, or just over 2 kilograms, of dough:

INGREDIENT	QUANTITY	BAKER'S PERCENTAGE
Flour	1,000 grams	100
Water	800 grams	80
Leaven	200 grams	20
Salt	20 grams	2
Total	2,020 grams	202

The equation is as follows:
Flour: (100 ÷ 202) x 2,020 = 1,000 grams
Water: (80 ÷ 202) x 2,020 = 80 grams
Leaven: (20 ÷ 202) x 2,020 = 20 grams
Salt: (2 ÷ 202) x 2,020 = 2 grams

Are you are still reading? Taking this even deeper, if you wanted to use baker's percentage to convert a bread formula from roller-milled flour to stone-ground flour, you would likely want to increase hydration to account for the higher percentage of soluble fiber in stone-ground flours, and perhaps reduce the leaven, as there is often higher enzymatic activity in stone-ground flours as well as a higher quantity of minerals and sugars, resulting in a more active dough. You could dive in deep with this, or simply proceed with the formulas as is and keep baking, since by far the best way to understand bread baking is by repetition.

Leavening

There are many ways to create natural leavening or a sourdough culture, each harnessing yeast and bacteria to leaven bread. We offer a couple different methods. The first, made from whole rye flour, is a liquid leaven; the second, made from whole-wheat flour, is a stiff leaven. *Liquid* and *stiff* refer to the amount of hydration, or water, in relation to the amount of flour. Although in the following pages, wheat leaven is called for in some recipes while rye leaven is called for in others, you don't need to keep two different cultures. The starter is the seed that, with the addition of flour and water, will become the leaven for your bread, and it can be pulled from either a wheat culture or a rye culture. That being said, for my Natural Bridge Bakery, I kept a wheat culture, a cracked rye culture, and a Khorasan (Kamut) culture, and at one point I also kept a rye flour culture and a spelt culture. Each had a different scent. They were part of my bakery's family. I could have whittled it down to one culture—I just didn't want to.

Now for the adventure to begin, Sharon Burns-Leader of Bread Alone Bakery sets the stage for us and then walks us through building a sourdough culture with rye flour. I bring up the rear with instructions for building a desem culture with whole-wheat flour.

Sharon's Pro Tips

FEED THE BABY: I call the daily refreshment of the sourdough "feeding the baby," as in, "Did you feed the baby?" It has been my personal experience that folks rarely forget to feed the baby, and if they do, bad things happen. "Feeding the mother," on the other hand, is a routinely overlooked kindness. Yes, this should change, but until it does—keep feeding that baby.

DISCARD AND FEED: Before you can "feed the baby," you will first discard or remove a portion of your sourdough. We discard before we feed so that the quantity of sourdough does not grow exponentially, and also, so that the proportion of fresh flour (or food for you sourdough) remains relatively the same.

Sourdough Thoughts

by Sharon Burns-Leader
Bread Alone Bakery, Boiceville, New York

Starting a culture is a bit of a misnomer. *You* aren't starting anything. You are a vehicle for creating conditions in which a culture can grow. Kind of like throwing a party.

If you want to have a successful party, you think about things like whom you will invite (two acerbic wits are one too many, for instance), what you will provide for refreshments (yes, Virginia, there is such a thing as too much mezcal), and where you will entertain your guests (maybe just close the door to the den). You think about what time folks will arrive and how long they will stay. If it's a hot time of year, you think about staying cool, or during the winter months, you center the activity around the fireplace.

In effect, you are creating the correct atmosphere for maximum fun. You are—if you'll permit a lame baker's pun—fermenting the fun.

Baking is just like that.

Baking with sourdough takes the party to the next level. Yes, perhaps a keg party was fun once, but now you enjoy craft beers made from elderberries and it's time to kick it up. Lose the commercially processed yeast and the wine coolers and learn how to party the old-fashioned way.

Natural leavening requires a maximum infusion of yeast cells grown in the organic manner: over time. This last item is the most important ingredient of all. Time. The other two ingredients—flour and water—need time applied by a conscientious human in order to maximize the potential for fermenting grain. Fermentation opens up a host of microbial and enzymatic activity, which together produce an edible, nourishing, endlessly flavorful baked item that can feed multitudes and cause grown women to cry—both from delight and from utter frustration. But enough about my life, let's get you started.

CONTAINERS WITH INSTRUCTIONS ON THE LID: Take two containers (I like Weck jars) that share one lid size. Using masking tape and a marker, put the feeding instructions on the lid. Try to feed the baby daily by using one clean container to add the starter, flour, and water according to the instructions on the lid. Discard (or use the leftover baby in Hemp Crisp Breads [page 128] or Cornmeal Crackers [page 153]) and replace the lid. Clean the soiled container for the next day's use.

FLOAT TEST: While this is not 100 percent accurate, it is a good indication that there is enough microbial activity in the flour-water network to rise a loaf of bread: Take a jar of water and place a teaspoon of ripe starter on the surface. If it floats, it may give you a nice loaf. The blob of starter should stay together in a blob and float. If it dissipates *and* floats, it's probably over-ripe and should be fed at least twice over a twenty-four-hour period to bring it back in balance.

NOBODY PUTS BABY IN A CORNER: If you need a break from feeding the baby, mix in twice the amount of flour you usually use to create a thick, dry starter. Place the baby in the refrigerator. When you feel up to feeding the baby as before, pull from the refrigerator and refresh it by adding water and flour as usual, keeping it on the counter at room temperature.

Building a Sourdough Culture

This process will take five days, or longer. Try to mix at the same time every day. Use a clear jar or container so you can see the fermentation. Keep the mixture covered and on the counter. Although you can use whatever flour you prefer, organic whole rye flour provides maximum potential for natural yeast presence. Use filtered water if your tap water is chlorinated.

DAY 1

INGREDIENT	QUANTITY	BAKER'S PERCENTAGE
Organic rye flour	60 grams	100
Water	80 grams	133

Mix the flour and water thoroughly.

DAY 2

Mix thoroughly, but no need to add any water or flour.

DAY 3

You should see tiny bubbles today. (If you don't see bubbles, mix again and wait until tomorrow to continue—just pretending it's still Day 3.) Now you start to "discard and feed" your culture.

INGREDIENT	QUANTITY	BAKER'S PERCENTAGE
Organic rye flour	60 grams	100
Water	80 grams	133
Baby	50 grams	83

In a clean jar, dissolve the baby (aka the Day 2 mixture) in the water. Add the flour.

DAY 4

INGREDIENT	QUANTITY	BAKER'S PERCENTAGE
Organic rye flour	60 grams	100
Water	80 grams	133
Baby	50 grams	83

In a clean jar, dissolve the baby (aka the Day 3 mixture) in the water. Add the flour.

DAY 5

INGREDIENT	QUANTITY	BAKER'S PERCENTAGE
Organic rye flour	60 grams	100
Water	80 grams	133
Baby	50 grams	83

In a clean jar, dissolve the baby (aka the Day 4 mixture) in the water. Add the flour.

Your sourdough baby may be ready to make a starter from today; 5 to 6 hours from the last time you fed the baby, do a float test (see page 96). Also smell and taste your starter: it should be sweet and tangy—musty and pungent are indications of a starter out of balance!

If your starter needs more time and attention (yes, sometimes it takes longer, due to temperature, available wild yeast, impurities in water, etc.), just keep up this daily feeding schedule:

DAYS 6–10

INGREDIENT	QUANTITY	BAKER'S PERCENTAGE
Organic rye flour	60 grams	100
Water	80 grams	133
Baby	50 grams	83

In the following bread recipes, to make the leaven, the starter is pulled from the "baby." Once your sourdough baby is mature, she can be stored in the refrigerator for up to 2 weeks without feeding, though she should be fed at a less hydrated state. One hundred percent hydration (equal parts flour and water) is a good measure, though she can be kept in even stiffer form if she is getting away from you before you are able to bake. By giving her more flour, or less water, you are slowing her down. By keeping her at cooler temperatures (in the refrigerator), you are slowing her down.

Dr. Erin McKenney on Sourdough

Humans have been baking bread for over fourteen thousand years. Bread has nourished us across the world and across time, making microbial cultures central to human culture. The microbes in sourdough starters digest sugars and starch to produce carbon dioxide, acids, and other flavors, transforming a glorified papier-mâché paste into a thriving microbial garden that increases the nutritional value and shelf life of bread. And those of us who keep starters are transformed, too. Of all the public science projects undertaken by the Rob Dunn Lab at North Carolina State University, the participants in the Sourdough Project are uniquely invested, not only in learning about their sourdough starters but also in the scientific process. Sourdough bakers tend to their starters daily, weekly, or biweekly. With that care over time, bakers build an intimate knowledge of their starter's behavior, its "preferences" for certain flour types, temperatures, and other conditions; they build a more direct, physical connection as well, as the starter is colonized with microbes from the home—in our dust and on our bodies—and it gives as much as it gets. Recent research by Dr. Anne Madden and Dr. Rob Dunn suggests that each baker bestows a personal microbial signature on their sourdough, which imparts unique flavors to their bread, and just as we change our sourdough starters, our starter changes us. When Anne and Rob studied the microbes on bakers' hands, they found that bakers harbor up to ten times more *Lactobacillus* compared to nonbakers!

The average modern Western human spends up to 23.5 hours per day inside. Megan Thoemmes's research comparing different styles of homes suggests that modern houses, so carefully sealed off from the outside environment, have become an echo chamber for bodily microbes and pathogens. Even something as simple as opening a window might help to let the outside in, to remind our immune systems what the world is like and help minimize risk of allergies. But how much more diverse the houses of bakers must be, with our sourdough microbes in the mix!

I have always loved bread. I grew my first sourdough starters as soon as I started my postdoctoral research on the Sourdough Project. But I continue to bake as a way to stay connected, both to other people who bake and to the daily wonder of microbial alchemy.

Building a Desem Culture

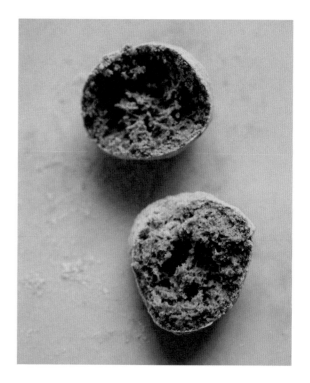

Not too long after discovering desem bread in *The Laurel's Kitchen Bread Book*, I came upon Thom Leonard's *The Bread Book*, in which he, too, devotes a chapter to this naturally leavened bread. Thom provides the most apt description of what makes the culture that leavens this bread so special: "Like good wine that is a product of the vineyard, fermented only by the indigenous organisms from the skin of the fruit, bread from this starter is truly a product of the wheat and of the earth from which it sprang."

Freshly milled flour is the first step in the process. From this flour, one creates a stiff dough ball of flour and water, then buries the ball in a sack of flour, which is then stored in a cellar or basement or any other location that maintains cool temperatures between 50° and 62°F. I use the term *naturally leavened* as opposed to *sourdough* to describe desem, as the scent of a desem culture is anything but sour. The desem culture should be fragrant, expressing a fruitiness that hints of apple cider. Begin with a 5-pound bag of stone-ground organic whole-wheat flour, and use filtered water if your tap water is chlorinated. It takes about two weeks to develop a culture; from there, she can be stored in the refrigerator.

INGREDIENT	QUANTITY	BAKER'S PERCENTAGE
Whole-wheat flour	50 grams	100
Water	25 grams	50

Measure the flour (drawing from your 5-pound bag) into a medium bowl and add the water. Mix and form into a stiff dough ball. Bury this ball deep into the bag of flour, about halfway down, so the dough is fully immersed and surrounded by flour. Close the bag and place it in a container such as a bucket or crock and cover with a lid. Store the container in a cool place, ideally a basement. You want the temperature to remain around 55°F (though if you end up with 62°F, that works, too—you will just have to feed her more often).

Every two or three days, retrieve the dough ball from the bag of flour. Initially, you'll notice the exterior of the ball beginning to dry out; eventually, a rind will form. Pre–rind stage, use both hands to pull open the dough ball and scoop out the dough from the center, discarding the dried-out exterior. (Eventually, you will be simply peeling away the rind to access the dough within.) Measure 25 grams of water into a medium bowl and dissolve the dough in the water.

Add 50 grams of flour (pulled from the 5-pound bag of flour). Mix and form into a stiff dough ball. Bury the ball into the bag of flour and store the bag as before.

Continue this process for two weeks. As the culture develops, take note of the scent. You're aiming for a floral scent. Sometimes the developing culture can initially have an off smell and then land in the floral zone after a few days, so don't worry if a few feedings don't smell quite right; however, if she begins to smell very wrong (trust your senses), discard most of the dough ball—all but about a dime's worth—dissolve the portion you've retained in 25 grams of water, and add 50 grams of flour. Mix and form into a dough ball, and continue the process as before, perhaps this time engaging with your developing culture daily, instead of every few days, to ensure success.

How will you know when your culture is fully developed? Trust your nose—as Sharon mentioned on page 98, musty and pungent are indications of a starter out of balance. And there's always the float test, described on page 96.

I refer to my desem culture as my "mother culture" aka sourdough culture, or as Sharon prefers, "sourdough baby." Once fully developed, she is stored in an airtight container in the refrigerator. In choosing the container, I personally prefer glass over plastic, and as a home baker, I use a half-pint mason jar, though a plastic pint container works, too. Place your mother culture in the container, then sprinkle a of flour on top, cover the container with a lid and store in the refrigerator.

To use, pull the required amount of starter directly from your mother culture. (The starter will then be extended to become the leaven for your dough.) To replenish what has been taken fro the mother culture, she will be fed at a more hydrated state than when she was stored in the basement. The increased hydration accounts for the fact that she is now being stored at a colder temperature.

MAINTAINING YOUR MATURE DESEM CULTURE

INGREDIENTS	QUANTITY	BAKER'S PERCENTAGE
Whole-wheat flour	25 grams	100
Water	18 grams	75

Before replenishing her, scoop out some of that excess flour that was sprinkled on top of the mother, plus about a heaping tablespoon of the mother culture and toss it (into the compost). Next, add water directly to the container with the culture, breaking apart the culture with a spoon (I prefer a tablespoon-size stainless-steel spoon). Then, add the flour and, using the spoon, mix into a cohesive form. Sprinkle flour on top, cover the container with a lid, and place the container back in the refrigerator. In the colder months, you may want to leave her out on the counter at room temperature for an hour or two just to wake her up a bit. You will establish a relationship with your culture and begin to understand her needs.

RESCUING YOUR DESEM CULTURE

INGREDIENTS	QUANTITY	BAKER'S PERCENTAGE
Whole-wheat flour	25 grams	100
Water	18 grams	75
Mother culture	7 grams	25

If your mother culture gets really out of balance or if it has been way too long since she has been replenished, you may need to rescue her. For this, get a separate container (another glass jar or plastic pint container), pull 7 grams from the center of your culture, and add it to your clean container along with 18 grams of water. Break apart the culture with a tablespoon-size spoon and then add 25 grams of flour and, using the spoon, mix into a cohesive form. Leave the container at room temperature; every 6 to 12 hours, scoop out and discard a heaping tablespoon of the mother culture, then replenish with 18 grams of water and 25 grams of flour. Continue this process until she comes back into good form. This may take three or four feedings, after which she can be drawn from as your starter, replenished, and placed back in the refrigerator.

Bread Method

I think what I love most about bread baking is that as long as you understand the basic principles, there is no one single method or sole approach. You can shape your baking schedule and adjust your methods to fit your particular set of circumstances. When I was apprenticing in Marin County, California, our conditions were ideal: we were tucked back in the hills above Tomales Bay and received daily four o'clock winds. It never got too warm, and while I was there, it was the dry season. The house where we baked hovered at a temperature of about 62°F, wonderful conditions for good fermentation (especially for baking desem, which loves cool temperatures). Our final proofing was done at 95°F and 100 percent humidity, an environment we created with a plastic-covered speed rack filled with proofing loaves and a hot plate at the base with a pot of boiling water producing steam.

When I left California to start my bakery in Tennessee, my ambient conditions were completely different. I ditched the final proofing setup and simply proofed my loaves at room temperature instead. After moving to North Carolina, I eventually added a cool room, so I could control some of my proofing conditions. My cool room's temperature ranged between

48° and 52°F, so I did my bulk fermentation in the cool room for 12 hours and my final proofing at room temperature for a shorter period, always responding to the changing seasons. In the winter, my final proof might require rolling the speed rack of proofing loaves up close to the oven; summertime might require that I roll the rack back into the cool room, if the final proofing needed slowing down. When I shifted roles from baker to miller, I had to learn how to become a home baker, which came with its own learning curve. Without a cool room, instead of a long, slow bulk fermentation at cool temperatures, I shifted to a shorter bulk fermentation at room temperature, applying a series of stretches and folds, again responding to the conditions around me.

Most of the bread recipes in this book follow this method. It's a good method, a solid foundation for a home baker, but if you want to veer from this path, do it. Experiment. This is just one method. The one golden rule with any approach is to be sure your leaven is fully developed before mixing the dough. Always pay attention to your baby.

Make the leaven

Measure the water into a clear container such as a Weck or mason jar (or even a clear plastic container; using a clear vessel allows you to see the fermentation in action), then add your starter (this is pulled from your mother culture or sourdough culture). Using a spoon (I prefer a tablespoon-size stainless-steel spoon) or your fingers, break apart the starter into the water. Add the flour and mix until fully incorporated. Cover with a lid and let stand at room temperature until fully developed before making the dough. This can take anywhere from 4 to 16 hours depending on how active your sourdough culture is, the temperature of your kitchen, and depending on the actual recipe—the amount of hydration, the amount of starter, and/or the particular flour called for in the recipe. All of these factors can affect the timeline. Using a clear container will help you understand what fully developed looks like, as you should see a series of bubbles and your leaven will have expanded, feeling aerated when scooped with a spoon. (Helpful hint: Place a rubber band around your jar to mark your undeveloped leaven so you can observe the growth in progress.)

Make the dough

STEP 1: MIX THE FLOUR, WATER, AND CULTURE (AUTOLYZE). Once your leaven is ready, measure your water into a large bowl, then add the leaven and dissolve it in the water. (For stiffer cultures, I squeeze the leaven between my fingers so that it breaks apart.)

Next, incorporate the flour: Add the flour to the bowl. Keep one hand clean and dry and use that hand to hold the edge of the bowl. With the other hand, take a flexible plastic scraper and scoop down underneath the ingredients, then fold them onto themselves. Continue this

Baker Michael Matson of Nashville, Tennessee.

process while rotating the bowl. With each scoop and fold, rotate the bowl, continuing until the ingredients are fully integrated and have become a homogenous dough, making sure no lumps or dry bits remain. Cover the bowl with a cotton or linen kitchen towel and let the dough rest at room temperature for 1 hour.

STEP 2: ADD THE SALT. Sprinkle the salt evenly over the dough. You want to fully incorporate the salt into the dough, and there are various ways to do this. My approach is to fold the dough over itself. Have a small bowl of water within reach, and wet your hands just enough so they don't stick to the dough, but shaking off any excess water so you are not incorporating too much water into the dough. Hold the edge of the bowl of dough with one hand, and use your other hand to fold the dough over itself, then repeat, rotating the bowl with each fold until you've done a full rotation (or four folds). Pour the dough out onto the counter and use the heel of one hand to push into the dough and with the other hand, fold the dough over itself, rotating the dough with each push-fold action; repeat until you've done a full rotation.

STEP 3: BULK FERMENTATION, WITH STRETCH AND FOLDS. Bulk ferment the dough at room temperature, applying a series of stretch and folds to the dough every 30 minutes to 45 minutes for the first 2 to 3 hours. (I highly recommend writing out your stretch-and-fold schedule on a piece of paper and placing it near the fermenting dough; mark each stretch and fold off the list as you go.) To do this, dip your hands in water to keep from sticking to the dough, but shake off any excess water so you are not incorporating too much water into the dough. With both hands, grab the underside of a section of dough and gently stretch it out until you feel resistance (but be careful not to tear the dough), then fold it over the top of the mass of dough. Rotate the bowl (or container) a quarter turn and repeat until you've done a full rotation, then turn the dough over so the folds are tucked underneath. By pulling and folding and resting in between over a period of time, you are strengthening the dough and building the gluten network necessary to provide shape and structure to your bread. With each stretch and fold, you should feel the dough develop strength, structure, and volume. After the last stretch and fold, if you are working with a particularly slack dough or weaker flour, you may want to add an additional fold, then allow the dough to rest until it has increased in volume by 20 to 30 percent and appears smooth and billowy. For this period, you can either leave the dough in the bowl and cover it with a cotton kitchen towel, or you can transfer the dough to a container with a lid—ideally a clear glass or plastic one, so you can see what is going on from the side of the container. Bread ferments from the bottom up, so having that side view is quite helpful. Choose a container large enough to allow the dough to expand, but not too large, so that as it expands, tension is created by constriction as the dough pushes against the container (this will not occur in a container that is too large). This period of bulk rise can take anywhere from 30 minutes to 2 hours, and sometimes longer, depending on the time of year.

STEP 4: PRESHAPING. The purpose of preshaping is to begin to form the eventual shape of the bread. This is done in stages in order to give the dough a chance to relax. To preshape, use a bench knife or your hands to drag the dough across your work surface to create surface tension while shaping it into a tight ball.

STEP 5: BENCH REST. This period of 15 to 30 minutes enables the dough to relax before the final shaping. *Bench rest* is definitely a term I learned once I became a home baker. In the bakery, bench rest just happens—during the time it takes to preshape all your loaves, the loaves have time to rest before their final shaping. At home, preshaping one to three loaves goes pretty quickly, so it is important to be mindful of allowing the dough to rest before its final shaping.

STEP 6: FINAL SHAPING. This really depends on the bread you are baking and/or the loaf shape you desire, but the aim is to create surface tension so the dough holds its form during the long proofing and baking periods that follow.

To shape the dough, flip your preshaped loaf onto a lightly floured surface, so that the seam side is up. Lightly pat down the dough just a bit (do not punch it down or flatten it—just give it a light and gentle patting down). Fold the bottom third of the dough up toward the center and then fold in the sides. Take the top of the dough and fold it down to the center. Then fold the bottom up past the center so the shaped loaf is now seam-side down with surface tension created. Allow the dough to rest for a few minutes so that the seam seals itself under the weight of the dough.

> **IF MAKING A HEARTH LOAF:** Generously dust a proofing basket with flour (rice flour, or a mixture of rice flour and another flour, works especially well for dusting proofing baskets, as it keeps the cloth from sticking to the dough) or line a proofing basket with a linen cloth and dust the cloth well with flour. Then transfer the dough seam-side up to the prepared basket.

> **IF MAKING A PAN LOAF:** With a pastry brush dipped in olive oil or melted butter (or a combination of both), grease a loaf pan. You can line the pan with parchment paper as well. To do so, cut parchment paper to fit the length of the pan and wide enough to cover the two long sides (you can allow the parchment to hang over the long sides of the pan for easy removal); grease the parchment as well. The narrow ends of the pan are left uncovered, so brush them with extra oil. Transfer the dough seam-side down to the prepared pan.

STEP 7: FINAL RISE OR FINAL FERMENTATION. Let the shaped loaves rise in the baskets or pans at room temperature for 2 to 3 hours, then transfer them to the refrigerator for an additional 8 to 24 hours of cold proofing. The long cold proof will provide the most complex flavor but some prefer the more mellow flavor profile of a same-day bake. If you opt to forgo the long cold proof and do a same-day bake, begin to look for visual cues that the bread is ready after 1½ to 2 hours. Dip your fingertip in flour and gently poke the dough. If the indentation slowly and evenly rises back, it is ready to bake.

STEP 8: BAKING IN A DUTCH OVEN. Place a Dutch oven on the lowest rack in a cold oven; place the lid on the rack as well. Preheat the oven to 500°F for 1 hour.

When ready to load the dough into the oven, cut a piece of parchment paper larger than your loaf but small enough to fit into the Dutch oven (it's okay if it comes up the sides of the pot). Sprinkle coarse flour, cornmeal, or semolina onto the parchment and then flip the loaf from the proofing basket onto the parchment, seam-side down. Score the loaf, ⅛-inch to ¼-inch deep, in whatever pattern you desire.

Using oven mitts, open the oven door, place the loaf (still on the parchment) in the preheated Dutch oven, and place the lid on the pot. Bake for 20 minutes, then remove the lid from the pot and lower the oven temperature to 450°F. Bake, uncovered, for an additional 15 to 20 minutes, until the bread has a deep golden hue and the internal temperature reads between 195° and 210°F, depending on the bread.

STEP 9: COOLING AND STORAGE. Remove from the oven and transfer the bread from the pot to a cooling rack (or if baking a pan bread, transfer from pan to cooling rack). Let cool as directed in the recipe (some loaves are best left to stand for 24 hours before slicing and serving, while others can be eaten after they've cooled completely.)

Wheat breads and rye breads are treated differently when it comes to short-term storage. In our household, we keep our bread (that is not rye), sliced side down on a cutting board covered with a linen cloth. If the loaf dries out, it can be revived by quickly running cold water over it to wet the crust (not soak, just wet), and placing in a hot oven (400°F) for 7 to 10 minutes, until the water has evaporated. This method works really well to bring life back into a loaf, but the bread must be eaten at one sitting or it will revert back to its dried-out state. High content rye breads, on the other hand, should be stored wrapped in plastic (or beeswax wrap) and placed in the refrigerator. This bread can keep for weeks, at least. For long-term storage, either bread—wheat or rye—can be frozen for up to 2 months. Be sure the loaves are fully cooled, and wrap as airtight as possible, in plastic or, as I prefer, in parchment paper and then plastic, before placing in the freezer.

ON TIME AND TEMPERATURE: Time and temperature play a huge role in bread baking, especially when baking with sourdough. Your leavening will develop at room temperature, but room temperature varies from home to home and from season to season. Colder temperatures slow down fermentation, and conversely, warmer temperatures speed up fermentation. The amount of time required to fully develop your leaven will not be static. Your ability to take note of your conditions—the ambient temperature, water temperature, and the condition of your sourdough culture—within the changing seasons will serve you and your breads.

For most of the following recipes, the suggested amount of time that one's leaven develops is overnight or for 8 to 10 hours but pay more attention to your own conditions than to the recipe at hand. For recipes that have many components—soakers and/or sprouting or a two-part feeding of the leaven—I have included timing in the ingredients list so that you can plan accordingly.

Hard Winter Wheat

Whole-Wheat Bread Flour

Stone-ground whole-wheat bread flour is hard winter wheat milled in its whole form. It is 100 percent whole grain. Nothing is removed or separated and recombined; it is milled intact—whole grain in, whole grain flour out—intact and whole.

High-Extraction Bread Flour

High-extraction flour is a sifted flour that still contains a high percentage of the whole grain. It can be 80 to 90 percent extraction, meaning 10 to 20 percent of the larger bran particles have been sifted out. By removing just the largest bran particles, most of the nutrients are preserved, but this flour provides extra loft to breads compared with 100 percent whole-grain flour. We call our high-extraction bread flour 85 bread flour, indicating that of the grain in the hopper, 85 parts become flour and 15 parts (the larger particles of bran) are sifted out, give or take.

75- Extraction Bread Flour

Within the realm of stone-milled regional flours, this is the closest version to a roller-milled white flour in terms of extraction rate, with about 25 parts sifted out. The flour is a creamy color, not actually white. Made from hard winter wheat, it is a medium-strong flour and is quite versatile. Unlike roller-milled flour, the germ is not removed, but is instead crushed into the starchy flour, spreading its oils and delivering a richness to the resulting baked goods. If you cannot find a 75-extraction flour, opt for using a high-extraction flour or "half white" stone-ground flour in its place in the following recipes. And if you so desire, you can hand-sift a high-extraction flour to get closer to a 75-extraction.

Whole White Wheat Flour

White wheats lack the tannins found in red wheats and so provide a wholly different flavor profile. White wheats can be hard wheat or soft wheat. We grow a variety of hard white wheat called Appalachian White. This is one of Dr. Marshall's varieties. Hard white wheat is lovely in bread applications, and any of the bread recipes in the Whole-Wheat Bread Flour section (pages 111–118) can be made with whole white wheat bread flour. But unlike whole wheat bread flour made from red wheat, white wheat excels in broad application, as the following recipes demonstrate.

FLEMISH DESEM BREAD

NATURAL BRIDGE BAKERY ◆ WALNUT, NORTH CAROLINA

My need for fresh stone-ground flour to make the culture that would leaven my breads—providing the foundation for my bakery—is where it all began for me as a baker, and really as a miller, too. And so it seems especially appropriate to place this recipe prominently at the very beginning. It is an apt place to begin, too, because this bread presents stone-ground whole-wheat flour in its best form. Through slow fermentation, the flour, water, and salt are transformed into a bread of lovely tooth and crumb, with a rich, bold flavor of red wheat. Perfect in its simplicity. The use of 100 percent whole grain flour accounts for the high percentage of water (or hydration) in this dough, as whole-grain flour absorbs more water than sifted flour. Don't worry if the dough seems especially wet during your initial mix. After a full hour of autolyze and the addition of salt, the dough will begin to come together nicely.

1 Make the leaven: Measure the water into a small clear container with a lid, such as a pint mason jar, then add the starter. Break apart the starter into the water, then add the flour and mix until fully incorporated. Cover and let stand at room temperature overnight or for 8 to 10 hours, until fully developed (see image on page 107).

2 Make the dough: Once the leaven is fully developed, measure the water into a large bowl, then add the leaven and dissolve it in the water. Add the flour and mix until fully incorporated (according to Step 1 on page 103). Cover with a cotton or linen kitchen towel and let the dough rest for 1 hour.

3 Sprinkle the salt evenly over the dough and then fully incorporate it into the dough (according to Step 2 on page 105). Cover the bowl with a cotton or linen kitchen towel.

4 Bulk ferment the dough: During bulk fermentation, apply a series of stretch and folds to the dough (according to Step 3 on page 105) every 45 minutes for 3 hours—four

series of folds total. With each stretch and fold, you should feel the dough develop in strength and structure. After the final fold, cover the dough with a kitchen towel or transfer to a container with a lid, and let rise, undisturbed, until it has increased in volume by 20 to 30 percent. This could take 1 to 3 hours depending on the time of year, the temperature of your kitchen, and how active your leavening is.

5 Preshape and bench rest: Turn the dough out onto your work surface and fold it over itself. Divide the dough into two equal portions weighing around 840 grams each. Preshape one portion of the dough at a time. Using a bench knife or your hands, drag the dough across the work surface to create surface tension while shaping it into a tight ball. Dust the dough with flour, cover with a kitchen towel, and let rest for 30 minutes.

CONTINUED

YIELD: 2 MEDIUM
LOAVES

LEAVEN

76g water

20g starter

80g whole-wheat
bread flour

DOUGH

713g water

158g leaven

792g whole-wheat
bread flour

17g fine sea salt

FLEMISH DESEM BREAD

CONTINUED

6 Final shaping: Line two 9-inch proofing baskets with a linen cloth and generously dust the cloth with flour. Perform the final shaping of the dough as directed on page 106. Sprinkle the top with flour, then place the dough seam-side up in the prepared basket.

7 Final rise: Cover the basket with a kitchen towel and let the dough rise at room temperature for 3 hours. Transfer loaves to the refrigerator to proof overnight.

8 Bake: In the morning, place two Dutch ovens on the lowest rack in a cold oven; place the lid on the rack as well. (If you don't have two Dutch ovens, leave one of your loaves in the refrigerator while the first loaf is in the oven.) Preheat the oven to 500°F for 1 hour.

9 Transfer each loaf to the Dutch oven (according Step 8 instructions on page 106) and place the lid on the pot. Bake for 20 minutes, then uncover the pot and lower the oven temperature to 475°F. Bake, uncovered, for an additional 15 to 20 minutes, until the bread is a deep dark bronze color, sounds hollow when you tap on the bottom, and the internal temperature reads between 204° and 210°F.

10 Remove from the oven and transfer the bread from the pot to a cooling rack. If you can wait, let the bread cool completely before slicing into it.

WALNUT DESEM AND WALNUT-RAISIN DESEM

NATURAL BRIDGE BAKERY ◆ WALNUT, NORTH CAROLINA

When I was running my Natural Bridge Bakery, this was my morning toast. I would make either a walnut or a walnut-raisin loaf each week. The addition of walnuts transforms the color of this dough to a beautiful mauve. The hydration is increased from the basic Flemish Desem Bread (page 111) to account for the add-ins. A full-hour autolyze assists in the absorption of the increased hydration. These are 1-pound loaves loaded with walnuts and raisins.

YIELD: 1 LARGE LOAF OR 2 SMALL LOAVES

LEAVEN

41g water

11g starter

43g whole-wheat bread flour

DOUGH

405g water

85g leaven

426g whole-wheat bread flour

115g walnuts, chopped into large pieces

9g fine sea salt

85g organic raisins (optional)

1 Make the leaven: Measure the water into a small clear container with a lid, such as a pint mason jar, then add the starter. Using a spoon or your fingers, break apart the starter into the water, then add the flour and mix until fully incorporated. Cover and let stand at room temperature overnight or for 8 to 10 hours, until fully developed (see image on page 107).

2 Make the dough: Once the leaven is fully developed, measure the water into a large bowl, then add the leaven and dissolve it in the water, breaking it apart with your fingers. Add the flour and walnuts and mix until fully incorporated (according to Step 1 on page 103). Cover with a cotton or linen kitchen towel and let the dough rest for 1 hour.

3 Sprinkle the salt evenly over the dough and then fully incorporate it into the dough (according to Step 2 on page 105). Cover the bowl with a cotton or linen kitchen towel.

4 Bulk ferment the dough: During bulk fermentation, apply a series of stretch and folds to the dough (according to Step 3 on page 105) every 45 minutes for 3 hours—four series of folds total. With each stretch and fold, you should feel the dough develop in strength and structure. After the final fold, cover the dough with a kitchen towel or transfer to a container with a lid, and let rise, undisturbed, until it has increased

in volume by 20 to 30 percent. This could take 1 to 3 hours depending on the time of year, the temperature of your kitchen, and how active your leavening is.

5 Preshape and bench rest: Turn the dough out onto your work surface and fold it over itself.

If making one large walnut loaf, using a bench knife or your hands, drag the dough across the work surface to create surface tension while shaping it into a tight ball. Dust the dough with flour, cover with a kitchen towel, and let rest for 30 minutes.

If making one walnut loaf and one walnut-raisin loaf, divide the dough into two equal portions weighing around 510 grams each. Preshape the first portion of the dough. Using a bench knife or your hands, drag the dough across the work surface to create surface tension while shaping it into a tight ball. Dust the dough with flour and cover with a kitchen towel. Lightly pat down the second portion of dough into a disk (do not flatten it—just pat it down somewhat) and place the raisins in the center. Fold the bottom edge of the dough up over the raisins, fold the sides in, then fold the top down over and past the bottom fold. Position the dough seam-side down, dust with flour, and cover with a kitchen towel. Let both portions of dough rest for 30 minutes.

CONTINUED

WALNUT DESEM AND WALNUT-RAISIN DESEM

CONTINUED

6 Final shaping: *If making one large walnut loaf,* line a 10-inch proofing basket with a linen cloth and generously dust the cloth with flour. Perform the final shaping of the dough as directed on page 106. Sprinkle the top with flour, then place the dough seam-side up in the prepared basket.

If making one walnut loaf and one walnut-raisin loaf, line two 8-inch proofing baskets with a linen cloth and generously dust the cloth with flour. Perform the final shaping of the walnut dough as directed in Step 6 on page 106. Sprinkle the top with flour, then place it seam-side up in one of the prepared baskets.

For the walnut-raisin loaf, flip the dough so it is floured-side down and gently pat it down. Fold the sides in and then gently pull the top of the dough away from you and, with the heel of your hand, press down on the very top of the dough, so that the top edge of the dough sticks to the counter, then roll the dough up from the bottom up and seal. Sprinkle the top with flour and then place the dough seam-side up in the second prepared basket.

7 Final rise: Cover the basket(s) with kitchen towel(s) and let the dough rise at room temperature for 3 hours, then transfer to the refrigerator to proof overnight.

8 Bake: In the morning, place two Dutch ovens on the lowest rack in a cold oven; place the lid on the rack as well. (If you don't have two Dutch ovens, you can bake one loaf at a time, leaving one of your loaves in the refrigerator until the first loaf is in the oven.). Preheat the oven to 500ºF for 1 hour. Pull the baskets from the refrigerator and set them on the counter; let the dough come to room temperature while the oven preheats.

9 Transfer each loaf to a Dutch oven according to Step 8 instructions on page 106 and place the lid on the pot. Bake for 20 minutes, then uncover the pot(s) and lower the oven temperature to 475°F. Bake, uncovered, for an additional 15 to 20 minutes, until the bread is a deep dark bronze color, sounds hollow when you tap on the bottom, and the internal temperature reads between 204° and 210°F.

10 Remove from the oven and transfer the bread from the pot(s) to a cooling rack. If you can wait, let the bread cool completely before slicing.

PIEDMONT LOAF

LA FARM BAKERY ◆ CARY, NORTH CAROLINA

YIELD: 1 (8 X 4-INCH) PAN LOAF

LEAVEN

50g water

10g starter

50g 75-extraction (stone-ground sifted) bread flour

DOUGH

320g water

100g leaven

266g whole-wheat bread flour

114g 75-extraction (stone-ground sifted) bread flour

9g fine sea salt

La Farm developed this bread to showcase the flour coming from our region. It is a 70/30 whole-grain/stone-ground sifted flour bread with its leavening fed with stone-ground sifted flour. The large percentage of whole-wheat delivers tooth and flavor, while the sifted flour provides the bread's loft. It is flavorful and spongy soft, the ideal choice for lunchbox sandwiches.

Note: This dough is baked the same day it is made, but it can be refrigerated overnight and baked in the morning. For the final rise, transfer the dough to the refrigerator after it has risen for about 2 hours, or when an indentation left by your fingertip only partially disappears.

1 Make the leaven: Measure the water into a small clear container with a lid, such as a ½ pint mason jar, then add the starter. Using a spoon or your fingers, break apart the starter into the water, then add the flour and mix until fully incorporated. Place the lid on the container and let sit overnight at room temperature or for 8 to 10 hours, until fully developed (see image on page 107).

2 Make the dough: Once the leaven is fully developed, measure the water into a large bowl, then add the leaven and dissolve it in the water. Add the whole-wheat and sifted bread flours and mix until fully incorporated (according to Step 1 on page 103). Cover with a cotton or linen kitchen towel and let rest for 1 hour.

3 Sprinkle the salt evenly over the dough and then fully incorporate it into the dough (as directed. Bread Method: Step 2 on page 105). Cover the bowl with a cotton or linen kitchen towel.

4 Bulk ferment the dough: During bulk fermentation, apply a series of stretch and folds to the dough (according to Step 3 on page 105) every 45 minutes for 3 hours—four series of folds total. With each stretch and fold, you should feel the dough develop in strength and structure. After the final fold, cover the dough with a kitchen towel or transfer to a container with a lid, and let rise, undisturbed, until it has increased in volume by 20 to 30 percent. This could take 1 to 2 hours depending on the time of year, the temperature of your kitchen, and how active your leavening is.

5 Preshape and bench rest: Turn the dough out onto your work surface and fold it over itself. Using a bench knife or your hands, drag the dough across the work surface to create surface tension while shaping it into a tight ball. Dust the dough with flour, cover with a kitchen towel, and let rest for 30 minutes.

6 With a pastry brush dipped in olive oil, grease an 8 x 4-inch loaf pan. Line the pan with parchment paper cut to fit the length of the pan and wide enough that it covers the two long sides, then grease the parchment as well. The narrow ends of the pan are left uncovered, so brush them with extra oil.

7 Final shaping: Perform the final shaping of the dough as directed in Step 6 on page 106 and place it seam-side down in the prepared pan.

8 Final rise: Cover and let the dough rise at room temperature for 2 to 3 hours. After 2 hours, begin checking the dough to see if it is ready to bake. Dip your fingertip in flour and gently poke the dough. If the indentation slowly and evenly rises back, it is ready to bake (see Note).

9 Bake: Position a rack in the bottom third of the oven and preheat the oven to 450°F.

10 Score the top of the dough as desired. Place the pan in the oven and bake for 35 to 40 minutes, until the bread is deep golden brown, sounds hollow when you tap on the bottom, and the internal temperature reads between 204° and 210°F.

11 Remove from the oven and immediately transfer the bread from the pan to a cooling rack. If you can wait, let the bread cool completely before serving.

WHOLE-WHEAT FLAX BREAD

WEAVER STREET MARKET BAKERY ◆ HILLSBOROUGH, NORTH CAROLINA

YIELD: 1 LARGE LOAF

LEAVEN (16 HOURS)

28g water

3g starter

43g 75-extraction
bread flour

SOAKER (16 HOURS)

146g water

50g flaxseeds

DOUGH

260g water

68g leaven

303g whole-wheat flour

124g 75-extraction
bread flour

196g soaker

38g hulled sunflower seeds

10g sea salt

This is another 70/30 whole wheat/sifted flour dough, this time with the addition of flax and sunflower seeds. The leaven for this bread is quite stiff and develops over a long period—16 hours. The flaxseeds, too, require 16 hours of soaking, after which their soaking liquid has transformed into a viscous elixir that adds an unbelievable silkiness to the dough (and the resulting crumb). It is flaxseed magic.

1 Make the leaven: Measure the water into a small clear container with a lid, such as a ½ pint mason jar, then add the starter. Using a spoon or your fingers, break apart the starter into the water, then add the flour and mix until fully incorporated. Cover and let stand at room temperature for 16 hours, or until fully developed (see image on page 107).

2 Make the soaker: In a container with a lid, stir together the water and flaxseeds. Cover and let stand at room temperature for 16 hours.

3 Make the dough: Once the leaven is fully developed, measure the water into a large bowl, then add the leaven and dissolve it in the water, breaking it apart with your fingers. Add both flours, the soaker, and the sunflower seeds and mix until fully incorporated (according to Step 1 on page 103). Cover with a cotton or linen kitchen towel and let the dough rest for 45 minutes to 1 hour.

4 Sprinkle the salt evenly over the dough and then fully incorporate it into the dough (according to Step 2 on page 105). Cover the bowl with a cotton or linen kitchen towel.

5 Bulk ferment the dough: During bulk fermentation, apply a series of stretch and folds to the dough (according to Step 3 on page 105) every 45 minutes for 3 hours—four series of folds total. With each stretch and fold,

you should feel the dough develop in strength and structure. After the final fold, cover the dough with a kitchen towel or transfer to a container with a lid, and let rise, undisturbed, until it has increased in volume by 20 to 30 percent. This could take 1 to 3 hours depending on the time of year, the temperature of your kitchen, and how active your leavening is.

6 Preshape and bench rest: Turn the dough out onto your work surface and fold it over itself. Using a bench knife or your hands, drag the dough across the work surface to create surface tension while shaping it into a tight ball. Dust the dough with flour, cover with a kitchen towel, and let rest for 30 minutes.

7 Final shaping: Line a 10-inch proofing basket with a linen cloth and generously dust the cloth with flour. Perform the final shaping of the dough as directed on page 106. Sprinkle the top with flour, then place the dough seam-side up in the prepared basket.

8 Final rise: Cover the basket with a kitchen towel and let the dough rise at room temperature for 3 hours, then transfer to the refrigerator to proof overnight.

9 Bake: In the morning, place a Dutch oven on the lowest rack in a cold oven; place the lid on the rack as well. Preheat the oven to 500°F for 1 hour. Pull the basket from the refrigerator

and set it on the counter; let the dough come to room temperature while the oven preheats.

10 Transfer the loaf to the Dutch oven according to the instructions on page 106 and place the lid on the pot. Bake for 20 minutes, then uncover the pot and lower the oven temperature to 450°F. Bake, uncovered, for an additional 15 to 20 minutes, until the bread has a deep dark golden hue, sounds hollow when you tap on the bottom, and the internal temperature reads between 204° and 210°F.

11 Remove from the oven and transfer the bread from the pot to a cooling rack. If you can wait, let the bread cool completely before slicing into it.

NORTH CAROLINA SOURDOUGH

FLAT ROCK VILLAGE BAKERY ◆ FLAT ROCK, NORTH CAROLINA

YIELD: 1 MEDIUM LOAF

LEAVEN

91g water

18g starter

91g whole-wheat
bread flour

DOUGH

271g water

181g leaven

376g high-extraction (85)
bread flour

12g fine sea salt

This is a bread that Flat Rock created to showcase our North Carolina bread wheat. Flat Rock was part of the original group of bakeries that helped launch Carolina Ground, and when they developed this bread, it was the first time I was able to experience what stone-ground high-extraction bread flour offers to our bakers. With just fifteen parts of the larger bran particles removed, this flour makes a bread with loft without compromising nutrients or flavor. The flavor is bold, but the crumb is open. This bread contains an especially high percentage of leaven (for a nonrye bread), creating an especially active dough with a complex flavor profile.

1 Make the leaven: Measure the water into a small clear container with a lid, such as a 1-pint mason jar, then add the starter. Using a spoon or your fingers, break apart the starter into the water, then add the flour and mix until fully incorporated. Cover and let stand at room temperature overnight or for 8 to 10 hours, until fully developed (see image on page 107).

2 Make the dough: Once the leaven is fully developed, measure the water into a large bowl, then add the leaven and dissolve it in the water, breaking it apart with your fingers. Add the flour and mix until fully incorporated (according to Step 1 on page 103). Cover with a cotton or linen kitchen towel and let the dough rest for 1 hour.

3 Sprinkle the salt evenly over the dough and then fully incorporate it into the dough (according to Step 2 on page 105). Cover the bowl with a cotton or linen kitchen towel.

4 Bulk ferment the dough: During bulk fermentation, apply a series of stretch and folds to the dough (according to Step 3 on page 105) every 45 minutes for 3 hours—four series of folds total. With each stretch and fold, you should feel the dough develop in strength and structure. After the final fold, cover the dough with a kitchen towel or transfer to a container with a lid, and let rise, undisturbed, until it has increased in volume by 20 to 30 percent. This could take 1 to 1½ hours depending on the time of year, the temperature of your kitchen, and how active your leavening is.

5 Preshape and bench rest: Turn the dough out onto your work surface and fold it over itself. Using a bench knife or your hands, drag the dough across the work surface to create surface tension while shaping it into a tight ball. Dust the dough with flour, cover with a kitchen towel, and let rest for 30 minutes.

6 Final shaping: Line a 9-inch proofing basket with a linen cloth and generously dust the cloth with flour. Perform the final shaping of the dough as directed on page 106. Sprinkle the top with flour, then place the dough seam-side up in the prepared basket.

7 Final rise: Cover the basket with a kitchen towel and let the dough rise at room temperature for 3 hours, then transfer to the refrigerator to proof overnight.

8 Bake: In the morning, place a Dutch oven on the lowest rack in a cold oven; place the lid on the rack as well. Preheat the oven to 500°F for 1 hour. Pull the basket from the refrigerator

and set it on the counter; let the dough come to room temperature while the oven preheats.

9 Transfer the loaf to the Dutch oven according to Step 8 on page 106 and place the lid on the pot. Bake for 20 minutes, then uncover the pot and lower the oven temperature to 475°F. Bake, uncovered, for an additional 15 to 20 minutes, until the bread is a deep dark bronze color,

sounds hollow when you tap on the bottom, and the internal temperature reads between 204° and 210°F.

10 Remove from the oven and transfer the bread from the pot to a cooling rack. If you can wait, let the bread cool completely before slicing into it.

NC MICHE

FLAT ROCK VILLAGE BAKERY ◆ FLAT ROCK, NORTH CAROLINA

YIELD: 1 EXTRA LARGE LOAF

LEAVEN STAGE 1

20g water

4g starter

20g whole-wheat bread flour

LEAVEN STAGE 2

43g stage 1 leaven

215g water

215g whole-wheat bread flour

DOUGH

645g water

430g leaven

896g high-extraction (85) bread flour

29g fine sea salt

When I first tasted this bread, I was amazed to learn it is actually made from the same dough as Flat Rock's North Carolina Sourdough (see page 120). It is extraordinary to see what happens when the size of a loaf is more than doubled. The difference in the ratio of crust to crumb from an 800-gram loaf to a 2-kilogram loaf and the increased baking time required for the larger loaf (which produces a much deeper caramelization of the crust) are enough to transform the same dough into a distinctly different bread. The leaven used in the dough is fed twice—timing-wise, this makes it a good bread to bring together over a long weekend: Do the initial feeding of the leaven midmorning on the first day and the second feeding that evening; mix your dough the next morning and put the shaped loaf in the refrigerator that evening; and finally bake the bread the following morning.

Note: The size of this bread requires a round proofing basket or banneton no less than 13 inches in diameter. You'll also need a Dutch oven no less than 13 inches in diameter, but if you don't have one, you can bake the dough on a pizza stone under a large stainless-steel bowl.

Note: This bread is shown on the book cover.

1 Make the leaven: This leaven will be build in two stages. For the first stage, measure the water into a small clear container with a lid, such as a pint-size mason jar, then add the starter. Using a spoon or your fingers, break apart the starter into the water. Add flour and mix until fully incorporated. Cover and let stand at room temperature for 6 to 8 hours.

2 Make stage 2 of the leaven: For the second stage, graduate to a larger container; a wide-mouth quart mason jar works well. Scoop the 43 grams of leaven (stage 1) into the jar and add the water, breaking the culture apart into the water, then adding the flour. Cover and let sit for 8 hours more before mixing the dough.

3 Make the dough: Once the leaven is fully developed, measure the water into a large bowl, then add the leaven and dissolve it in the water, breaking it apart with your fingers.

Add the flour and mix until fully incorporated (according to Step 1 on page 103). Cover with a cotton or linen kitchen towel and let the dough rest for 1 hour.

4 Sprinkle the salt evenly over the dough and then fully incorporate it into the dough (according to Step 2 on page 105). Cover the bowl with a cotton or linen kitchen towel.

5 Bulk ferment the dough: During bulk fermentation, apply a series of stretch and folds to the dough (according to Step 3 on page 105) every 45 minutes for 3 hours—four series of folds total. With each stretch and fold, you should feel the dough develop in strength and structure. After the final fold, cover the dough with a kitchen towel or transfer to a container with a lid, and let rise, undisturbed, until it has increased in volume by 20 to 30 percent. This could take 1 to 3 hours depending on the time of year, the

temperature of your kitchen, and how active your leavening is.

6 Preshape and bench rest: Turn the dough out onto your work surface and fold it over itself. Using a bench knife or your hands, drag the dough across the work surface to create surface tension while shaping it into a tight ball. Dust the dough with flour, cover with a kitchen towel, and let rest for 30 minutes.

7 Final shaping: Line a round 13-inch proofing basket with a linen cloth and dust the cloth well with flour. Flip the dough onto your work surface, floured-side down. Pull each corner of dough toward the center, making a round. Seal the seam on the bottom by rolling the dough on its side and pinching the bottom between the work surface and the palm of your hand. Sprinkle the top of the dough with flour, then place it seam-side up in the prepared basket.

8 Final rise: Cover the basket with a kitchen towel and let the dough rise at room temperature for 2 hours, then transfer to the refrigerator to proof overnight.

9 Bake: In the morning, place an extra-large Dutch oven (no less than 13 inches in diameter) on the lowest rack in a cold oven; place the lid on the rack as well. (If you don't have a large enough Dutch oven, place a large baking stone on the lowest rack instead, and have a stainless-steel bowl at least 13 inches in diameter and 5 inches deep handy.) Preheat the oven to 500°F for 1 hour. Pull the basket from the refrigerator and set it on the counter; let the dough come to room temperature while the oven preheats.

10 *If you have a large enough Dutch oven,* transfer the loaf to the Dutch oven according to Step 8 on page 106 and place the lid on the pot.

11 *If you are baking on a stone,* cut a piece of parchment paper larger than the loaf but smaller than the baking stone. Sprinkle the parchment with coarse flour, cornmeal, or semolina, then flip the loaf seam-side down onto the parchment. Score the loaf in whatever pattern you desire (four slashes making a square works well on a miche). Using oven mitts, open the oven door and place the loaf, still on the parchment, on the baking stone. Quickly cover the loaf with a large stainless-steel bowl and close the oven door. (Note: If you have a pizza peel, forgo the parchment and load the loaf directly onto the baking stone.)

12 Bake for 20 minutes, then uncover the pot (if using a Dutch oven) or remove the bowl (wearing oven mitts and using the tip of a knife to carefully lift the bowl so you can remove it) and lower the oven temperature to 400°F. Bake, uncovered, for an additional 40 minutes, or until the bread is a deep dark bronze, sounds hollow when you tap on the bottom, and the internal temperature reads between 206° and 210°F.

13 Remove from the oven and transfer the bread from the pot to a cooling rack. Let cool completely before slicing.

HIPPIE DESEM (AKA SEEDED WHEAT)

OSONO BREAD • ATLANTA, GEORGIA

YIELD: 1 LARGE LOAF

LEAVEN

34g water

17g starter

49g whole-wheat
bread flour

DOUGH

321g water

73g leaven

23g maple syrup

367g high-extraction (85)
bread flour

92g whole-wheat
bread flour

10g fine sea salt

37g hulled pumpkin seeds,
plus more for coating

37g hulled sunflower seeds,
plus more for coating

14g flaxseeds,
plus more for coating

14g poppy seeds,
plus more for coating

14g sesame seeds,
plus more for coating

mixed seeds, for coating

Betsy Gonzalez, baker/owner of Osono Bread, explains the origins of this bread, "The 'Hippie' name comes from my time interning at Bread by Bike—Andy Strang, the owner, named his seedy sourdough loaf the Hippie loaf after his father said bread with seeds was for 'hippies.' The desem part comes from the emphasis of whole-grain and high-extraction flour both from the starter and dough, but mainly from my time in Bokrijk, Belgium, at Egt Brood, where desem is Dutch for leaven.' The name was really an homage to my time interning at Bread by Bike and Egt Brood."

Note: The process for this bread diverges a bit from the Bread Method on page 103 in that the initial autolyze is without the leaven and is 2 hours long. Also note that all of those hippie seeds will be added 1 hour into the bulk fermentation phase.

1 Make the leaven: Measure the water into a small clear container with a lid, such as a ½-pint mason jar, then add the starter. Using a spoon or your fingers, break apart the starter into the water, then add the flour and mix until fully incorporated. Cover and let stand at room temperature for 6 to 8 hours, until fully developed (see image on page 107).

2 Make the dough: Two hours before the leaven is mature, measure the water into a large bowl, then add the maple and both flours. Mix until fully incorporated (according to Step 1 on page 103). Cover with a cotton or linen kitchen towel and let the dough rest for 1 hour.

3 After 2 hours, add the leaven to the dough, incorporating it by squeezing it into the dough and folding the dough over itself. Allow the dough to rest for 20 minutes.

4 Sprinkle the salt evenly over the dough and then fully incorporate it into the dough (according to Step 2 on page 105). Cover the bowl with a cotton or linen kitchen towel.

5 Bulk ferment the dough: During bulk fermentation, apply a series of stretch and folds to the dough every 30 minutes for 1½ to 2½ hours (three to six series of folds total), until the dough feels strong (see page 105 for detailed stretch-and-fold instructions), incorporating the seeds by folding them into the dough as part of the second fold. With each stretch and fold, you should feel the dough developing strength and structure. After the final fold, cover the dough with a kitchen towel or transfer to a container with a lid, and let rise, undisturbed, until it has increased in volume by 20 to 30 percent. This could take 1 to 3 hours depending on the time of year, the temperature of your kitchen, and how active your leavening is.

6 Preshape and bench rest: Turn the dough out onto your work surface and fold it over itself. Using a bench knife or your hands, drag the dough across the work surface to create surface tension while shaping it into a tight ball. Dust the dough with flour, cover with a kitchen towel, and let rest for 20 to 30 minutes.

7 Final shaping: Line a 10-inch proofing basket with a linen cloth and dust the cloth well with flour. Combine the remaining mixed seeds on a large plate. Perform the final shaping of the dough as directed in Step 6 on page 106, then roll the shaped dough in the mixed seeds and place it seam-side up in the prepared basket.

8 Final rise: Cover the basket with a kitchen towel and let the dough rise at room temperature for 3 hours, then transfer to the refrigerator to proof overnight.

9 Bake: In the morning, place a Dutch oven on the lowest rack in a cold oven; place the lid on the rack as well. Preheat the oven to 500°F for 1 hour. Pull the basket from the refrigerator and set it on the counter; let the dough come to room temperature while the oven preheats. (If your kitchen is cold, place your loaf near your oven.)

10 Transfer the loaf to the Dutch oven according to Step 8 on page 106 and place the lid on the pot. Bake for 20 minutes, then uncover the pot and lower the oven temperature to 450°F. Bake, uncovered, for an additional 15 to 20 minutes, until the bread is deep golden brown, sounds hollow when you tap on the bottom, and the internal temperature reads between 204° and 210°F.

11 Remove from the oven and transfer the bread from the pot to a cooling rack. If you can wait, let the bread cool completely before slicing into it.

CIABATTA SANDWICH ROLLS

BEACH HOUSE RESTAURANT ◆ BRADENTON BEACH, FLORIDA

Teddy Louloudes developed this recipe specifically for the grilled veggie sandwich served at Beach House, a sandwich inspired by the organically raised vegetables grown fifteen minutes down the road from their kitchen at Gamble Creek Farms. This is one of the few yeast-leavened breads in this book, but the dough includes a pre-ferment called a biga—a small portion of the flour, water, and yeast left to ferment overnight. Stretching out the fermentation time further highlights flavor-forward flours; this can be done in a yeasted bread by the use of a pre-ferment. Here the biga contributes complexity to the bread's flavor and crumb.

YIELD: 8 SANDWICH ROLLS

BIGA

103g water

¼ teaspoon yeast, instant or active-dry

154g high-extraction (85) bread flour

DOUGH

395g water

1¾ teaspoons yeast, instant or active-dry

258g biga

428g high-extraction (85) bread flour

48g whole-wheat bread flour

10g fine sea salt

semolina, for dusting

1 Make the biga: Measure the water into a small clear container with a lid, such as a 1-pint mason jar, then add the yeast and flour and mix until fully incorporated. Cover and let stand at room temperature overnight.

2 Make the dough: The next morning, measure the water into a large bowl. Add the yeast, biga, and both flours and mix until fully incorporated. Cover with a cotton or linen kitchen towel and let the dough rest for 45 minutes.

3 Sprinkle the salt evenly over the dough and then fully incorporate it into the dough as directed on page 103. Cover the bowl with cotton or linen kitchen towel.

4 Bulk ferment the dough: Let the dough ferment at room temperature for 1 hour, stretching and folding the dough every 20 minutes (see page 105 for detailed stretch and fold instructions). With each stretch and fold, you should feel the dough developing strength and structure. After the final fold, cover the dough with a kitchen towel and let rise, undisturbed, until it has increased in volume by 20 to 30 percent. This could take 30 minutes to 1½ hours, depending on the time of year.

5 Preshape and bench rest: Turn the dough out onto your work surface and fold it over itself. Using a bench knife, divide the dough into eight equal pieces weighing around 138 grams each. Preshape one piece of the dough at a time: Using a bench knife or your hands, drag the dough across the work surface to create surface tension while shaping into a tight ball. Dust the dough with flour and set aside. Repeat to preshape the remaining pieces of dough, then cover them all with a kitchen towel and let rest for 20 minutes.

6 Final shaping: Dust a couche (linen cloth well) with flour. Working with one ball of dough at a time, perform the final shaping as directed on page 106, creating little baby loaves. Roll each in flour and them place on the prepared cloth, seam-side down, four rows of two end to end with a folded crease of cloth dividing the rows.

7 Final rise: Cover the rolls with a kitchen towel and let rise for 30 minutes to 1½ hours.

8 Bake: Preheat a convection oven to 475°F or a standard oven to 480°F. Lightly dust a baking sheet with semolina.

9 Carefully transfer the rolls to the prepared baking sheet. Bake for 12 to 14 minutes, until they begin to turn golden and their internal temperature reads 195°F. Transfer to a cooling rack.

HEMP CRISP BREADS

BEACH HOUSE RESTAURANT ◆ BRADENTON BEACH, FLORIDA

YIELD: ABOUT 30 CRISP BREADS

142g water

42g sourdough culture (see Note)

227g high-extraction (85) flour

57g whole-wheat bread flour

37g hemp hearts

7g sea salt

This is a great use for extra sourdough culture. These crisp breads keep incredibly well, a solid approach to stocking the pantry with house-made crackers. I love that Teddy chose our high-extraction flour for these, as the flavor of the flour and the flavor of the hemp hearts combine beautifully. At Beach House, these crisp breads are served with their smoked fish dip and house-made ferments made from organic vegetables grown just down the road from their kitchen. Teddy adapted this recipe from Chad Robertson's *Tartine Book No. 3.*

Note: This recipe uses extra sourdough culture. If you don't have any, measure 19 grams water into a small clear container with a lid, such as a ½-pint mason jar, then add 4 grams starter. Using a spoon or your fingers, break apart the starter into the water. Add 19 grams flour (this can be whole grain or sifted, wheat or rye) and mix until fully incorporated. Cover and let stand at room temperature for 6 to 8 hours, until fully developed (see image on page 107).

1 In a large bowl, combine the water, sourdough culture, both flours, the hemp hearts, and the salt and mix until just incorporated. Remove from the bowl and wrap tightly with plastic wrap. Refrigerate overnight.

2 The next day, preheat the oven to 400°F. Line a baking sheet with parchment paper.

3 Turn the dough out onto your work surface. Divide it into three equal pieces weighing around 170 grams each. The dough for these crisp breads can be rolled out by hand or with a hand-crank pasta roller (without the cutting attachment).

4 *To roll out the dough by hand,* cut two 18 x 13-inch sheets of parchment paper. Place one piece of the dough between the parchment sheets and roll it out with a rolling pin to the edges of the parchment, rotating 90 degrees as needed to extend each side. You want to roll out the dough as thin as possible; if it is resisting, let it rest for 10 minutes, then try again. Transfer the dough to the prepared baking sheet.

To roll out the dough using a pasta maker, feed one piece of dough through the pasta roller on the number 1 setting (I like to do this a couple of times before moving on to the thinner settings). Change the setting to 2 and feed the sheet of dough through; continue to the number 6 setting, then transfer the sheet of dough to the prepared baking sheet.

5 Bake for 7 to 10 minutes, making sure the center is crisp and fully baked through. Keep an eye on these, as they definitely can jump from golden to burnt quickly.

6 Remove the baking sheet from the oven and transfer the crisp bread to a cooling rack. Let cool completely, then break into smaller pieces and store in an airtight container at room temperature. These crackers keep really well, at least a week, though we've never let them last that long.

HIGH-EXTRACTION FOCACCIA

WALNUT SCHOOLHOUSE ◆ WALNUT, NORTH CAROLINA

Brennan Johnson's Walnut Schoolhouse is a wood-fired bakery located in the space that was formerly occupied by my Natural Bridge Bakery. Baking in a wood-fired oven means considering which breads can best utilize the range of heat produced in a single firing: flatbreads (pita, pizza, and focaccia) on one end—when the hearth is too hot for loaves of bread that will take at least 25 minutes to bake—and on the other end, when the heat is waning, 100 percent rye breads that can bake for hours at low temperatures. Brennan developed this focaccia—made from a wet and airy dough meant to be baked hot—in order to take the high heat, cooling down his hearth enough for the loaves of bread to follow. This focaccia also translates well to a baking sheet and home oven. Top it with any number of ingredients, such as sage and other fresh herbs, sliced shallots, garlic, thinly sliced potatoes, and (always) flaky sea salt.

YIELD: 1 (18 X 13-INCH) FOCACCIA

LEAVEN

86g water

17g starter

86g high-extraction (85) bread flour

DOUGH

765g water

170g leaven

850g high-extraction (85) bread flour

21g fine sea salt

43g olive oil, plus more for drizzling

TOPPINGS

flaky sea salt

2 cups (prepped) vegetables, such as thinly sliced shallots, tomatoes, or garlic

1 cup fresh herbs, such as basil, flat-leaf parsley, or sage, whole or slivered

1   Make the leaven: Measure the water into a small clear container with a lid, then add the starter. Using a spoon or your fingers, break apart the starter into the water, then add the flour and mix until fully incorporated. Cover and let stand at room temperature for about 8 hours, until fully developed (see image on page 107).

2   Make the dough: Once the leaven is fully developed, measure the water into a large bowl, then add the leaven and dissolve it in the water, breaking it apart with your fingers. Add the flour and mix until fully incorporated (according to Step 1 on page 103). Sprinkle on the salt and pour the olive oil over. Cover with a cotton or linen kitchen towel and let the dough rest for 45 minutes.

3   Mix the olive oil and salt into the dough (as directed on page 103). Cover with plastic wrap, or transfer it to a container with a lid.

4   Bulk ferment the dough: Let the dough ferment at room temperature for 3 hours, stretching and folding the dough every 30 minutes

(see page 105 for detailed stretch-and-fold instructions). After the final fold, cover the bowl or container, then transfer to the refrigerator to proof overnight.

5   Final rise: The next day, grease a baking sheet well. Pour the dough out onto the prepared baking sheet and let proof at room temperature for 3 to 4 hours, until very bubbly.

6   Bake: Preheat the oven to 550°F, or as high as your oven will go.

7   Using wet fingers, dimple the dough, consolidating the small air bubbles into bigger ones and leaving indentations from your fingers in between them. Drizzle with olive oil and sprinkle with flaky salt, then fill the indentations with any desired toppings.

8   Bake for 20 to 30 minutes, until deeply browned.

9   Remove the baking sheet from the oven, place on a cooling rack for 7 to 10 minutes, and then remove focaccia from the baking sheet and transfer to a cooling rack.

SOURDOUGH SWEET BUNS

WALNUT SCHOOLHOUSE ◆ WALNUT, NORTH CAROLINA

YIELD: 24 BUNS

LEAVEN

66g water

11g starter

55g high-extraction (85)
bread flour

DOUGH

170g unsalted butter

140g milk

140g heavy cream

1 tablespoon ground
cardamom

1 egg

70g granulated sugar

120g leaven

240g high-extraction (85)
bread flour

120g Trinity Blend flour (or
your own blend; see page 238)

1 teaspoon fine sea salt

FILLING

150g unsalted butter,
at room temperature

90g granulated sugar

1½ tablespoons
ground cardamom

GLAZE AND TOPPINGS

2 tablespoons syrup (either
golden syrup, honey, sorghum)

1 tablespoon water

flaky sea salt, for finishing

granulated sugar, for finishing
(optional)

This is a naturally leavened version of a sweet Scandinavian wheat bun similar to what we know as a sticky bun in the United States, though a bit more refined—less sweet, less sticky, with a fragrant cardamom-forward flavor. This dough calls for both high-extraction flour and a flour we call our Trinity Blend, a mix of rye flour, pastry flour, and bread flour that has been sifted. If you don't have this blend, you can use a 50/50 mix of stone-ground light rye flour and sifted pastry flour. I've also had success making this recipe using just high-extraction (stone-ground) all-purpose flour—a blend of bread flour and pastry flour. Don't be afraid to experiment.

1 Make the leaven: Measure the water into a small clear container with a lid, such as a ½-pint mason jar, then add the starter. Using a spoon or your fingers, break apart the starter into the water. Add the flour and mix until fully incorporated. Cover and let stand at room temperature for 6 to 8 hours, until fully developed (see image on page 107).

2 Make the dough: In a small saucepan, combine the butter, milk, cream, and cardamom and heat over low heat, stirring, until the butter has melted. Pour the mixture into a large bowl and let cool, then whisk in the egg and sugar. Add the leaven, both flours, and the salt, and mix and knead until the dough is smooth and shiny. Cover with a cotton or linen kitchen towel.

3 Bulk ferment at room temperature applying a series of stretch and folds to the dough every hour (according to Step 3 instructions on page 105) for 3 hours. Cover the bowl with a kitchen towel and transfer to the refrigerator to proof overnight.

4 Make the filling: In the morning, line a baking sheet with parchment paper. Remove the dough from the fridge. While the dough is coming to room temperature (or at least warming up enough to become malleable), make the filling in a medium bowl, combining the butter, sugar, and cardamom. Mix well to make a spreadable paste.

5 Shape and fill the buns: Turn the dough out onto your work surface. Divide it into two equal pieces. Working with one piece of dough at a time, roll it out into a rectangle about 5 inches wide, 12 inches long, and ¼ inch thick. Orient the dough so one long side is parallel with the edge of your counter. Spread the filling over the bottom half of the dough (the side closest to you). Fold down the unfilled top half to enclose the filling, forming a rectangle 2½ inches wide and 12 inches long. Cut the rectangle crosswise into twelve 1-inch-wide strips and cut a slit in each strip so it looks like a pair of trousers. Twist the trouser legs around each other and then wrap the last bit around the whole pastry. Place the buns on the prepared baking sheet. Repeat to roll out, fill, and shape the second piece of dough. Cover with a kitchen towel and let proof at room temperature for about 45 minutes.

6 Bake: Preheat the oven to 425°F.

7 Bake the buns for 20 to 23 minutes, until golden along the edges.

8 Meanwhile, make the glaze: In a small bowl, whisk together the syrup and water until smooth.

9 Remove the buns from the oven and transfer to a cooling rack. While cooling, baste them with the syrup. Sprinkle with flaky salt and sugar, if desired.

PORRIDGE BREAD

OWL BAKERY ◆ ASHEVILLE, NORTH CAROLINA

This bread has a lovely texture, loaded with porridge and seeds—a combination of buckwheat, barley, oats, and sunflower seeds—all ingredients that can come off the same fields as our wheat and rye. Rich, diverse crop rotations are good for the soil and for the farmer (think diversified portfolio). Incorporated into bread, this diversity adds flavor, texture, and increased nutritional value. This bread is baked from a wet dough that is well served by using a bread pan, though it can be done in a very well-floured basket. The recipe involves both an overnight soaker and a cooked porridge, which should be at room temperature when it is incorporated into the dough (the porridge can be made the day before, refrigerated, and then pulled out of the fridge 3 to 4 hours before using). This recipe yields three loaves, as OWL's co-owner Maia Surdam considers this the perfect number to bake at home: "One to eat, one to freeze, and one to give away."

1 Make the leaven: Measure the water into a small clear container with a lid, such as a widemouthed 1-pint mason jar, then add the starter. Using a spoon or your fingers, break apart the starter into the water. Add the flour and mix until fully incorporated. Cover and let stand at room temperature or overnight for 8 to 10 hours, until fully developed (see image on page 107).

2 Make the soaker: In a container with a lid, stir together the flaxseeds and hot water. Cover and let stand at room temperature overnight or for 8 to 10 hours.

3 Make the porridge: In a large pot, combine the barley groats, buckwheat groats, oats, water, and salt. Stir well and bring to a boil over high heat, then reduce the heat to low. Cook, stirring regularly so the porridge doesn't burn on the bottom of the pan, until the porridge has thickened considerably but not become dry, 10 to 20 minutes. If your porridge is hot, wait about 10 minutes and then cool it down by

spreading it out on a baking sheet and covering with plastic wrap so it doesn't dry out as it cools.

4 Make the dough: This dough likes patient hydration. Pour 600 grams of the water into a large bowl, then add the leaven and dissolve it in the water, breaking it apart with your fingers. Add both flours and mix until fully incorporated (according to Step 1 on page 103). Cover with a cotton or linen kitchen towel and let the dough rest for 45 minutes to 1 hour.

5 Sprinkle the salt evenly over the dough, splash on the remaining 40 grams water, and then fully incorporate the salt and water into the dough using a squeezing motion to pass the dough between your fingers to ensure that the salt is distributed evenly. Fold in the porridge, then the soaker, and then sunflower seeds, again using a squeezing motion to incorporate each into the dough. Cover the bowl with a cotton or linen kitchen towel.

CONTINUED

YIELD: 3 (8 X 4-INCH) PAN LOAVES OR MEDIUM-SIZE HEARTH BREADS

LEAVEN (8 TO 10 HOURS)

83g water

14g starter

83g whole-wheat bread flour

SOAKER (8 TO 10 HOURS)

100g flaxseeds

100g hot water

PORRIDGE

70g barley groats

70g buckwheat groats

100g rolled oats

525g water

pinch fine sea salt

DOUGH

640g water

160g leaven

640g 75-extraction bread flour

160g whole-wheat bread flour

20g fine sea salt

about 600g porridge

200g soaker

100g hulled sunflower seeds, toasted

PORRIDGE BREAD

CONTINUED

6 Bulk ferment the dough: Let the dough ferment at room temperature for 2 hours, stretching and folding the dough every 30 minutes (according to Step 3 on page 105). With each stretch and fold, you should feel the dough developing strength and structure. After the final fold, transfer to a container (with a lid), large enough to allow for expansion, and place in the refrigerator to proof for 12 to 18 hours.

7 Preshape and bench rest: The next day, pull dough from the refrigerator and turn it out onto your work surface. Using a bench knife, divide it into three equal pieces weighing about 840 grams each. Using a bench knife or your hands, drag the dough across the work surface to create surface tension while shaping it into a tight ball. Dust the dough with flour, cover with a kitchen towel, and let rest for 30 minutes.

8 With a pastry brush dipped in olive oil, grease three 8 x 4-inch bread pans. Line each with parchment paper cut to fit the length of the pan and wide enough to cover the two long sides. Grease the parchment as well; the narrow ends of each pan are left uncovered, so brush them with extra oil.

9 Final shaping: Working with one piece of dough at a time, perform the final shaping as directed on page 106, then place the dough seam-side up in one of the prepared pans.

10 Final rise: Cover the pans with kitchen towels and let the dough rise at room temperature until the dough is ready. This can take as little as 1 hour or as much as 3 hours or more depending on the time of year and the strength of your leaven. To gauge whether the dough is fully proofed, dip your fingertip in flour and gently poke the dough. If the indentation slowly rises back, leaving behind a slight dip, it is ready to bake. If the dough bounces right back, let proof for another 15 minutes, then test it again.

11 Bake: Position a rack in the bottom third of the oven and preheat the oven to 450°F.

12 Score the top of the dough as desired. Place the pans in the oven and bake for 35 to 45 minutes, until the bread is deep golden brown, sounds hollow when you tap on the bottom, and the internal temperature reads between 204° and 210°F.

13 Remove the pans from the oven and immediately transfer the loaves to a cooling rack. Let cool completely before serving.

PIEDMONT MICHE

WEAVER STREET MARKET BAKERY ◆ HILLSBOROUGH, NORTH CAROLINA

From Weaver Street baker Jon McDonald: "This dough defies logic a bit by pre-fermenting a rather large percentage of the flour. The bread includes a wheat and a rye starter and should have a beautiful dark, shiny mahogany color coming out of the oven. The crust is redolent of fresh ground coffee and butterscotch. The flavor is robust but not super acidic. The crumb should have a medium consistency."

This is a large, over 3-pound loaf that requires a round basket or banneton at least 10 inches in diameter and an 11-inch-diameter Dutch oven; if you don't have a Dutch oven large enough, you can bake the dough on a pizza stone under a large stainless-steel bowl.

1 Make the rye leaven: Measure the water into in a small clear container with a lid, such as a widemouthed 1-pint mason jar, then add the starter. Using a spoon or your fingers, break apart the starter into the water. Add the flour and mix until fully incorporated. Cover and let stand at room temperature for 16 hours, or until fully developed (see image on page 107).

2 Make the wheat leaven: Measure the water into a container (with a lid) large enough to allow for expansion, but not too large (this is a lot of leaven and requires a container that's ideally about 3.5 liters), then add the starter. Using a spoon or your fingers, break apart the starter into the water, then add the flour and mix until fully incorporated. Cover and let stand at room temperature for 16 hours, or until fully developed (see image on page 107).

3 Make the dough: Once the leaven is fully developed, measure the water into a large bowl, then add both leavens and dissolve them in the water, breaking them apart with your fingers. Add both flours and mix until fully incorporated.(according to Step 1 on page 103). Cover with a cotton or linen kitchen towel and let the dough rest for 1 hour.

4 Sprinkle the salt evenly over the dough and then fully incorporate it into the dough (according to Step 2 on page 105). Cover the bowl with a cotton or linen kitchen towel.

5 Bulk ferment the dough: During bulk fermentation, apply a series of stretch and folds to the dough (according to Step 3 on page 105) every 45 minutes for 3 hours—four series of folds total. With each stretch and fold, you should feel the dough develop in strength and structure. After the final fold, cover the dough with a kitchen towel and let rise, undisturbed, for 30 minutes, until it has increased in volume by 20 to 30 percent. If not, continue bulk fermentation for another hour or more. Because of the higher percentage of leavening in this dough, it will likely develop more quickly than doughs with less leavening.

CONTINUED

YIELD: 1 LARGE ROUND LOAF

RYE LEAVEN (16 HOURS)

128g water

5g starter

135g whole-rye flour

WHEAT LEAVEN (16 HOURS)

322g water

39g starter

489g 75-extraction bread flour

DOUGH

178g water

798g wheat leaven

242g rye leaven

160g whole-wheat bread flour

106g 75-extraction bread flour

16g fine sea salt

PIEDMONT MICHE

CONTINUED

6 Preshape and bench rest: Turn the dough out onto your work surface and fold it over itself. Using a bench knife or your hands, drag the dough across the work surface to create surface tension while shaping it into a tight ball. Dust the dough with flour, cover with a kitchen towel, and let rest for 30 minutes.

7 Final shaping: Line a 10-inch-round proofing basket with a linen cloth and dust the cloth well with flour. To shape the miche, flip the dough floured-side down onto your work surface. Pull each corner of dough toward the center, making a round. Seal the seam on the bottom by rolling the dough on its side and pinching the bottom between the work surface and the palm of your hand. Sprinkle the top of the dough with flour, then place it seam-side up in the prepared basket.

8 Final rise: Cover the basket with a kitchen towel and let rise at room temperature for 2 hours, then transfer to the refrigerator to proof overnight.

9 Bake: In the morning, place a large Dutch oven (at least 11 inches in diameter) on the lowest rack in a cold oven; place the lid on the rack as well. Preheat the oven to 500°F for 1 hour.

10 Transfer the dough to the Dutch oven according to the instructions on page 106 and place the lid on the pot. After you've placed the bread in the oven, lower the oven temperature to 440°F. Set a timer for 30 minutes. When it goes off, uncover the pot and lower the oven temperature to 420°F. Bake, uncovered, for an additional 30 to 40 minutes, until the bread is a deep dark mahogany color, sounds hollow when you tap on the bottom, and the internal temperature reads between 206° and 210°F.

11 Remove from the oven and transfer the bread from the pot to a cooling rack. If you can wait, let the bread cool completely before slicing into it.

MICHE BABY

TARA JENSEN ◆ POUND, VIRGINIA

YIELD: 1 MEDIUM LOAF

RYE LEAVEN

28g water

7g starter

28g whole-rye flour

WHEAT LEAVEN

28g water

7g starter

28g whole-wheat
bread flour

DOUGH

332g warm water
(about 85°F)

55g wheat leaven

55g rye leaven

313g 75-extraction
bread flour

39g whole-rye flour

39g whole-spelt flour

8g fine sea salt

I was intrigued by this recipe because, like Weaver Street's miche (see page 137), it calls for two different starters and, additionally, a blend of flours, with each baker's choice of flour defining the bread. In Tara's miche, 80 percent of the flour is 75-extraction bread flour, and her choice of adding 10 percent whole rye and 10 percent whole spelt contributes tenderness to the crumb. With this recipe, Tara shares, "Traditional miche can weigh anywhere between 1.5 and 5 kilograms. The heavy weight reflects a time when bread was baked in a communal oven and a family would eat from a single loaf for the week. Often the loaf was round and would be cut into wedges. This version is scaled down to a standard 840-gram loaf." Miche baby.

1 Make the rye leaven: Measure the water into a small clear container with a lid, such as a ½-pint mason jar, then add the starter. Using a spoon or your fingers, break apart the starter into the water, then add the flour and mix until fully incorporated. Cover and let stand at room temperature overnight or for 8 to 10 hours, until fully developed (see image on page 107).

2 Make the wheat leaven: Measure the water into a small clear container with a lid, such as a ½-pint mason jar, then add the starter. Using a spoon or your fingers, break apart the starter into the water, then add the flour and mix until fully incorporated. Cover and let stand at room temperature overnight or for 8 to 10 hours, until fully developed (see image on page 107).

3 Make the dough: Once the leaven is fully developed, measure the water into a large bowl, then add both leavens and dissolve them in the water, breaking them apart with your fingers. Add the bread flour, rye flour, and spelt flour and mix until fully incorporated (according to Step 1 on page 103). Cover with a cotton or linen kitchen towel and let the dough rest for 1 hour.

4 Sprinkle the salt evenly over the dough and then fully incorporate it into the dough (according to Step 2 on page 105). Cover the bowl with cotton or linen kitchen towel.

5 Bulk ferment the dough: During bulk fermentation, apply a series of stretch and folds to the dough (according to Step 3 on page 105) every 30 minutes for 1½ hours. With each stretch and fold, you should feel the dough develop in strength and structure. After the third fold, if it feels like a fourth fold will serve your dough, do it, then cover the dough with a kitchen towel or transfer to a container with a lid, and let rise, undisturbed, until it has increased in volume by 20 to 30 percent. This could take 1 to 3 hours depending on the time of year, the temperature of your kitchen, and how active your leavening is.

6 Preshape and bench rest: Turn the dough out onto your work surface and fold it over itself. Using a bench knife or your hands, drag the dough across the work surface to create surface tension while shaping it into a tight ball. Dust the dough with flour, cover with a kitchen towel, and let rest for 25 to 35 minutes.

7 Final shaping: Line an 9-inch-round (or oval) proofing basket with a linen cloth and dust the cloth well with flour. To shape the miche, flip the dough floured-side down onto your work surface. Pull each corner of dough toward the center, making a round. Seal the seam on the bottom by rolling the dough on its side and pinching the bottom between the work surface and the palm of your hand. Sprinkle the top of the dough with flour and then place it seam-side up in the prepared basket.

8 Final rise: Cover the basket with a kitchen towel and let the dough rise at room temperature for 3 hours, then transfer to the refrigerator to proof overnight.

9 Bake: In the morning, place a Dutch oven on the lowest rack in a cold oven; place the lid on the rack as well. Preheat the oven to 500°F for 1 hour.

10 Transfer the loaf to the Dutch oven according to Step 8 on page 106 and place the lid on the pot. Bake for 20 minutes, then uncover the pot and lower the oven temperature to 475°F. Bake, uncovered, for an additional 15 to 20 minutes, until the bread is a deep golden brown, sounds hollow when you tap on the bottom, and the internal temperature reads between 204° and 210°F.

11 Remove from the oven and transfer the bread from the pot to a cooling rack. If you can wait, let the bread cool completely before slicing into it.

RUSTIC PEASANT BREAD

NATURAL BRIDGE BAKERY ◆ WALNUT, NORTH CAROLINA

YIELD: 1 MEDIUM LOAF

CRACKED RYE LEAVEN

32g water

6g starter

32g coarsely cracked rye

SCALD

99g coarsely cracked rye

119g hot water

DOUGH

246g water

61g leaven

218g scald

307g 75-extraction bread flour

7g fine sea salt

When I first began my Natural Bridge Bakery, I made just one bread—100 percent whole-grain desem bread. I had a few customers ask if I'd considered offering a little variety, but I wasn't inspired by any other bread until we traveled up to Glover, Vermont, and met Peter Schumann of the Bread and Puppet Theater. He was making a bread that was half cracked rye and half sifted wheat flour. I was so intrigued by the flavor, texture, and nose of this bread. At the time, I had no interest in sifted flour, but the cracked rye gave the sifted flour flavor and texture, and the sifted flour provided structure and crumb to the cracked rye. As soon as I made it back to my bakery, I began experimenting until I landed on this recipe. I then called Peter Schumann and asked if I could name my bread after him. He told me that was a ridiculous idea, as he did not invent the bread. He said it was gray bread, or graubrot, and that that was what I ought to call it. I was not sure if anyone would want to buy a bread called "grey bread," so I called it my Rustic Peasant.

Note: The cracked rye scald must be soaked overnight.

1 Make the leaven: Measure the water into a small clear container with a lid, such as a ½-pint mason jar, then add the starter. Using a spoon or your fingers, break apart the starter into the water. Add the flour and mix until fully incorporated. Cover and let stand at room temperature overnight or for 8 to 10 hours, until fully developed (see image on page 107).

2 Make the cracked rye scald: In a medium bowl, stir together the coarsely cracked rye and hot water. Cover with a cotton kitchen towel and let sit overnight.

3 Make the dough: Once the leaven is fully developed, measure the water into a large bowl, then add the leaven and dissolve it in the water, breaking it apart with your fingers. Add the scald and the flour and mix until fully incorporated (according to Step 1 on page 103). Cover with a cotton or linen kitchen towel and let the dough rest for 45 minutes to 1 hour.

4 Sprinkle the salt evenly over the dough and then fully incorporate it into the dough (according to Step 2 on page 105). Cover the bowl with a cotton or linen kitchen towel.

5 Bulk ferment the dough: During bulk fermentation, apply a series of stretch and folds to the dough (according to Step 3 on page 105) every 30 minutes for 1½ hours. With each stretch and fold, you should feel the dough develop in strength and structure. After the third fold, if it feels like a fourth fold will serve your dough, do it, then cover the dough with a kitchen towel or transfer to a container with a lid, and let rise, undisturbed, until it has increased in volume by 20 to 30 percent. This could take 1 to 3 hours depending on the time of year, the temperature of your kitchen, and the strength of your leaven.

6 Preshape and bench rest: Turn the dough out onto your work surface and fold it over itself. Using a bench knife or your hands, drag the dough across the work surface to create surface tension while shaping it into a tight ball. Dust the dough with flour, cover, and let rest for 30 minutes.

7 Final shaping: Line a 9-inch proofing basket with a linen cloth and dust the cloth well with flour. Perform the final shaping of the dough as directed on page 106. Sprinkle the top with flour, then place the dough seam-side up in the prepared basket.

8 Final rise: Cover the basket with a kitchen towel and let the dough rise at room temperature for 3 hours, then transfer to the refrigerator to proof overnight.

9 Bake: In the morning, place a Dutch oven on the lowest rack in a cold oven; place the lid on the rack as well. Preheat the oven to 500°F for 1 hour. Pull the basket from the refrigerator and set it on the counter; let the dough come to room temperature while the oven preheats. (If your kitchen is cold, place your loaf near your oven.)

10 Transfer the loaf to the Dutch oven according to Step 8 on page 106 and place the lid on the pot. Bake for 20 minutes, then uncover the pot and lower the oven temperature to 475°F. Bake, uncovered, for an additional 15 to 20 minutes, until the bread is a deep golden brown, sounds hollow when you tap on the bottom, and the internal temperature reads between 204° and 210°F.

11 Remove from the oven and transfer the bread from the pot to a cooling rack. If you can wait, let the bread cool completely before slicing into it.

SOUTHEAST SOURDOUGH

FOLK ◆ NASHVILLE, TENNESSEE

**YIELD: 1 LARGE
HEARTH LOAF**

**LEAVEN (AKA MOM,
SEE NOTE)—
4 TO 6 HOURS**

36g water

7g starter

36g whole-wheat
bread flour

DOUGH

358g water

51g leaven

316g 75-extraction
bread flour

84g whole white
wheat bread flour

219g whole-rye flour
(or rye meal)

11g fine sea salt

Michael Matson developed this bread while running the bread program at Folk. His choice of flours in this bread provide the ideal balance of what he sought to achieve: a simple loaf where the flour is the most important facet of the bread. Whole-grain hard white wheat provides tooth without adding the bold flavor of whole-grain red wheat. Rye lends a silkiness to the crumb, as well as delivers flavor. And the 75-extraction bread flour provides the loft.

Note: Michael refers to his leaven as "Mom."

1 Make the leaven: Measure the water into a small clear container with a lid, such as a widemouthed 1-pint mason jar, then add the starter. Using a spoon or your fingers, break apart the starter into the water. Add the flour and mix until fully incorporated. Cover and let stand at room temperature for 4 to 6 hours, until fully developed (see image on page 107).

2 Make the dough: Once the leaven is fully developed, measure the water into a large bowl, then add the leaven and dissolve it in the water, breaking it apart with your fingers. Add the bread flour, whole-wheat flour, and rye flour and mix until fully incorporated (according to Step 2 on page 105). Cover with a cotton or linen kitchen towel and let the dough rest for 45 minutes to 1 hour.

3 Sprinkle the salt evenly over the dough and then fully incorporate it into the dough (according to Step 2 on page 105). Cover the bowl with a cotton or linen kitchen towel.

4 Bulk ferment the dough: During bulk fermentation, apply a series of stretch and folds to the dough (according to Step 3 on page 105) every 30 minutes for 2 hours—four series of folds total. With each stretch and fold, you should feel the dough develop in strength and structure. After the final fold, cover the dough

with a kitchen towel or transfer to a container with a lid, and let rise, undisturbed, until it has increased in volume by 20 to 30 percent. This could take 30 minutes to 2 hours depending on the time of year, the temperature of your kitchen, and the strength of your leaven.

5 Preshape and bench rest: Turn the dough out onto your work surface and fold it over itself. Preshape the dough, using a bench knife or your hands to drag the dough across the work surface to create surface tension while shaping it into a tight ball. Dust the dough with flour, cover with a kitchen towel, and let rest for 30 minutes.

6 Final shaping: Line a 10-inch proofing basket with a linen cloth and dust the cloth well with flour.

7 Perform the final shaping of the dough as directed on page 106. Sprinkle the top with flour and place seam-side up in the prepared basket.

8 Final rise: Cover with a kitchen towel and let the dough rise at room temperature for 1 to 2 hours, then transfer to the refrigerator to proof for 12 to 24 hours.

9 Bake: Place a large Dutch oven on the lowest rack in a cold oven; place the lid on the rack as well. Preheat the oven to 500°F for 1 hour. Pull the loaf from the refrigerator and let the dough come to room temperature while the oven preheats.

10 Transfer the dough to the Dutch oven according to the instructions on page 106 and place the lid on the pot. Bake for 20 minutes, then uncover the pot and lower the oven temperature to 450°F. Bake, uncovered, for an additional 15 to 20 minutes, until the loaf has a deep dark golden hue, sounds hollow when you tap on the bottom, and the internal temperature reads between 204° and 210°F.

11 Remove the Dutch oven from the oven and immediately transfer the loaf to a cooling rack. If you can wait, let cool completely before slicing.

A Word about Pizza and Cold-Milled Stone-Ground Flour

Using exclusively cold-milled stone-ground flour in pizza dough can certainly result in exceptional pies—crisp and chewy—but expect a deeper flavor in the crust and perhaps not quite as much light, open crumb. Pizza dough made from stone-ground flavor-forward flours can influence one's choice of toppings, perhaps opting for a simpler selection of toppings that further accentuate instead of overshadow the flavor of the crust.

In the following pages I have included two pizza dough recipes: the first, Michael Matson developed while he was with Folk in Nashville (see page 148), and the second from Gregory Seymour of Pizzeria Gregario in Safety Harbor, Florida (see page 149). There are similarities between the two recipes, but where they diverge demonstrates each baker's choice and vision for their particular pie.

Shelter-in-Place Pizza

These were the last recipes I tested for this book. I'm not a pizza maker and was intimidated by the task at hand until my husband, Scott, suggested we do this together. Scott actually co-owns and runs a wood-fired pizza restaurant, West First Wood-Fired, in downtown Hendersonville, North Carolina, so I was in good hands. He was home from work because we all were. The whole country was sheltering in place. Our ingredients were limited to what we already had in the kitchen. We topped our pizzas with a quick tomato sauce (see sidebar on the opposite page), fresh mozzarella, anchovies, capers, and, once out of the oven, fresh arugula.

The following is a basic method for making a pizza once your dough is ready.

Place a pizza stone on the upper rack in the oven and preheat the oven to 500°F (or as high as your oven will allow). We happened to have had a stack of firebrick (because Scott had just done some repairs to his oven at West First) so he filled two baking sheets with firebrick and placed one on the lowest rack of the oven and the other on the upper rack, about 8 inches from the broiler, where we actually baked our pizza. Because of the density of the firebrick, he preheated the oven for 2 hours. With a pizza stone, you just need to preheat the oven for 1 hour (similar to a Dutch oven, though on the upper rack for pizza.)

If you're using the All Stone-Ground Pizza Dough (page 148), pull it from the refrigerator about 20 minutes before you are ready to bake and set it on the counter.

Flour your work surface and lightly flour the top of your dough. Gently transfer the dough to your work surface, being careful not to de-gas it as you transfer it. Cup your hands around the dough to gently reshape it into a round (if it has lost some of its roundness). Using the pads of your fingers, start to flatten the dough, keeping the edges thicker and being careful not to make the center too thin. Rotate the dough as you simultaneously gently press down and stretch out, using the pads of your fingers at first and then, as the dough increases in size, using the outer edge of your hands.

If you have a pizza peel, flour the peel and then scoop up the dough onto your peel. (If you don't have a peel—as we, ironically, did not—just use the back of your hands to transfer the dough onto a floured rimless baking sheet.) Build your pie with the dough on the peel (or baking sheet).

In building your pie, go easy on the toppings. Spread your sauce to about ½ inch to 1 inch from the edge. Distribute your toppings evenly, being careful not to pile too much in the very center of the dough, as you risk ripping a hole in the dough when you transfer it to the stone. Less is more when balancing the flavor elements of stone-ground flour along with its reduced tensile strength.

Transfer the pizza from the peel (or baking sheet) onto the hot pizza stone and bake until the crust is browned and the topping is bubbling. Ovens vary greatly, but expect no more than 10 minutes of baking time. (We found success with baking at 500°F for a little more than 5 minutes and then switching the oven to broil for a final 3 minutes.)

Remove the pizza from the oven and place on a cooling rack for a minute or two before transferring to a cutting board to slice and serve.

Quick and Simple Tomato Sauce

2 cups canned or jarred whole plum tomatoes (we prefer Jovial brand organic tomatoes)

1 tablespoon extra-virgin olive oil

Fine sea salt and freshly ground black pepper

2 tablespoons chopped fresh oregano

Puree the tomatoes with an immersion blender. Add the olive oil and season with salt and pepper. Stir in the oregano.

ALL STONE-GROUND PIZZA DOUGH

FOLK ◆ NASHVILLE, TENNESSEE

YIELD: ENOUGH
DOUGH FOR 6
(12-INCH) PIZZAS

LEAVEN

76g water

15g starter

76g whole white
wheat bread flour

DOUGH

585g water

151g leaven

843g 75-extraction
bread flour

44g whole white
wheat flour

27g fine sea salt

Michael Matson developed this pizza dough with the goal of creating a dough that used 10 percent cold-milled stone-ground flour. His choice of whole white wheat for his leaven and as a small percentage of the flour in the dough provides tooth without the added bitter undertone that the tannins in whole red wheat express, contributing a butteriness in flavor instead.

1 Make the leaven: Measure the water into a small clear container with a lid, such as a 1-pint mason jar, then add the starter. Using a spoon or your fingers, break apart the starter into the water. Add the flour and mix until fully incorporated. Cover and let stand at room temperature for 4 to 6 hours or more, until fully developed (see image on page 107).

2 Make the dough: Measure the water into a large bowl, then add the leaven and dissolve it in the water, breaking it apart with your fingers. Add both flours and mix until fully incorporated (according to Step 2 on page 105). Cover with a cotton or linen kitchen towel and let the dough rest for 45 minutes.

3 Sprinkle the salt evenly over the dough and then fully incorporate it into the dough (according to Step 2 on page 105). Cover the bowl with plastic wrap or transfer the dough to a container with a lid.

4 Bulk ferment the dough: During bulk fermentation, apply a series of stretch and folds to the dough (according to Step 3 on page 105) every 45 minutes for 3 hours—four series of folds total. With each stretch and fold, you should feel the dough develop in strength and structure. After the final fold, cover the dough with a kitchen towel and let rise, undisturbed, until it has increased in volume and feels billowy.

5 Divide and preshape: Turn the dough out onto your work surface and fold it over itself. Divide it into six equal pieces weighing about 275 grams each. Preshape one portion of the dough at a time: Using a bench knife or your hands, drag the dough across the work surface to create surface tension while shaping it into a tight ball. Place dough balls on a parchment-lined and floured baking sheet. Dust the dough with flour, cover with a kitchen towel, and let rest for 2 hours, then transfer the dough to the refrigerator to proof for 6 to 8 hours.

6 Bake: Place a pizza stone on the upper rack in a cold oven. Preheat the oven to as hot as it will go for 1 hour. Remove the dough from the refrigerator about 20 minutes before you are ready to bake.

7 Working with one portion of the dough at a time, follow the instructions on page 146 to shape the dough, top it, and transfer it to the pizza stone. Bake for 5 minutes and then switch to broil for 2 to 3 minutes. You want to see the crust browned and the topping bubbling. If the crust seems like it needs a little more time after 3 minutes on broil, switch back to bake. Ideally, total bake time should be no more than 10 minutes.

8 Remove the pizza from the oven and place on a cooling rack for a minute or two before transferring to a cutting board to slice and serve.

GREGARIO'S CAROLINA GROUND PIZZA DOUGH

PIZZERIA GREGARIO | SAFETY HARBOR, FLORIDA

Pizzeria Gregario is an unexpected find in Safety Harbor, Florida. The pizzas are made with 100 percent cold-milled stone-ground flour, a portion of which the restaurant's chef/baker/owner, Gregory Seymour, mills in-house, hand-sifts, and then blends with our flour. Walking into this small wood-fired pizza restaurant, one is greeted by a large sign spelling out his ethos. At the top, it reads: "Ingredients Matter." A second sign lists his purveyors. And a third sign shows a chart of the costs of goods sold: In the far left column are his ingredients—flour, mozzarella, tomatoes, sausage, chorizo, prosciutto, bacon; the center column displays the national brands' prices for these items; and the right column shows the prices from his purveyors. Total transparency.

Gregory is part chef, part mad scientist when it comes to pizza dough. He does two versions of his dough at his restaurant. One is made with a blend of heritage grains that he mills in-house and then hand-sifts to his desired extraction. And the second one, the one that we are providing here, is his more basic approach to a dough, although compared to most, it is hardly basic.

Khorasan wheat, otherwise known as Kamut, is an ancient relative of the durum wheat. It is a lovely spring wheat with a good amount of protein. Sadly, it is not grown in our part of the country, but Gregory's choice is with intention. The Khorasan wheat provides added elasticity to his dough, along with a buttery flavor and inviting tooth. Using the Khorasan to build his leaven is helpful in the Florida heat, as the Khorasan develops at a more controlled pace (attributed to its higher protein count). The sifted spelt lends a nutty flavor and a delicate crumb.

CONTINUED

GREGARIO'S CAROLINA GROUND PIZZA DOUGH

CONTINUED

1 Make the leaven: Measure the water into a small clear container with a lid, such as a ½-pint mason jar, then add the starter. Using a spoon or your fingers, break apart the starter into the water. Add the flour and mix until fully incorporated. Let stand at room temperature for 8 to 10 hours, until fully developed (see image on page 107).

2 Make the dough: Once the leaven is fully developed, measure the water into a large bowl, then add the leaven and dissolve it in the water, breaking it apart with your fingers. Add the bread flour, spelt flour, and Khorasan flour and mix until fully incorporated (according to Step 1 on page 103). Cover with a cotton or linen kitchen towel and let the dough rest for 45 minutes.

3 Sprinkle the salt evenly over the dough and then fully incorporate it into the dough (according to Step 2 on page 105). Cover the bowl with a cotton or linen kitchen towel.

4 Bulk ferment the dough: Let the dough ferment at room temperature for 3 hours, stretching and folding the dough every 30 minutes (according to Step 3 on page 105). After the final fold, cover the dough with a kitchen towel and let rise, undisturbed, until it has increased in volume and feels billowy. Once the dough has risen sufficiently, transfer it to the refrigerator to proof overnight.

5 Preshape and final proof: Turn the dough out onto your work surface and fold it over itself. Divide it into five portions weighing about 225 grams each. Preshape one portion of the dough at a time: Using a bench knife or your hands, drag the dough across the work surface to create surface tension while shaping it into a tight ball. Dust the dough balls with flour, cover with a kitchen towel, and let proof at room temperature for 3 hours before shaping and topping.

6 Bake: Place a pizza stone on the upper rack in a cold oven. Preheat the oven to as hot as it will go for 1 hour.

7 Working with one portion of the dough at a time, follow the instructions on page 146 to shape the dough, top it, and transfer it to the pizza stone. Bake for 5 minutes and then switch to broil for 2 to 3 minutes. You want to see the crust browned and the topping bubbling. If the crust seems like it needs a little more time after 3 minutes on broil, switch back to bake. Ideally, total bake time should be no more than 10 minutes.

8 Remove the pizza from the oven and place on a cooling rack for a minute or two before transferring to a cutting board to slice and serve.

YIELD: ENOUGH DOUGH FOR 5 (12-INCH) PIZZAS

LEAVEN

23g water

5g starter

23g whole Khorasan wheat (Kamut) flour

DOUGH

480g water

45g leaven

448g 75-extraction bread flour

122g sifted spelt (85) flour

70g whole Khorasan wheat (Kamut) flour

14g fine sea salt

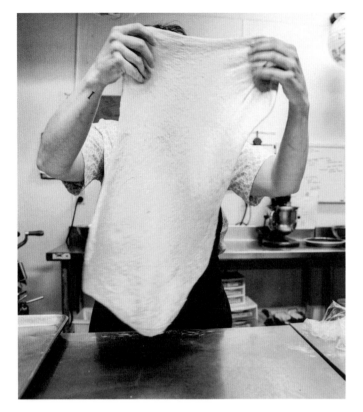

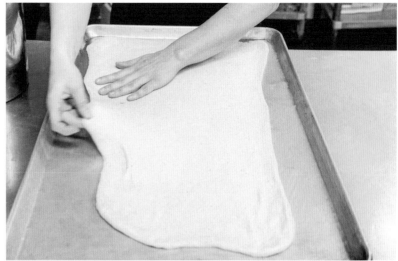

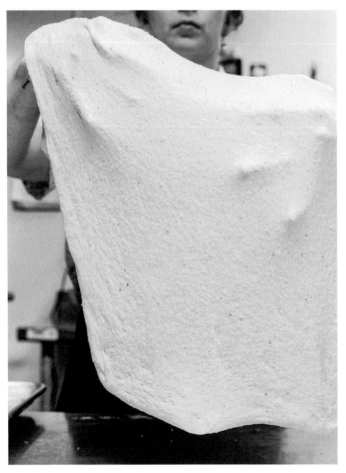

CORNMEAL CRACKERS

ASHLEY CAPPS ◆ ASHEVILLE, NORTH CAROLINA

The combination of sourdough culture and cornmeal gives this cracker a cheeselike flavor, made even better when served with pimiento cheese, though they are quite addictive on their own, too. This recipe is a good use for extra sourdough culture, as it calls for such a small amount. The crackers are stretched windowpane thin and baked low and slow.

YIELD: ABOUT 30 CRACKERS

125g (½ cup) warm water (90°F)

42g (3 tablespoons) milk, warmed (90°F)

56g (¼ cup) unsalted butter, melted

7g (1½ teaspoons) olive oil

½ teaspoon honey

20g (2 tablespoons) sourdough culture (see Note, page 128)

225g (2 cups) 75-extraction bread flour

56g (⅓ cup) fine cornmeal, plus more for topping

1½ teaspoons fine sea salt, plus more for topping

1½ teaspoons freshly ground black pepper

1 In a large bowl, stir together the water, milk, melted butter, olive oil, and honey. Add the sourdough culture and dissolve it in the liquid.

2 In a separate bowl, combine the flour, cornmeal, salt, and pepper. Add the dry ingredients to the wet ingredients and mix until fully incorporated and a dough forms.

3 Cover the bowl and let the dough ferment at room temperature for 1 hour, stretching and folding the dough every 30 minutes (according to Step 3 on page 105).

4 Turn the dough out onto your work surface. Divide it into three pieces, weighing around 180 grams each. Preshape one portion at a time: Using a bench knife or your hands, drag the dough across the work surface to create surface tension while shaping it into a tight ball. Transfer all three balls of dough into a container with a lid. Cover the container, transfer to the refrigerator, and let proof overnight or for 24 to 36 hours.

5 The next day (or the following day), pull the dough from the refrigerator. Working with one portion at a time, roll out the dough with a rolling pin to ½ inch thick to lengthen and stretch it—don't force the dough or it will tear. Transfer the slab of dough to a piece of parchment paper and top with a second piece of parchment; cover with a kitchen towel to prevent a skin from forming. Repeat to roll out the remaining dough, stacking the slabs on top of each other, separated with parchment. Let rest, covered, for 1 hour to relax the gluten so that you can stretch the dough further.

6 Preheat the oven to 300°F.

7 Pick up a slab of dough and use rounded knuckles to gently tug and stretch it (see the photo on the opposite page) as thin as possible. Place the dough on a baking sheet and use your fingers to pull and press the edges to thin out the dough as needed. Repeat with the remaining dough, placing each slab on a separate baking sheet.

8 Mist the sheets of dough with water and sprinkle the tops evenly with cornmeal and salt. Mist water again to hydrate the cornmeal and salt.

9 Bake one baking sheet at a time (depending on the size of your oven) for 25 to 35 minutes, until the crackers are evenly golden brown and crisp.

10 Remove from the oven and place on a cooling rack. Let cool, then break into shards as desired. Stored in an airtight container at room temperature, these crackers will keep for at least a couple of weeks.

ALMOND CANTUCCI

ANISETTE ◆ RALEIGH, NORTH CAROLINA

**YIELD: ABOUT
15 COOKIES**

240g (2 cups) 75-extraction
bread flour

232g (1¼ cups)
granulated sugar

¾ teaspoon baking powder

⅛ teaspoon fine sea salt

¼ teaspoon ground
anise seed

3 eggs

½ teaspoon pure
vanilla extract

75g (½ cup) roasted
almonds

Cantucci are cookies of Tuscan origin similar to biscotti, though their texture is a bit different from that of biscotti in that they have a chew to them. Like biscotti, cantucci are twice baked and are perfect for dunking into coffee or tea. Stored in an airtight container, they will keep for weeks. This recipe lacks butter or oil, which is traditional for this centuries-old cookie. The choice of bread flour in this application works well, as this rustic cookie is all about the tooth.

1 Preheat the oven to 350°F. Line a baking sheet with parchment paper.

2 In the bowl of a stand mixer fitted with the paddle attachment, combine the flour, sugar, baking powder, salt, and anise and mix on low speed for 30 seconds to combine.

3 Separate one of the eggs, placing the yolk in a medium bowl; set the egg white aside. Add the remaining two eggs and the vanilla to the bowl and whisk to combine. Add the egg mixture to the mixer bowl and mix on low until the dry ingredients are evenly moistened. Stop and scrape down the sides and bottom of the bowl, then mix on low for 2 minutes. Add the almonds; mix on low for 2 minutes.

4 Turn the dough out onto your work surface. Divide it into two equal portions, weighing around 340 grams each. Form each portion into a 12-inch log. Place the logs on the prepared baking sheet with about 4 inches between them and brush them with the egg white.

5 Bake the logs for 25 minutes. Remove from the oven and let cool for 10 minutes, then slice each log on an angle into 1-inch-thick cookies. Return the cookies to the baking sheet, cut-side down, and bake for 10 minutes more, or until golden. Transfer to a cooling rack. Once fully cooled, store in an airtight container at room temperature for a few weeks.

BREAKFAST COOKIE

LYDIA STAMM ◆ ASHEVILLE, NORTH CAROLINA

YIELD: 18 LARGE COOKIES

300g (2⅓ cups) whole white wheat flour

1 teaspoon baking powder

1 teaspoon baking soda

1 teaspoon fine sea salt

113g (½ cup) unsalted butter, at room temperature

260g (1¼ cups), packed light brown sugar

2 eggs

120g (½ cup) plain yogurt

1 tablespoon pure vanilla extract

340g (3½ cups) rolled oats

28g (2 tablespoons) barley malt flour (see first Note)

283g (10-ounce bag) dark chocolate (at least 60% cacao) chips or chunks

30g tart unsweetened frozen fruit (see second Note)

Lydia Stamm, miller, queen of our online store, keeper of chickens, bees, dogs and cats, developed this cookie, inspired by a recipe she found while still in high school and continued to adapt over the years since. She explains, "I grew up reading cookbooks and baking for a large family, so I was always modifying recipes according to available ingredients and everyone's dietary preferences. The sour cherries were added on a whim—we had many fruit trees and berry bushes, and we picked, pitted, froze, and cooked fruit all summer long. I took some out of the freezer, chopped them up, and added two kinds of chocolate. Since it was the low-fat '90s, I was obliged to cut some of the butter with yogurt. Here, it makes for a magical consistency, soft, a little chewy, and a little cakey. Recently, I revisited this recipe when nothing was living up to my ideal oatmeal cookie. I often use bread flour in heartier cookies to get the structure I'm looking for, and I thought our Appalachian white whole-wheat bread flour would be a nice complement, with some crisp sturdiness and a mild flavor that wouldn't overpower the fruit. The stone-ground flour and thick oats help soak up some of the moisture from the yogurt and berries and end up with just enough chewiness. I also added NC Malt flour for another hint of earthy flavor, but if you don't have it, make these cookies anyway."

Notes: If you omit the barley malt flour, you may need an additional 2 tablespoons bread flour.

Use tart (unsweetened) fruit such as cherries, raspberries, or cranberries. Although fresh fruit can be used, frozen fruit mixes in a little more easily without liquifying.

1 Preheat oven to 360°F. Line a baking sheet with parchment paper.

2 In a medium bowl, sift together the flour, baking powder, baking soda, and salt; set aside.

3 In the bowl of a stand mixer fitted with the paddle attachment, cream the butter and sugar on medium speed until light and fluffy, stopping frequently to scrape down the sides of the bowl.

4 With the mixer on low speed, slowly add the eggs, one at a time, and mix thoroughly. Add yogurt and vanilla, then stop and scrape down the bowl. Mix on high speed until fully incorporated and light in color, then stop and scrape down the bowl.

5 With the mixer on low speed, add the dry ingredients all at once and mix until just incorporated, making sure that no streaks of butter are remaining and stopping to scrape down the bowl as needed—do not overmix. Add the oats, barley malt flour, and chocolate and mix on low speed just to combine. Remove the bowl from the mixer and gently fold in the fruit.

6 Pack the dough into a ⅓ cup measure to scoop. Evenly space six cookies on the prepared baking sheet. Bake the cookies, up to 2 sheets at a time, for approximately 14 to 18 minutes, or until just slightly wet looking in the center. Check a few minutes early, as ovens vary and you don't want to overbake these. Transfer to a cooling rack. Repeat with the remaining dough.

7 These cookies do not store well at room temperature because of the high moisture content, but they do store especially well in the freezer and are actually a lovely summer treat directly from the freezer. Once completely cooled, place in a single layer in a zip-top bag. Squeeze out any air and seal before placing in the freezer for up to 3 months.

DECADENT CHOCOLATE CHIP COOKIES

ASHLEY CAPPS ◆ ASHEVILLE, NORTH CAROLINA

I am obsessed with this cookie. I was torn between putting this in the rye section or here in the wheat section because the recipe was originally written for rye and the flavors work so well with rye, but I have a love affair with our Appalachian White wheat and wanted to see how this cookie would work using that instead of the rye. I found that white wheat (whole grain) seemed to elevate this cookie even more (if that were even possible). It lends tooth and brightness, whereas rye is grassier and more tender. If you do choose to make this with rye, a medium-rye works well. Just reduce your baking time to 12 to 15 minutes.

Note: All the ingredients should be at room temperature.

1 In a medium bowl, sift together the flour, baking powder, baking soda, and salt; set aside.

2 In the bowl of a stand mixer fitted with the paddle attachment, cream the butter and both sugars on medium speed until light and fluffy, about 10 minutes, stopping frequently to scrape down the sides of the bowl.

3 With the mixer on low speed, slowly add the honey, eggs, milk, sour cream, and vanilla, then stop and scrape down the bowl. Mix on high speed until fully incorporated and light in color, then stop and scrape down the bowl.

4 With the mixer on low speed, add the dry ingredients all at once and mix until just incorporated, making sure that no streaks of butter are remaining and stopping to scrape down the bowl as needed—do not overmix. Add the chocolate and mix on low speed just to combine. Remove the bowl from the mixer, cover, and refrigerate the dough overnight.

5 The next day, line a baking sheet with parchment paper.

6 Use a 1-ounce cookie scoop or a heaping tablespoon to scoop the dough onto the prepared baking sheet, spacing the cookies 1½ inches apart. Top the cookies with flaky salt, cacao nibs, and chopped chocolate as desired, pressing the toppings lightly against the dough to adhere. Then cover the baking sheet with plastic wrap and put into the freezer for 30 minutes to 1 hour or longer.

7 Preheat the oven to 325°F.

8 Bake the cookies for 15 to 17 minutes, rotating the pan once during baking.

9 Remove the pan from the oven and transfer to a cooling rack. Once fully cooled, store in an airtight container at room temperature for up to a week.

YIELD: 3 DOZEN COOKIES

DOUGH

360g (2¾ cups) whole white wheat flour

1 teaspoon baking powder

½ teaspoon baking soda

½ teaspoon fine sea salt

212g (¾ cup + 3 tablespoons) unsalted butter, at room temperature

190g (¾ cup + 2 tablespoons) light brown sugar

90g (½ cup) granulated sugar

2 teaspoons honey

2 eggs, at room temperature

30g (⅛ cup) milk, at room temperature

30g (⅛ cup) sour cream, at room temperature

1 teaspoon pure vanilla extract

170g (6 ounces) dark chocolate (at least 60% cacao), chopped into large chunks

56g (2 ounces) milk chocolate, chopped into large chunks

TOPPINGS

flaky sea salt

cacao nibs

chopped chocolate

WHITE WHEAT CAKE

CAROLINA GROUND ◆ ASHEVILLE, NORTH CAROLINA

YIELD: 1 (7-INCH) ROUND CAKE

57g (¼ cup + 1 tablespoon) granulated sugar

56.5g (¼ cup) unsalted butter

1 large egg, separated

2 heaping tablespoons apricot jam

104g (¾ cup) whole white wheat flour

¾ teaspoon baking powder

¼ teaspoon baking soda

⅛ teaspoon fine sea salt

82g (⅓ cup) buttermilk

¾ teaspoon almond extract

¼ teaspoon pure vanilla extract

45g (1.5 ounces) bittersweet chocolate (at least 60% cacao), coarsely chopped

Inspired by the flavors of a Sachertorte, with bitter chocolate, apricot jam, and almond extract and the texture of an Italian semolina cake, I originally developed this recipe using Khorasan (Kamut) wheat, but it has evolved to embrace the availability of North Carolina–grown Appalachian White wheat. If you live out west, Khorsan or White Sonora works well—whatever you have available to you. I chose to make this a small (7-inch) cake, because I find that I tend to only make large cakes for celebrations, but a small cake like this is a lovely dessert any time. To increase the size of the cake, just double the recipe and bake the batter in a 9-inch springform pan.

1   Preheat the oven to 350°F. Line the bottom of a 7-inch springform pan with parchment paper cut to fit, then grease the pan and dust it with flour, tapping out any excess.

2   In the bowl of a stand mixer fitted with the paddle attachment, cream the sugar and butter on high speed until light and fluffy. Adjust to low speed and add the egg yolk and jam, then increase the speed and mix until fluffy.

3   In a medium bowl, sift together the flour, baking powder, baking soda, and salt.

4   Measure the buttermilk into a bowl and stir in the almond and vanilla extracts.

5   Add the flour mixture and the buttermilk mixture to the butter mixture in two additions, mixing only until incorporated after each addition. Add the chocolate and mix until just incorporated.

6   In a separate medium bowl, whip the egg white until it holds stiff peaks. By hand, gently fold the beaten egg white into the batter, then pour the batter into the prepared pan. Smooth the top with a spatula.

7   Bake until the cake springs back when you touch the center lightly and a toothpick inserted into the middle comes out clean, about 35 minutes.

8   Remove the pan from the oven and place on a cooling rack. Allow to cool 5 to 7 minutes before removing from springform pan. Cool completely on cooling rack before serving.

9   Store covered in the refrigerator for 5 to 6 days.

Rye

RYE BREADS

Danish Rye 165

Dark Rye with Caraway, Fennel,
and Cardamom 166

100% Sourdough
Coffee Can Rye 167

Seeded Rye 168

Rugbrød 170

Volkornbrot with Fenugreek
and Brown Sesame 171

Seeded Rye with Kvass 173

Russian Scalded Rye 176

Whole Rye 179

Nordic Rye with Beer
and Sorghum 180

Sprouted and Seeded Rye 182

RYE: SWEET

Chocolate Rye Brownies 185

Vegan Double Chocolate Cookies
with Rye and Olive Oil 186

Salted Cane Syrup Tart with
Rye-and-Oat Cookie Crust 189

Rye Hand Pies 190

Rye Chocolate Chip Sablés 193

Rye Shortbread 194

Jam Tart with Rye Crust 197

Upside-Down Rye Cake
with Seasonal Fruit 198

Salted Rye Cookies 201

Rye Shortbread with Mascarpone
and Lemon Curd 202

Salted and Malted Cookies 203

North Carolina Rye Custard 205

Rye: In the Field

It was on Billy Carter's (pages 52 and 190) farm that I first noticed the pronounced difference between rye and wheat in the field. In the bakery, the difference is obvious. Whole-rye flour looks and feels distinctive, with a bluish hue and a powdery texture interspersed with larger bran flakes, compared to whole-wheat flour, which has a more uniform consistency. Rye mixes differently, absorbs more liquid, and ferments quicker. Lovely bread can be made from 100 percent rye, but this will be a denser loaf than wheat, with a tight, moist crumb. Having experienced these differences as a baker, I wasn't much surprised to see the evidence in the field on Billy's farm. His rye fields appeared to have more personality than the adjacent fields of wheat. Some of the rye stalks stood out, taller than the rest, whereas the wheat grew in a near uniform manner. Manifest in the field is the difference between a cross-pollinating cereal and a self-pollinating cereal. Wheat is self-pollinating, reproducing itself at close to 100 percent pure progeny, whereas rye is an outcrosser, or a cross-pollinating cereal, meaning that pollination occurs between two plants of the same species. A variety of rye is actually a population, so there literally is more personality in a field of rye than a field of wheat. This diversity also likely contributes to rye's resilience. Rye can grow in poor soil and under adverse conditions. And because it is easy to grow, it has been an ideal crop to push forward the regional grains movement.

Rye: In the Bakery

In my mind, there is no other grain that is as well served by stone milling than rye. Industrial roller-milled rye flour is a faint shadow of its former self, its flavor having been mistaken for caraway. Freshly stone-ground rye is extraordinary, and our Southern-grown Wrens Abruzzi delivers deep and rich flavors. Although rye is considered a gluten-containing grain, it is a different kind of gluten than wheat. Whereas wheat's gluten-forming proteins—gliadin and glutenin—provide the structure to dough, the glutenin, which contributes elasticity, is not present in rye. Instead, starch and non-starch complex carbohydrates play a significant role in forming the structure of rye breads. These complex carbohydrates, collectively called pentosans, have high water-binding capacity, which is why rye flour can absorb more water than wheat flour. The high water absorption transforms complex carbohydrates into starchlike gel, and through fermentation, a three-dimensional network of soluble proteins, starch, and pentosans enable the gas-holding capacity of rye flour. The starchlike gel performs a similar function to gluten but does not dry out like gluten and thus also contributes to the keeping quality of rye bread.

DANISH RYE

JOE BOWIE ◆ COLUMBIA, SOUTH CAROLINA

This is an extraordinary recipe—straightforward and accessible for any level of baker. It will take a full 48 hours from start to slicing into this bread, so time this right to work for you. Building the leaven and soaking seeds right before going to sleep is a good schedule. The next morning, mix the dough and pan the bread, allowing the loaf to rise at room temperature throughout the day. Joe notes, "The amount of proof time really depends on how active your starter is (and the temperature of your home)." Joe loves this bread with salted vegan butter or cultured butter.

Also note that Joe's formula for leaven produces 25 grams more than the dough requires. Having extra leaven is a good safety measure, and for some, this is the seed for the next bake. You can use this extra culture in Hemp Crisp Breads (page 128), Mississippi Market Galettes (page 228), or Cornmeal Crackers (page 153).

YIELD: 1 (8 X 4-INCH) PAN LOAF

LEAVEN (8 TO 12 HOURS)
150g water
75g starter
100g whole-rye flour

SOAKER (8 TO 12 HOURS)
150g hulled pumpkin seeds
75g hulled sunflower seeds
100g cold water

DOUGH
100g warm water (about 85°F)
200g leaven
200g whole-rye flour
1½ teaspoons sorghum syrup
10g fine sea salt
soaker (above), drained

1 Make the leaven: Measure the water into a small clear container with a lid, such as a widemouthed 1-quart mason jar, then add the starter. Using a spoon or your fingers, break apart the starter into the water. Add the flour and mix until fully incorporated. Cover and let stand at room temperature for at least 8 to 12 hours (it's possible to let it go even longer, say, 14 hours), until fully developed (see image on page 107).

2 Make the soaker: In a container with a lid, stir together the sunflower seeds, pumpkin seeds, and cold water. Cover and let stand at room temperature for 8 to 12 hours, then drain and set aside.

3 Make the dough: Once the leaven is fully developed, measure the water into a large bowl, then add the leaven and dissolve it in the water, breaking it apart with your fingers. Add the flour, sorghum syrup, salt, and drained soaker and mix until fully incorporated, squeezing and mixing all the ingredients together vigorously to make a smooth, claylike dough.

4 Final rise: Grease an 8 x 4-inch standard loaf pan with olive oil or butter (if you're not vegan, the butter is more commonly used in this Danish bread).

5 Place the dough directly in the prepared pan, using wet hands to smooth the top of the loaf. Cover with a cotton or linen kitchen towel and proof at room temperature for 4 to 8 hours, until small holes appear in the top of the loaf. (The final proof time depends on how active your leaven is and the temperature of your kitchen.)

6 Bake: Preheat the oven to 450°F. Bake for 10 minutes, then lower the oven temperature to 350°F and bake for another 45 minutes, or until the internal temperature reads 206°F.

7 Remove from the oven and immediately transfer the bread from the pan to a cooling rack. Let cool completely, ideally for 24 hours, before slicing. If you would like a softer crust, remove the loaf from the pan and let cool for 10 minutes, then return it to the pan and let it cool completely.

DARK RYE WITH CARAWAY, FENNEL, AND CARDAMOM

WEAVER STREET MARKET BAKERY ◆ HILLSBOROUGH, NORTH CAROLINA

YIELD: 1 (9 X 4-INCH PULLMAN) LOAF

LEAVEN (14 HOURS)

154g water

13g starter

163g whole-rye flour

DOUGH

288g water

314g leaven

219g 75-extraction bread flour

165g whole-rye flour

11g fine sea salt

1 teaspoon bread spice (see Note)

This bread was inspired by our Wrens Abruzzi rye flour. Weaver Street was excited to highlight the flavor of this Southern rye grown less than an hour's drive from the bakery, so they created this bread. There is a beautiful simplicity to it—a moist crumb with the addition of a blend of cardamom, caraway, and fennel rounding out the flavor of the rye. This bread has become a staple in our household, lovely with cheese and ferments, or with tahini and orange marmalade, my morning favorite.

Note: For the bread spice, use a mixture of 2 parts freshly ground caraway seed, 1 part fennel seed, and 1 part cardamom.

1   Make the leaven: Measure the water into a small clear container with a lid, such as a widemouthed 1-quart mason jar, then add the starter. Using a spoon or your fingers, break apart the starter into the water. Add the flour and mix until fully incorporated. Cover and let stand at room temperature for at least 14 hours, until fully developed (see image on page 107).

2   Make the dough: Once the leaven is fully developed, measure the water into a large bowl, then add the leaven and dissolve it in the water, breaking it apart with your fingers. Add both flours, the salt, and the bread spice and mix until fully incorporated. Once everything is mixed, either leave the dough in the bowl and cover with a cotton or linen kitchen towel, or transfer it to a container with a lid.

3   Bulk ferment the dough: Let the dough ferment at room temperature for 3 to 4 hours, stretching and folding the dough every 45 minutes (according to Step 3 on page 105). Although this is a rye dough, which does not have the elasticity or pliability of wheat, there

is enough wheat in this dough that it will begin to develop strength and elasticity with each stretch and fold.

4   Final rise: With a pastry brush dipped in olive oil or melted butter (or a combination of both), grease a 9 x 4-inch Pullman loaf pan thoroughly. Place the dough in the prepared pan, then use wet hands to smooth the top of the loaf. Cover and proof at room temperature for 2 to 4 hours, until small holes appear in the top of the loaf.

5   Bake: Preheat the oven to 475°F.

6   Bake for 25 minutes, then lower the oven temperature down to 460°F and bake for another 20 to 30 minutes, until the internal temperature of the bread reads 206°F.

7   Remove from the oven and immediately transfer the bread from the pan to a cooling rack. Let cool completely, ideally for 12 hours, before slicing.

100% SOURDOUGH COFFEE CAN RYE

CHICKEN BRIDGE BAKERY ◆ PITTSBORO, NORTH CAROLINA

This bread is baked in a 15-ounce coffee can, producing a cylindrical loaf and perfectly round slices. Made with mostly light (sifted) rye flour, it has a smooth texture and moist crumb. Its stripped-down simplicity is the beauty of this 100 percent rye bread—with no add-ins, and just fennel, caraway, and anise to enhance the flavorful rye. If you are without a coffee can but would like to make this bread, doubling this recipe yields one 9 x 4-inch Pullman loaf.

1 Make the leaven: Measure the water into a small clear container with a lid, such as a widemouthed 1-pint mason jar, then add the rye starter. Using a spoon or your fingers, break apart the starter into the water. Add the flour and mix until fully incorporated. Cover and let stand at room temperature for 4 hours, or until fully developed (see image on page 86).

2 Make the dough: Once the leaven is fully developed, measure the water into a large bowl, then add the leaven and dissolve it in the water, breaking it apart with your fingers. Add both flours, the malt, salt, caraway, anise, and fennel and mix until fully incorporated. Cover with a cotton or linen kitchen towel.

3 Bulk ferment the dough: Let the dough ferment at room temperature for 3 to 4 hours, depending on the ambient temperature. The dough will appear to have expanded at about 1.5 to 2 times.

4 Final rise: With a pastry brush dipped in olive oil or melted butter (or a combination of both), grease a clean empty 15-ounce metal coffee can generously. Scoop the dough into the prepared can, then use wet hands to smooth the top of the loaf. Cover with a kitchen towel and proof at room temperature for 2 hours, or until the dough has risen to the rim of the can and the surface has cracked.

5 Bake: Preheat the oven to 500°F.

6 Bake for 20 minutes, then lower the oven temperature to 450°F and bake for another 20 minutes, or until the internal temperature of the bread reads 209°F.

7 Remove from the oven and immediately transfer the bread from the can to a cooling rack. Let cool completely, ideally for 24 hours, before slicing.

YIELD: 1 CYLINDRICAL LOAF

LEAVEN (4 HOURS)

82g warm water (about 85°F)

21g rye starter

82g whole-rye flour

DOUGH

190g water

152g leaven

190g light rye flour

63g whole-rye flour

12.5g malt

5.2g fine sea salt

3g caraway seeds

1g anise seeds

1g fennel seeds

SEEDED RYE

MICHAEL MATSON ◆ NASHVILLE, TENNESSEE

YIELD: 1 (13 X 4-INCH
PULLMAN) LOAF

**SOAKER
(12 TO 24 HOURS)**

242g cracked rye

97g hulled sunflower seeds

97g sesame seeds

48.5g hulled pumpkin seeds

194g nut milk, unsweetened

96g brewed coffee,
room temperature

24g sorghum syrup

**LEAVEN
(14 TO 16 HOURS)**

159g water

32g starter

159g whole-wheat flour

DOUGH

513g water

315g leaven

242g whole-wheat
bread flour

121g whole-rye flour

121g 75-extraction
bread flour

799g soaker

15g fine sea salt

This bread is mostly seeds and cracked rye, though it contains enough wheat flour, along with a wheat leaven, to enable it to build strength and structure with each stretch and fold. Michael Matson developed this bread, inspired by a rye bread he used to make during his time spent in Newport, Maine, at Zu Bakery. This bread is meant to be sliced thin and pairs beautifully with cured meats, cheeses, and ferments.

1 Make the soaker: In a container with a lid, stir together the cracked rye, sunflower seeds, sesame seeds, pumpkin seeds, nut milk, coffee, and sorghum syrup. Cover and let stand at room temperature for 12 to 24 hours.

2 Make the leaven: Measure the water into a small clear container with a lid, such as a widemouthed 1-quart mason jar, then add the starter. Using a spoon or your fingers, break apart the starter into the water. Add the flour and mix until fully incorporated. Cover and let stand at room temperature for 4 to 6 hours, until fully developed (see image on page 107).

3 Make the dough: Once the leaven is fully developed, measure the water into a large bowl, then add the leaven and dissolve it in the water, breaking it apart with your fingers. Add the whole-wheat bread flour, whole-rye flour, and 75 bread flour and mix until incorporated (according to Step 1 on page 103). Cover with a cotton or linen kitchen towel and let the dough rest for 30 minutes.

4 Add the soaker and salt and mix until fully incorporated. Cover with a kitchen towel.

5 Bulk ferment the dough: Let the dough ferment at room temperature for 3½ hours, applying a series of stretch and folds at 1-hour intervals for the first 2 hours (see page 105 for detailed stretch-and-fold instructions). After the final fold, cover the dough with a kitchen towel and let rise, undisturbed, for another 30 minutes.

6 Final rise: With a pastry brush dipped in olive oil or melted butter (or a mixture of both), grease a 13 x 4-inch Pullman loaf pan thoroughly. Scoop the dough into the prepared pan, then use wet hands to smooth the top of the loaf. Cover and proof at room temperature for 1½ to 2 hours, then refrigerate for 16 to 24 hours.

7 Bake: Preheat the oven to 375°F.

8 Place the loaf in the oven directly from the refrigerator and bake for 1½ hours, until the internal temperature reads 210°F.

9 Remove from the oven and immediately transfer the bread from the pan to a cooling rack. Ideally, wait 24 hours before slicing into the bread.

RUGBRØD

CHICKEN BRIDGE BAKERY ◆ PITTSBORO, NORTH CAROLINA

YIELD: 1 (9 X 4-INCH
PULLMAN) LOAF

LEAVEN (4+ HOURS)

49g warm water
(about 85°F)

12g starter

49g whole-rye flour

SOAKER (4+ HOURS)

142g coarsely cracked rye
(rye chops)

224g hot water

DOUGH

153g water

101g leaven

366g soaker

52g buttermilk

7g sorghum syrup

127g whole-wheat flour

47g whole-rye flour

9g barley malt

68g flaxseeds

33g sesame seeds

30g hulled sunflower seeds

30g hulled pumpkins seeds

6g fine sea salt

coarsely cracked rye, for
sprinkling

Rob Segovia-Welsh relays the story behind this bread: "We had a Danish customer who came to me one market day saying that she was homesick for the traditional rye bread she grew up with. She asked me if I would try making it if she translated a formula for me. I had never made a rye bread that looked anything like this. So much hydration, so much sourdough culture, more whole grains and seeds than flour! As I mixed it for the first time, I thought, 'No way could this be right!' There was no shaping, just scooping the dough into bread tins. But it turned out all right. With more practice and some weeks, she gave me her stamp of approval. It has turned into one of my most favorite breads to make and eat and is our most popular whole-grain loaf by far."

1 Make the leaven: Measure the water into a small clear container with a lid, such as a widemouthed 1-pint mason jar, then add the rye starter. Using a spoon or your fingers, break apart the starter into the water. Add the flour and mix until fully incorporated. Cover and let stand for 4 hours, or until fully developed (see image on page 107).

2 Make the soaker: Put the coarsely cracked rye in a medium bowl and pour over the hot water. Cover and let stand at room temperature for 4 hours.

3 Make the dough: Once the leaven is fully developed, measure the water into a large bowl, then add the leaven and dissolve it in the water, breaking it apart with your fingers. Add the soaker, buttermilk, sorghum syrup, both flours, the malt, flaxseeds, sesame seeds, sunflower seeds, and pumpkin seeds and mix until fully incorporated. Cover with a cotton or linen kitchen towel and let the dough rest for 30 minutes.

4 Sprinkle the salt evenly over the dough and mix by hand until fully incorporated. Cover with a kitchen towel.

5 Bulk ferment the dough: Let the dough ferment at room temperature for 3 to 4 hours. It will appear to have expanded somewhat, but because of the add-ins, rely more on the temperature of your kitchen, the clock, and your senses to judge when it is ready.

6 Final rise: With a pastry brush dipped in olive oil or melted butter (or a combination of both), grease a 9 x 4-inch Pullman loaf pan thoroughly. Scoop the dough into the prepared pan, then use wet hands to smooth the top of the loaf. Sprinkle the top of the loaf with coarsely cracked rye. Let proof at room temperature for 2 to 3 hours, until small holes appear in the top of the loaf.

7 Bake: Preheat the oven to 500°F.

8 Bake for 20 minutes, then lower the oven temperature to 450°F and bake for another 25 minutes, or until the internal temperature of the bread reads 209°F.

9 Remove from the oven and immediately transfer the bread from the pan to a cooling rack. Let cool completely, ideally for 24 hours, before slicing.

VOLKORNBROT WITH FENUGREEK AND BROWN SESAME

PIZZERIA GREGARIO ◆ SAFETY HARBOR, FLORIDA

I thought we had enough rye recipes in this book, really. I had no intention of adding another. But then I visited Gregory Seymour in Safety Harbor, Florida, and he handed me a slice of this bread, and I knew I needed to include this one, too! The taste combination of spice and depth of our Wrens Abruzzi rye with the unexpected notes that the fenugreek contributes, and the tooth provided by the addition of the sesame seeds—in the layers of flavor and texture, I was reminded that Gregory, before becoming a baker, was and always will be a chef.

1 Make the leaven: Measure the water into a large clear container with a lid, then add the starter. Using a spoon or your fingers, break apart the starter into the water. Add the rye meal and mix until fully incorporated. Cover and let stand at room temperature for 15 to 20 hours, until fully developed (see image on page 107).

2 Make the soaker: In a container with a lid, stir together the rye meal, sesame seeds, fenugreek, water, and salt. Cover and let stand at room temperature for 12 hours.

3 Make the dough: Once the leaven is fully developed, measure the water into a large bowl, then add the leaven and dissolve it in the water, breaking it apart with your fingers. Add the soaker and then the flour and mix until fully incorporated. Cover the bowl with a cotton or linen kitchen towel.

4 Bulk ferment the dough: Let the dough ferment at around 78°F for 2 hours (longer in a cooler environment—in my kitchen in North Carolina, I would likely go another hour). The dough will appear to have expanded.

5 Final rise: With a pastry brush dipped in olive oil or melted butter (or a combination of both), grease a 13 x 4-inch Pullman loaf pan thoroughly. Scoop the dough into the prepared pan, then use wet hands to smooth the top of the loaf. Sprinkle rye flour over the top. Let proof at room temperature for 1½ to 3 hours, until small holes appear in the top of the loaf.

6 Bake: Preheat the oven to 450°F.

7 Bake for 20 minutes, then lower the oven temperature to 425°F and bake for another 55 minutes, or until the internal temperature reads 204°F.

8 Remove from the oven and immediately transfer the bread from the pan to a cooling rack. Let cool completely, ideally for 24 hours, before slicing into the bread.

YIELD: 1 (13 X 4-INCH PULLMAN) LOAF

LEAVEN (15 TO 20 HOURS)

324g water

34g starter

341g rye meal

SOAKER (12 HOURS)

322g rye meal

150g brown sesame seeds, toasted

50g fenugreek, whole

435g water

21g fine sea salt

DOUGH

151g water

644g leaven

977g soaker

280g whole-rye flour, plus more for dusting

SEEDED RYE WITH KVASS

OWL BAKERY ◆ ASHEVILLE, NORTH CAROLINA

Maia Surdam, co-owner of OWL, baker, and historian, developed this recipe while pursuing her research project on the history between beer and bread, a project inspired by a collaboration between OWL and a local brewery. Maia explains, "At OWL, our adventures with kvass began when our friends at Fonta Flora Brewery asked us if they could make a beer with our bread. They wanted three hundred pounds of our country sourdough bread to make it! Their version included a mixed-culture yeast and spent strawberries, resulting in a delightfully tart and fruity beer. This modern-day kvass spoke to the collaborative and creative spirit of our community, but only partially resembled the kvass of ancient times. Indeed, kvass has a long history, particularly in the Slavic areas of Eastern Europe, where, some claim, it has been consumed since the Middle Ages. People typically made it from stale rye bread. Over the centuries, people of all classes drank it, but it was especially popular among working people. Easily and quickly made at home, it was a nutritious, flavorful, and refreshing addition to the diet of peasants."

Note: This recipe involves a leaven, soaker, pre-ferment, and dough. Read through the recipe before proceeding so you can plan for the timing of this bread. Making the leaven and soaker in the morning, the preferment in the evening, and the dough the following morning is a suggested schedule to follow. If you don't have access to store-bought kvass, not to worry—this bread can be made with beer or water instead of the kvass. We've also included a recipe for making kvass (a great use of old bread). This recipe will produce extra leaven. Save it to use in a later batch of kvass or to make Hemp Crisp Breads (page 128) or Cornmeal Crackers (page 153).

YIELD: 2 (9 X 4-INCH PULLMAN) LOAVES

LEAVEN (8 TO 10 HOURS)
70g warm water (about 85°F)

14g starter

70g whole-rye flour

SOAKER (8 TO 10 HOURS)
47g sorghum molasses

133g hulled pumpkin seeds

133g hulled sunflower seeds

47g flaxseeds

23g sesame seeds

340g hot water

PRE-FERMENT (8 TO 10 HOURS)
252g warm water

134g leaven

722g soaker

420g whole-rye flour

25g fine sea salt

DOUGH
234g kvass (recipe on page 175), beer, or water

1,554g pre-ferment

306g coarsely cracked rye

150g whole-wheat bread flour

100g water (if needed)

1 Make the leaven: In the morning, measure the water into a small clear container with a lid, such as a widemouthed 1-pint mason jar, then add the starter. Using a spoon or your fingers, break apart the starter into the water. Add the flour and mix until fully incorporated. Cover and let stand at room temperature for 8 to 10 hours, until fully developed (see image on page 107).

2 Make the soaker: In a bowl, combine the sorghum, pumpkin seeds, sunflower seeds, flaxseeds, and sesame seeds, then pour over the hot water. Cover and let stand at room temperature for 8 to 10 hours.

3 Make the pre-ferment: In the evening, measure the warm water into a large bowl, then add the leaven and dissolve it in the water, breaking it apart with your fingers. Add the soaker and stir with your hands to combine it with the leaven. Add the flour and salt and mix until the dough is fully hydrated and uniform. Cover with a cotton or linen kitchen towel and let rest overnight.

4 Make the dough: Add the kvass to the pre-ferment. Add the coarsely cracked rye and whole-wheat bread flour. Mix until the ingredients are fully incorporated. The dough

CONTINUED

SEEDED RYE WITH KVASS

should be stiff but evenly moist. You may need to add 100 grams more water to hydrate the dough.

5   Final rise: With a pastry brush dipped in olive oil or melted butter (or a combination of both), grease two 9 x 4-inch Pullman loaf pans thoroughly. Divide the dough into two pieces, weighing about 1,120 grams each. Scoop the dough into the prepared pans, then use wet hands to smooth the top of each loaf. Be sure to get the dough all the way into the corners of the pans. Dust the tops of the loaves with flour. Cover each pan loosely with a kitchen towel so the tops of the loaves don't dry out.

6   Let proof at room temperature for 2 to 4 hours. The exact proofing time will depend on the temperature of your dough as well as the room temperature. Watch for signs that the bread is ready: it will nearly fill up the pan with a dome and small cracks will start to form along the surface.

7   Bake: Preheat the oven to 375°F.

8   Bake for 15 minutes, then lower the oven temperature to 350°F and bake for about 1½ hours more, until the internal temperature of each loaf reads 203°F.

9   Remove from the oven and transfer the loaves from the pans to a cooling rack. Allow to sit out, uncovered, for 24 hours before cutting into.

KVASS

(ADAPTED FROM OLIA HERCULES'S *MAMUSHKA*)

Maia explains the origins of this recipe: "Like other traditional beverages once made exclusively in homes, kvass has undergone changes over time. In parts of Eastern Europe today, one can buy kvass from street vendors, although it tends to be sweet, more closely resembling a commercial soft drink than a naturally fermented beverage. OWL baker Lola Borovyk grew up drinking this style of kvass in the Ukrainian city of Kamianske. She found it refreshing, but Lola's mother always praised the homemade kvass made by her grandfather, which she remembered as less sweet and more complex through his use of raisins and spices.

"Lola made OWL's first batch of kvass using Olia Hercules's recipe as a guide. To obtain a deeper flavor reminiscent of her great-grandfather's kvass, she uses OWL's 100 percent sourdough rye bread (made with Carolina Ground flour), sweetens it with honey and raisins, and adds coriander and caraway. We have since made several batches of kvass, each a bit different, and use it when we make the Seeded Rye Kvass bread."

YIELD: 1 LITER (1000 GRAMS)

200g to 250g dried toasted bread (rye is traditional but any kind of whole-grain sourdough bread will work)

1,360g (48 ounces) boiling water

1 tablespoon mixture of coriander, cardamom, and caraway (optional)

2 tablespoon honey

1½ teaspoons leaven

70g mixture of raisins, dates, and dried figs

1 Place the dried bread in a ½-gallon heat-tempered jar such as a mason jar and pour the boiling water over it. Add the spices and cover with a cloth. Let sit at room temperature for 1 to 2 days.

2 Strain the mixture into a clean jar. (At OWL, they compost the soaked bread.) Add the honey, leaven, and dried fruit and stir well. Cover with a cloth, and set aside in a warm, dark place for 24 to 36 hours.

3 Taste the kvass and see if you like the flavor. Let it ferment longer if you want a tangier flavor.

4 When the flavor is to your liking, transfer the kvass to the refrigerator to slow fermentation. Its flavor will continue to evolve over time, becoming more sour and tangy. Serve cold, over fresh mint, if possible, and enjoy!

RUSSIAN SCALDED RYE

WALNUT SCHOOLHOUSE ◆ WALNUT, NORTH CAROLINA

YIELD: 1 LARGE ROUND
(OR 13 X 4-INCH
PULLMAN) LOAF

**LEAVEN STAGE 1
(6 TO 8 HOURS)**

330g warm water
(about 85°F)

16g starter

165g whole-rye flour

**LEAVEN STAGE 2
(10 TO 12 HOURS)**

275g whole rye flour

511g stage 1 leaven (above)

**SCALD
(12 TO 16 HOURS)**

250g rye meal

469g boiling water

DOUGH

300g water

715g leaven

719g scald

350g whole-rye flour

18g fine sea salt

This is a unique bread that involves a two-stage rye leaven build as well as a scald of a portion of your flour. The result is a rye bread of complex flavor with hints of coffee and chocolate. Brennan Johnson adapted the recipe from Stanley Ginsberg's *The Rye Baker*. It requires a large (5.5-quart) Dutch oven for baking or can be made in a large pullman loaf pan.

1 Make the stage 1 leaven: Measure the warm water into a large container with a lid (about 3.5 liters), then add the starter. Using a spoon or your fingers, break apart the starter into the water. Add the flour and mix until fully incorporated. Cover and let stand in a warm spot for 6 to 8 hours, until very active and bubbly. (This leaven will have a liquid, batterlike consistency.)

2 Make the stage 2 leaven: Stir the rye flour into the stage 1 leaven; the mixture will be quite stiff. Let stand for 10 to 12 hours, until it has visibly expanded, cracked on top, and smells sour.

3 Make the scald: Put the rye meal in a medium bowl and pour over the boiling water. Cover and let stand overnight or for 12 to 16 hours to develop sweetness.

4 Make the dough: Once the leaven is fully developed, in a large bowl, combine the water, leaven, scald, flour, and salt and mix until combined, folding the dough over itself a few times to develop structure. This bread will not need any intense kneading. Let sit for 15 minutes.

5 With a pastry brush dipped in olive oil or melted butter (or a combination of both), grease a Dutch oven. Shape the dough into a flattened ball that will fit inside the Dutch oven, place the dough in the pot, and smooth out the top with a plastic dough scraper. (Alternately, scoop the dough into greased 13 x 4-inch Pullman loaf pan, then use wet hands to smooth the top of the loaf.) Cover and let proof in a warm environment for 2½ to 3 hours, until small cracks are visible over the surface. For a decorative appearance, dip the dough scraper in water and use it to score patterns on top of the loaf.

6 Preheat the oven to 500°F.

7 Bake for 15 minutes, then lower the oven temperature to 400°F and bake for another hour or more, until the bread is deeply browned and fragrant and its internal temperature reads 206° to 209°F.

8 Remove from the oven and transfer the bread from the pot to a cooling rack. Let stand for at least 24 hours before slicing.

WHOLE RYE

FOLK ◆ NASHVILLE, TENNESSEE

This recipe takes some planning, as one must sprout the rye berries and soak old bread and seeds before mixing the dough, but the results are worth it. Soaking old bread and incorporating it into the next bake not only enables one to recycle old bread, but also the soaker contributes a depth of flavor to the bread and an improved keeping quality. Michael Matson suggests using the strained liquid from the soaker as part of the water in the dough, as it becomes dark and syrupy and contributes even more flavor. The sprouted berries lend a sweetness, and with the long bake time, the sugars in the crust caramelize, resulting in layers of flavor.

YIELD: 1 (13 X 4-INCH PULLMAN) LOAF

RYE SPROUTS (60 TO 72 HOURS)

70g rye berries

SOAKER (24 HOURS)

112.5g old bread

33g hulled sunflower seeds

LEAVEN (14 TO 16 HOURS)

446g water

22g starter

446g whole-rye flour

DOUGH

434g water, as needed

836g leaven

140g sprouted rye berries

146g soaker

557g whole-rye flour, plus more for dusting

14g fine sea salt

1 Sprout the rye: Place the rye berries in a widemouthed quart mason jar and add cold water to cover. Cover the jar with cheesecloth or a screen and soak the rye berries for 12 hours. Drain and rinse thoroughly, then return the rye berries to the jar. Rinse and drain the rye twice a day until they sprout and the tail is about the length of the grain itself. It should take 2 to 3 days.

2 Make the soaker: In a bowl, combine the old bread and sunflower seeds and add just enough water to cover. Cover the bowl and let stand at room temperature for 24 hours, then drain the liquid into a container, reserving it for later use, and set aside the soaker until you're ready to mix the dough.

3 Make the leaven: Measure the water into a large container with a lid (this will make a lot of leaven and requires a container that's about 3.5 liters to allow for expansion), then add the starter. Using a spoon or your fingers, break apart the starter into the water. Add the flour and mix until fully incorporated. Cover and let stand at room temperature for 14 to 16 hours, until fully developed (see image on page 107).

4 Make the dough: Drain the liquid from the soaker into a medium bowl and place on scale. Add enough water to make 434 grams liquid total.

Once the leaven is fully developed, pour this liquid into a large bowl, then add the leaven and dissolve it in the liquid, breaking it apart with your fingers. Add the drained soaker, sprouted rye berries, flour, and salt and mix until fully incorporated. Cover with a cotton or linen kitchen towel.

5 Bulk ferment the dough: Let the dough ferment at room temperature for 45 minutes to 1 hour.

6 Final rise: With a pastry brush dipped in olive oil or melted butter (or a combination of both), grease a 13 x 4-inch Pullman loaf pan thoroughly. Scoop the dough into the prepared pan, then use wet hands to smooth the top of the loaf. Dust the top with rye flour. Let proof at room temperature for 1½ to 3 hours, until small holes appear in the top of the loaf.

7 Bake: Preheat the oven to 475°F.

8 Bake for 15 minutes, then lower the oven temperature to 375°F and bake for another 1 hour 15 minutes, or until the internal temperature reads 209°F.

9 Remove from the oven and immediately transfer the bread from the pan to a cooling rack. Let let cool completely, ideally for 24 hours, before slicing.

NORDIC RYE WITH BEER AND SORGHUM

BOULTED BREAD ◆ RALEIGH, NORTH CAROLINA

YIELD: 1 (13 X 4-INCH) PULLMAN LOAF

SEED SOAKER (12 TO 16 HOURS)

177g water

88g flaxseeds, lightly toasted

88g hulled sunflower seeds, lightly toasted

88g sesame seeds, lightly toasted

RYE BREAD SOAKER (12 TO 16 HOURS)

48g old rye bread

48g water

LEAVEN STAGE 1 (3 TO 4 HOURS)

54g warm water

27g starter

54g whole-rye flour

LEAVEN STAGE 2 (3 TO 4 HOURS)

271g warm water

135g stage 1 leaven (above)

271g whole-rye flour

PORRIDGE

183g dark beer

88g rye berries

Joshua provides the origins of this bread: "We first baked this loaf for Olly Olly 2017, a gathering of craft beer brewers we (luckily) were invited to attend. This is our classic Nordic Rye formula with additions of dark beer and sorghum to bolster, but not mask, the flavor of North Carolina–grown Wrens Abruzzi rye."

This recipe is involved but surprisingly fun. It really builds upon all the other rye bread recipes that came before it. With a very high portion of leaven, it requires two leaven builds and also has two soakers—plus a porridge. Be sure to read through the entire recipe before proceeding, to make sure you capture all the steps. The first time I made this, I did not read through the entire recipe (I know…). By the time I was ready to mix the final dough, I was so proud of myself that I poured myself a glass of beer—as there seemed to be beer left over. And then I realized, not quite soon enough, that that leftover beer was actually meant to be used as the liquid in the final dough.

1 Make the seed soaker: In a container with a lid, stir together the water, flaxseeds, sunflower seeds, and sesame seeds. Cover and let stand at room temperature for 12 to 16 hours.

2 Make the rye bread soaker: Put the bread in a bowl and pour over the water. Cover and let stand at room temperature for 12 to 16 hours.

3 Make stage 1 leaven: Measure the water into a large clear container with a lid, such as a 1,750 ml Weck jar, then add the starter. Using a spoon or your fingers, break apart the starter into the water. Add the flour and mix until fully incorporated. Cover and let stand at room temperature for 3 to 4 hours until fully developed (see image on page 107).

4 Make stage 2 leaven: Measure the water into a separate large clear container with a lid and add the leaven. Using a spoon or your fingers, break apart the leaven into the water. Add the flour and

mix until fully incorporated. Cover and let stand at room temperature for 3 to 4 hours until fully developed (see image on page 86).

5 Make the porridge: In a medium saucepan, combine the beer and rye berries. Bring to a boil over medium-high heat. Once the rye berries swell, reduce the heat to low and cook until the rye berries have absorbed all the liquid. Remove from the heat.

6 Make the dough: Once the stage 2 leaven is fully developed, measure the beer into a large bowl, then add the leaven and dissolve it in the beer, breaking it apart with your fingers. Add both soakers, the porridge, sorghum syrup, flour, and salt and mix until fully incorporated.

7 Final rise: With a pastry brush dipped in olive oil or melted butter (or a combination of both), thoroughly grease a 13 x 4-inch Pullman loaf pan with a lid. Scoop the dough into the prepared pan, then use wet hands to smooth the top of the loaf. Dust the top with rye flour.

8 Let proof at room temperature for 2 to 3 hours or more, until small holes appear in the top of the loaf.

9 Bake: Preheat the oven to 420°F.

10 Bake with the lid of the pan closed for 2 hours, then remove the lid and bake for another 15 minutes, or until the internal temperature of the bread reads 205°F.

11 Remove from the oven and immediately transfer the bread from the pan to a cooling rack. Let cool completely, ideally for 24 hours, before slicing.

DOUGH

240g dark beer

615g leaven

96g rye bread soaker

441g seed soaker

271g porridge

29g sorghum syrup

343g whole-rye flour, plus more for dusting

17g fine sea salt

SPROUTED AND SEEDED RYE

OSONO BREAD • ATLANTA, GEORGIA

YIELD: 1 (9 X 4-INCH PULLMAN) LOAF

RYE SPROUTS

40g rye berries

BUCKWHEAT SPROUTS (24 TO 36 HOURS)

23g buckwheat groats

LEAVEN (6 TO 8 HOURS)

64g warm water (about 85°F)

13g starter

64g whole-rye flour

DOUGH

257g water

89g buttermilk

31g beer

13g honey

125g leaven

255g medium-rye flour, plus more for dusting

6g fine sea salt

89g rye sprouts

64g buckwheat sprouts

25g hulled sunflower seeds, toasted

25g hulled pumpkin seeds, toasted

10g flaxseeds, toasted

10g sesame seeds, toasted

TOPPING

mixture of sunflower, pumpkin, flax, and sesame seeds (optional)

This was one of the last recipes I tested. I pushed it to the end because honestly, I was intimidated. The recipe requires sprouting both rye berries and buckwheat groats. I often sprout grains in the mill room to test germination rate, but for some reason, translating this to the kitchen seemed complex. The reality is, sprouting is quite simple and in a way is like taking care of a sourdough culture. One is simply providing the right conditions, and the rest just happens.

Note: Start the rye sprouts 72 hours before you make the final dough. The sprouts are ready when they have just begun to show a tail and can be used until the shoots are about the length of the seed. Going further creates a stringy, not-so-appetizing addition to a loaf of bread. The amount of time it takes the grains to sprout depends on what is being sprouted and how warm or cool your kitchen is.

1 Sprout the rye: Place the rye berries in a widemouthed quart mason jar and add cold water to cover. Cover the jar with a screen and soak the rye berries for 12 hours. Drain and rinse thoroughly, then return the rye berries to the jar. Rinse and drain the rye twice a day until they sprout and the tail is about the length of the grain itself. It should take 2 to 3 days.

2 Sprout the buckwheat: Buckwheat takes much less time to sprout and requires less soaking time. Rinse the buckwheat thoroughly, then place it in a widemouthed quart mason jar and add cold water to cover. Cover the jar with a screen and soak the buckwheat for 30 minutes. Drain and rinse thoroughly, then return the buckwheat to the jar. Rinse and drain every 12 hours for 24 to 36 hours.

3 Make the leaven: Thirty-six hours after beginning the sprouting process, measure the water into a small clear container with a lid, then add the starter. Using a spoon or your fingers, break apart the starter into the water. Add the flour and mix until fully incorporated. Cover and let stand at room temperature for 6 to 8 hours, until fully developed (see image on page 107).

4 Make the dough: Once the leaven is fully developed, in a large bowl, stir together the water, buttermilk, beer, and honey. Add the leaven and dissolve it in the liquid, breaking it apart with your fingers. Add the flour and salt and mix to incorporate. This dough should be batterlike. Cover with a cotton or linen kitchen towel and let stand at room temperature for 20 minutes.

5 Add both sprouts and the seeds to the dough and mix until fully incorporated.

6 Final rise: With a pastry brush dipped in olive oil or melted butter (or a combination of both), thoroughly grease a 9 x 4-inch Pullman loaf pan. Scoop the dough into the prepared pan, then use wet hands to smooth the top of the loaf. Sprinkle the top with a mixture of seeds or rye flour. Let proof in a warm spot for 2 to 3 hours or more, until small holes appear in the top of the loaf.

7 Bake: Preheat the oven to 450°F. Bake for 45 to 55 minutes, until the internal temperature of the bread reads 205°F.

8 Remove from the oven and immediately transfer the bread from the pan to a cooling rack. Let cool completely, at least 12 hours, before slicing.

CHOCOLATE RYE BROWNIES

JOE BOWIE ◆ COLUMBIA, SOUTH CAROLINA

This is a quick and simple recipe that is a serious crowd-pleaser. For an especially beautiful touch, I top these brownies with Fossil River charcoal salt flakes, which adds black specks to the crust. If one chooses to use Dutch-process cocoa (either Dutch-process or natural cocoa powder will work in this recipe), the color of the brownies will be near black, and if topped with an even deeper black charcoal salt flake, they are stunning.

YIELD: 12 LARGE, 24 SMALL, OR 48 BITE-SIZE BROWNIES

150g (⅔ cup) unsalted butter

300g (11 ounces) dark chocolate (at least 60% cacao), broken into pieces or chopped

50g (½ cup) unsweetened cocoa powder (natural or Dutch-process)

200g (2 cups) whole-rye flour

½ teaspoon aluminum-free baking powder

1 teaspoon fine sea salt

200g (1 cup) granulated pure cane sugar

200g (1 cup + 2 tablespoons) light brown sugar

4 eggs

1 tablespoon pure vanilla extract

flaky sea salt, for sprinkling

1 Preheat the oven to 350°F. Butter a 9 x 13-inch baking pan and line it with parchment paper, leaving a few inches overhanging the sides of the pan. Butter the parchment as well.

2 Bring a few inches of water to a simmer in a saucepan. Combine the butter and chocolate in a heatproof bowl and set it over the pan (the bottom of the bowl should not touch the water). Heat, stirring occasionally, until the butter and chocolate have melted and the mixture is well combined.

3 In a medium bowl, whisk together the cocoa powder, flour, baking powder, and salt.

4 In the bowl of a stand mixer fitted with the whisk attachment, combine the sugars, eggs, and vanilla and whisk on medium-high speed until light and fluffy, about 5 minutes. Switch to the paddle attachment. With the mixer on low speed, slowly add the chocolate mixture, followed by the dry ingredients. Mix just enough to combine.

5 Pour the batter into the prepared baking pan. Smooth the top with an offset or rubber spatula, then sprinkle with flaky salt.

6 Bake for 20 to 25 minutes, until the brownies are set. Be careful not to overbake. Let the brownies cool completely in the pan, then use the overhanging parchment to lift them from the pan and transfer to a cutting board. Cut into 12, 24, or 48 pieces, depending on what size brownie you prefer. Once fully cooled, store cut brownies in an airtight container at room temperature for 1 or 2 days, in the refrigerator up to 1 week, or wrapped well (or in an airtight container) in the freezer for up to 3 months.

VEGAN DOUBLE CHOCOLATE COOKIES WITH RYE AND OLIVE OIL

LEVEE BAKING CO. ◆ NEW ORLEANS, LOUISIANA

YIELD: 2 DOZEN COOKIES

225g (1⅓ cups) light rye flour

63g (⅔ cup) unsweetened dark cocoa powder

1 teaspoon baking soda

½ teaspoon fine sea salt

80g (⅓ cup) canola oil

44g (¼ cup) olive oil

100g (½ cup) unsweetened nut milk

2 teaspoons pure vanilla extract

300g (1½ cups) granulated pure cane sugar

80g (½ cup) dark chocolate, coarsely chopped

A crisp exterior with a soft, rich, and chocolaty interior, this is an excellent cookie that also happens to be vegan. Rye adds a depth of flavor, well paired with chocolate. At Levee, this cookie is made with Carolina Ground Wren Abruzzi rye and dark chocolate from Acalli Chocolate, a New Orleans–based small-batch bean-to-bar chocolate company that maintains direct relationships with their farmers at origin.

1 Into a medium bowl, sift together the rye flour, cocoa powder, baking soda, and salt. Set aside.

2 In the bowl of a stand mixer fitted with the whisk attachment (or in a large bowl by hand), whisk together the canola oil, olive oil, nut milk, and vanilla. Add the sugar and whisk very well until emulsified.

3 Switch to the paddle attachment. With the mixer on low speed, add the dry ingredients and mix just until incorporated; do not overmix. Pulse a few times and then fold in the chocolate by hand.

4 Line a baking sheet with parchment paper. Using a 1-ounce cookie scoop or a heaping tablespoon, scoop the dough onto the prepared baking sheet, spacing the cookies 1½ inches apart. Cover the baking sheet with plastic wrap and refrigerate for at least 1 hour or preferably overnight.

5 Preheat the oven to 350°F.

6 Bake for 12 to 14 minutes, until the cookies are crackly on top. Remove from oven and transfer to a cooling rack. Once fully cooled, store in an airtight container at room temperature.

SALTED CANE SYRUP TART WITH RYE-AND-OAT COOKIE CRUST

LEVEE BAKING CO. ◆ NEW ORLEANS, LOUISIANA

Cane syrup is to Louisiana what sorghum syrup is to Tennessee. These flavor-forward Southern sweeteners act as the defining element in a recipe. Here the salted cane syrup and the rye-and-oat cookie crust provide the perfect balance of flavor and texture to this iteration of a classic chess pie.

1 Preheat the oven to 350°F. Line a baking sheet with parchment paper.

2 Make the crust: In a small bowl, combine the flour, oats, salt, and baking powder; set aside.

3 In the bowl of a stand mixer fitted with the paddle attachment, cream the butter and both sugars on medium-high speed until light and fluffy, about 5 minutes. Scrape down the sides of the bowl with a rubber spatula.

4 With the mixer running on low speed, add the egg and mix until fully combined. Add the dry ingredients in two parts and mix until just incorporated, scraping down the bowl as needed and making sure that no streaks of butter remain; do not overmix.

5 Scrape the dough out onto the prepared baking sheet. Spread it in an even layer about ¼ inch thick and bake until golden brown and crispy, 15 to 18 minutes.

6 Remove the cookie from the oven and let cool completely; keep the oven on. Break up the cookie and transfer it to a food processor, then pulse until broken down into crumbs (alternatively, transfer the cookie pieces to a zip-top bag and crush into crumbs with a rolling pin).

7 Grease a 10-inch tart pan with a removable bottom. Transfer the cookie crumbs to a bowl and stir in the melted butter until the mixture resembles wet sand. Press the crumbs evenly over the bottom and up the sides of the prepared pan.

8 Bake for 8 to 10 minutes, until set. If the sides sag a little, use a clean kitchen towel to press up the sides while the crust is still hot. Remove from the oven and let cool completely before filling; keep the oven on.

9 Make the filling: In a large bowl, whisk together both sugars, the dry milk powder, and the salt, breaking up any lumps. Add the melted butter, cream, and cane syrup. Whisk to emulsify. Add the vanilla seeds, then the egg yolks and whisk slowly until incorporated. You don't want to add any air to the filling.

10 Pour the filling into the cooled crust. Bake for 35 to 45 minutes, rotating the pan halfway through, until the custard is just set. Let cool completely, then remove the tart from the pan, sprinkle flaky salt on top, and serve. Store covered in the refrigerator for up to 4 days.

YIELD: 1 (10-INCH) TART

CRUST

80g (¾ cup) light rye flour

120g (1 cup + 1 tablespoon) rolled oats, toasted

½ teaspoon fine sea salt

¼ teaspoon baking powder

113g (½ cup) unsalted butter, at room temperature

75g (⅓ cup) dark brown sugar

2 teaspoons granulated sugar

1 egg, whisked

25g (2 tablespoons) unsalted butter, melted

FILLING

90g (⅓ cup) dark brown sugar

75g (⅓ cup) granulated sugar

24g (¼ cup) dry milk powder

½ teaspoon fine sea salt

112g (¼ cup) butter, melted

80g (⅓ cup) heavy cream, at room temperature

75g (¼ cup) cane syrup

½ vanilla bean, split lengthwise and seeds scraped out

4 egg yolks, at room temperature

flaky sea salt, for sprinkling

RYE HAND PIES

LA FARM BAKERY ● CARY, NORTH CAROLINA

YIELD: ABOUT 6 LARGE (3 X 5-INCH) HAND PIES

250g (2⅛ cups) high-extraction all-purpose flour (85AP)

50g (½ cup) whole-rye flour

15g (¼ cup) unsweetened cocoa powder

15g (1½ tablespoons) granulated sugar, plus more for sprinkling

1 teaspoon fine sea salt

227g (1 cup) unsalted butter, cubed and chilled

egg white from 1 egg

30g (2 tablespoons) milk, cold

1 pint fresh strawberries

90g (¼ cup + 2 tablespoons) chocolate-hazelnut spread

1 egg yolk

1 tablespoon milk

A couple years into milling, around harvest, Billy Carter, Lionel Vatinet, and I came together—farmer, baker, and miller—at Billy's farm. Lionel brought Billy a loaf of bread and pastries from his bakery. We talked about grain and flour, and about our kids. It is these human connections that provide the foundation for regional milling endeavors. Our Wrens Abruzzi rye comes from Billy Carter's farm. This recipe, developed in order to showcase our Wrens Abruzzi rye, arose out of La Farm's desire to bring this story back to their customers. And who doesn't love a hand pie? These are classically French in that there is very little sugar in the dough, but a healthy amount of butter, which brings forward the rye flavor. Think of a Pop-Tart and then imagine the best version. Here's the recipe.

1 In the bowl of a stand mixer fitted with the paddle attachment, combine both flours, the cocoa powder, sugar, and salt. With the mixer on medium speed, add the butter one cube at a time and mix until the mixture resembles coarse crumbs, 2 to 3 minutes.

2 In a separate bowl, mix together the egg whites and milk. With the mixer on low speed, pour in the egg mixture and beat until the dough just starts to come together.

3 Remove the dough from the mixer bowl and divide it in half. Press each half flat into a rectangle. Wrap in plastic wrap and chill for at least 2 hours or up to overnight.

4 Position a rack in the center of the oven and preheat the oven to 350°F. Line two baking sheets with parchment paper.

5 Wash the strawberries and pulse a few times in a food processor, or chop by hand into small ⅛ to ¼-inch pieces.

6 To make an egg wash, in a small bowl, whisk together the egg yolks and milk.

7 Remove one portion of the dough from the refrigerator. Working quickly, roll out the dough into a ⅛-inch-thick rectangle. Use bench scraper or pastry knife to cut it into 3 x 5-inch rectangles. Transfer to the prepared baking sheet and refrigerate. Repeat with the remaining dough; transferring the rectangles to the second baking sheet and refrigerate.

8 Remove the first set of rectangles from the refrigerator. Spread 1 heaping tablespoon of the chocolate-hazelnut spread on half the rectangles, leaving a ¼-inch border. Top with 1 heaping tablespoon of strawberries, being careful not to overfill. Brush the edges with the egg wash and top with the remaining rectangles of dough. Press the edges to seal. Use a fork to crimp the edges and prick the tops to allow steam to escape. Brush the tops with the egg wash and then sprinkle with sugar. Repeat with the second set of rectangles.

9 Bake on the center rack for 25 to 30 minutes, until the hand pies are golden around the edges. Transfer to a cooling rack and allow to cool for at least 15 minutes before diving in.

RYE CHOCOLATE CHIP SABLÉS

LA FARM BAKERY ◆ CARY, NORTH CAROLINA

These are another product La Farm developed to showcase our Wrens Abruzzi rye. They are less sweet than they are rich, bringing forward the flavor and mouthfeel of the whole-rye flour. Lovely served with tea.

1 In a medium bowl, combine the rye and all-purpose flours. Set aside.

2 In the bowl of a stand mixer fitted with the paddle attachment, cream the butter and sugar on medium speed until fluffy, 4 to 5 minutes. With the mixer on low speed, add the salt, then add the flour in three increments, mixing until just incorporated after each addition before adding the next; be careful not to overmix. Add the chocolate and mix until evenly distributed.

3 Divide the dough in half and press each portion into a squared-off disk. Wrap each disk in plastic wrap and refrigerate for at least 4 hours or up to overnight.

4 Preheat the oven to 350°F. Line a baking sheet with parchment paper.

5 Remove the dough from the refrigerator and let it come to room temperature. Roll out the dough to ½ inch thick and cut it into 2-inch squares. Place them on a baking sheet 1 inch apart. Sprinkle the tops generously with sugar.

6 Bake for 12 to 14 minutes, until golden brown on the edges. Remove from oven and transfer to a cooling rack. Once fully cooled, store in an airtight container at room temperature for up to a week.

YIELD: ABOUT 40 COOKIES

240g (2⅔ cups) whole-rye flour

270g (2¼ cups) high-extraction all-purpose flour (85AP)

390g (1¾ cups) unsalted butter, at room temperature

180g (1 cup) granulated sugar, plus more for sprinkling

½ teaspoon fine sea salt

100g (4 ounces) bittersweet chocolate, chopped

RYE SHORTBREAD

BOULTED BREAD ◆ RALEIGH, NORTH CAROLINA

**YIELD: ABOUT
30 COOKIES**

401g (1¾ cups) unsalted
butter, at room temperature

150g (¾ cup)
granulated sugar

1 egg

1 teaspoon pure
vanilla extract

500g (5⅛ cups) medium
or light rye flour

1 teaspoon fine sea salt

60g (½ cup) cacao nibs

Like La Farm's Rye Chocolate Chip Sablés (page 193), these rye shortbreads are less sweet than they are rich. These are made with 100 percent sifted rye, delivering a lovely sandy tooth and full flavor. Pairs well with red wine.

1 In the bowl of a stand mixer fitted with the paddle attachment, cream the butter and sugar on medium speed until fluffy, 4 to 5 minutes. Stop the mixer and scrape down the sides of the bowl with a rubber spatula.

2 With the mixer on low speed, add the egg and vanilla. Increase the speed to medium-high and mix until fully incorporated. With the mixer on low speed, add the flour and salt and mix until just incorporated. Pulse in the cacao nibs until evenly dispersed.

3 Remove the bowl from the mixer, cover, and refrigerate for 30 minutes.

4 Preheat the oven to 425°F. Line a baking sheet with parchment paper.

5 Roll out the dough to ½ inch thick and cut it into 1 x 3-inch rectangles. Place them on the prepared baking sheet 1 inch apart.

6 Bake for 14 minutes, or until golden brown. Transfer to a cooling rack. Once fully cooled, store in an airtight container at room temperature for up to a week.

JAM TART WITH RYE CRUST

ANISETTE • RALEIGH, NORTH CAROLINA

Jason drives from Raleigh once a month to pick up flour. Sometimes I see him, which is always great. Oftentimes we miss each other, but he leaves treats that Nicole sends with him in the mill room. This tart was one of those treats. It was summertime, and the tart was filled with a rhubarb jam. Everyone who came into the mill room that day got a slice. We all wanted the recipe, so here it is.

Note: If you'd like to make your own jam for the filling, the formula Nicole likes to use is 3 parts fruit (already washed and chopped) to 1 part sugar by weight. Cook the mixture in a saucepan over medium heat, stirring to ensure the sugar is dissolved. Once dissolved, continue cooking (without stirring) until it reaches 220°F. Let cool before using to fill the tart.

YIELD: 1 (8-INCH) TART

220g (2¼ cups) light rye flour

58g (¼ cup) granulated sugar

⅛ teaspoon fine sea salt

113g (½ cup) unsalted butter, cubed and chilled

1 egg

lemon zest from half a large lemon

200g (¾ cup) jam (see Note)

1 In a medium bowl, whisk together the flour, sugar, and salt. Add the butter and use a pastry blender to cut it into the dry ingredients until the mixture resembles a coarse meal.

2 Make a well in the center of the mixture. Place the egg and lemon zest in the well and use a fork to gradually incorporate the flour and combine all the ingredients.

3 Divide the dough into two portions, one weighing approximately 275 grams and the other approximately 165 grams, and form them into disks (the smaller disk will be used for the lattice top). The dough will be crumbly, but will come together as you gather it to form the disks. Wrap each disk in plastic wrap and refrigerate for at least 30 minutes and up to 2 days.

4 Preheat the oven to 375°F.

5 On a lightly floured work surface or a sheet of parchment paper, roll out the larger disk of dough to a 9-inch round. Transfer the dough to an 8-inch tart pan with a removable bottom, gently pressing it into the corners, and prick with a fork. Freeze the tart shell for 15 minutes.

6 Roll out the smaller disk of dough into a round slightly larger than 8 inches in diameter and cut it into 1-inch-wide strips (or cut out decorative shapes).

7 Remove the tart shell from the freezer and fill it with the jam, spreading it evenly. Carefully place the dough strips parallel to one another over the top of the tart, spacing them about 1 inch apart (or top the tart with the decorative cutouts). The strips are delicate, and it's best to lift them with a long, slim knife so they don't break.

8 Bake for 35 to 45 minutes, until the jam is bubbling and the edges of the crust are starting to lightly brown. Remove from oven and transfer to a cooling rack. Let cool completely, then remove the tart from the pan.

UPSIDE-DOWN RYE CAKE WITH SEASONAL FRUIT

OWL BAKERY • ASHEVILLE, NORTH CAROLINA

YIELD: 1 (9-INCH) ROUND UPSIDE-DOWN CAKE OR ONE (13 X 4-INCH PULLMAN) LOAF

300g (1½ cups) granulated sugar

150g (1¼ cups) high-extraction all-purpose flour (85AP)

105g (1 cup) light rye flour

1½ teaspoons baking powder

1 teaspoon fine sea salt

390g (1¾ cups) unsalted butter, at room temperature

6 eggs

100g (½ cup) heavy cream

1 tablespoon pure vanilla extract

FOR PREPARING THE PAN

80g (6 tablespoons) unsalted butter

80g (⅓ cup + 1 tablespoon) light brown sugar

2 to 3 cups seasonal fruit (see second Note)

At OWL, they use blackberries as the fruit layer during the summer and then incorporate minced fresh thyme (about 2 tablespoons) into the dough. Other seasonal ideas that pair well with rye are apples in the fall and thinly sliced oranges in the winter.

Notes: This recipe can be made as a simple rye pound cake loaf instead of an upside-down cake. Butter a 13 x 4-inch loaf pan and line it with parchment paper. Prepare the batter as directed, then pour it into the prepared pan. Bake for 1 hour.

If you'll be using stone fruits, apples, or pears to make this upside-down cake, be sure to slice them thinly.

1 Preheat the oven to 350°F. Butter a 9-inch-round cake pan and line the bottom with parchment paper cut to fit.

2 In the bowl of a stand mixer fitted with the paddle attachment, combine the granulated sugar, both flours, the baking powder, and the salt until incorporated. Add the butter and mix on medium speed for 5 minutes. Add the eggs one at a time, stopping to scrape down the bowl with a rubber spatula after each addition. Add the cream and vanilla and mix until incorporated.

3 In a small bowl, mix the 80 grams of butter and brown sugar into a paste and spread the mixture evenly over the bottom of the prepared pan. Add the fruit, covering the entire bottom of the pan, then pour the batter over the fruit.

4 Bake for 1 hour 40 minutes, until the cake springs back when pressed and a toothpick inserted into the center comes out clean.

5 Let cool in the pan for 2 to 3 minutes, then place a large plate over the pan and invert the pan and plate together to turn the cake out onto the plate. Store covered in the refrigerator for up to 5 to 6 days.

SALTED RYE COOKIES

CAROLINA GROUND ◆ ASHEVILLE, NORTH CAROLINA

This is a recipe that I adapted from Liana Krissoff's *Whole Grains for a New Generation*. I became sort of obsessed with making this cookie, pulling back on the sugar each time. This is where I landed. The combination of buttery, salty, and sweet carried by our flavor-forward rye strikes just the right balance for me.

1 In a small bowl, whisk together the flour and ¼ teaspoon of the salt; set aside.

2 In the bowl of a stand mixer fitted with the paddle attachment, cream the butter and granulated sugar on medium speed until fluffy, 4 to 5 minutes. Add the egg and vanilla and beat on medium-low speed until fully incorporated. With mixer running on low speed, add the flour mixture and mix until just incorporated, making sure that no streaks of butter are remaining; do not overmix.

3 Lightly dust a sheet of parchment paper with flour. Turn the dough out onto the parchment, wrap, and refrigerate for 20 minutes, until the dough feels cold.

4 Unwrap the dough, reserving the parchment, and form it into a log about 1½ inches in diameter. Wrap the log in the parchment and freeze for 10 to 15 minutes.

5 Line a baking sheet with parchment paper. On a second piece of parchment paper, combine the sparkling sugar and the remaining salt. Unwrap the dough and roll it in the sugar-salt mixture to coat well. Place the log on a cutting board and cut it crosswise into ¼-inch-thick rounds, placing them 1 inch apart on the prepared baking sheet. Place the baking sheet in the freezer for 15 minutes.

6 Preheat the oven to 350°F.

7 Bake for 20 to 22 minutes, until the edges begin to brown. Transfer the cookies to a cooling rack and let cool completely. They will crisp up as they cool. Once fully cooled, store in an airtight container at room temperature for up to a week.

YIELD: AT LEAST
30 COOKIES

260g (2⅔ cups) whole- or medium-rye flour

1¼ teaspoons fine sea salt

200g (¾ cup + 2 tablespoons) unsalted butter, cubed and chilled

125g (⅔ cup) granulated sugar

1 egg

1 teaspoon pure vanilla extract

3 tablespoons sparkling sugar

RYE SHORTBREAD WITH MASCARPONE AND LEMON CURD

CAROLINA GROUND • ASHEVILLE, NORTH CAROLINA

YIELD: ABOUT
10 COOKIES

200g (¾ cup +
2 tablespoons) unsalted
butter, at room
temperature

100g (½ cup)
granulated sugar

1 teaspoon pure
vanilla extract

¼ teaspoon fine sea salt

1 egg

260g (2⅔ cups) light
rye flour

8-ounces mascarpone
cheese

100g (⅓ cup) lemon curd

This cookie was our creative solution to a mistake in the mill room. It was the first year we were milling. Tara Jensen was working with me in the mill room and we were milling whole rye. Neither of us noticed that the slide gate for the bucket elevator was open, diverting some of our flour to the bolter (the machine that sifts our flour). Once I realized the issue (it did not take long, as the amount of whole-grain flour we were producing was reduced), I turned on the bolter and we ran the rye flour over the screens that were in the bolter at the time—our finest screens. I had no idea what to do with this flour, so Tara took some home and came back the next day with these shortbread cookies, or something quite similar. (She didn't write down the recipe, so the two of us collaborated on reviving the recipe.) And because of this cookie, we started producing our light rye flour.

1 In a food processor, combine the butter, sugar, vanilla, and salt and process until smooth. Scrape down the sides of the processor bowl, then add the egg and process until fully incorporated. Add the flour and pulse about 10 times, until a consistent dough forms. Scrape the dough into a medium bowl, cover, and refrigerate for 3 hours.

2 Line a baking sheet with parchment paper. Turn the dough out onto a lightly floured work surface and roll it out to ¼ inch thick. With a 2¾-inch-round cookie cutter, stamp out cookies and transfer them to the prepared baking sheet.

3 Place a heaping tablespoon of the mascarpone in the center of half of the cookies and slightly spread the cheese, leaving a ½-inch border. Add a heaping teaspoon of the lemon curd on top of the mascarpone.

4 Using a 1½-inch circular cutter, stamp out the centers of the unfilled cookies and place the leftover rings on top of the filled cookies. (The stamped out centers can be baked into simple rye cookies.) Using a small fork, crimp the edges all the way around. Freeze for 25 minutes.

5 Preheat the oven to 350°F.

6 Bake for 25 to 30 minutes, until golden around the edges. Remove from the oven and transfer to a cooling rack and let cool completely before diving in.

SALTED AND MALTED COOKIES

KIM THOMPSON ◆ ASHEVILLE, NORTH CAROLINA

Kim Thompson is the second miller Carolina Ground has produced. Within minutes of meeting her, I knew she would be a great fit. She'd served in the military and had majored in philosophy, which seemed like the perfect ingredients for a miller—mighty and reflective. Kim used to bring various iterations of this cookie to the mill to share. We all became obsessed.

Note: Although this recipe is written with medium-rye as the flour, whole rye or light rye also work well here. It took a lot to get Kim to actually commit this recipe to paper, as it was historically inspired by whatever flour she happened to have in her kitchen.

1 In a medium bowl, sift together the flour, cocoa powder, baking soda, baking powder, and sea salt. Add the malt and coffee. Set aside.

2 In the bowl of a stand mixer fitted with the paddle attachment (or in a large bowl using a sturdy wooden spoon), cream the butter and both sugars on medium-high speed until fluffy. Stop the mixer and scrape down the sides of the bowl with a rubber spatula.

3 In a small bowl, whisk together the eggs and vanilla.

4 With the mixer on low speed, add the egg mixture, then increase the speed to medium-high and mix until fully incorporated. Stop the mixer and scrape down the bowl. With the mixer on low speed, add the dry ingredients and mix until just incorporated, scraping down the bowl as needed and making sure no streaks of butter remain; do not overmix. With the mixer on low speed, add the chocolate chips and mix just to combine.

5 Remove the bowl from the mixer, cover, and refrigerate overnight.

6 Line a baking sheet with parchment paper. Remove the dough from the refrigerator. Divide the dough into 28-gram portions (or use a 1-ounce cookie scoop) and shape into balls. Place them on the prepared baking sheet, spacing them 1½ inches apart. Generously top with cacao nibs and flaky salt, pressing them gently into the dough. Cover the baking sheet with plastic wrap and freeze for at least 1 hour or even overnight before baking.

7 Preheat the oven to 350°F.

8 Bake the cookies for 14 minutes, rotating the pan halfway through. (Depending on if you're a fan of crispy or chewy cookies, let them go for longer or shorter. For Kim, 14 minutes seems to be the sweet spot.)

9 Remove from the oven and slide the cookies, still on the parchment, onto a cooling rack. Once fully cooled, store in an airtight container at room temperature for up to a week.

YIELD: ABOUT 42 COOKIES

326g (3⅓ cups) medium-rye flour (see Note)

42.5g (½ cup) unsweetened dark cocoa powder

1½ teaspoons baking soda

½ teaspoon aluminum-free baking powder

½ teaspoon fine sea salt

71g (¼ cup) malt flour

1¾ teaspoons finely ground coffee or instant espresso powder

218g (¾ cup + 3 tablespoons) unsalted butter, at room temperature

227g (1 cup + 1 tablespoon) light brown sugar

227g (1¼ cup) granulated pure cane sugar

2 eggs

1 tablespoon pure vanilla extract

340g (12 ounces) dark chocolate chips

cacao nibs, for topping

flaky sea salt, for topping

NORTH CAROLINA RYE CUSTARD

ASHLEY CAPPS ◆ ASHEVILLE, NORTH CAROLINA

Ashley developed this recipe for the launch of Asheville's farm-to-table restaurant Rhubarb. As pastry chef, she was set to the task of creating a dessert that incorporated rhubarb and rye, two Southern-grown favorites. Ashley explains, "One of the first desserts we opened up Rhubarb with was called Rhubarb + Rye—it was poached rhubarb, rye shortbread, rye custard, and rhubarb sorbet." This is a rich custard that is best used as an accompaniment—a dollop or two—to elevate a dessert or a bowl of fruit. Consider using this as a topping for the White Wheat Cake (page 160).

Note: This recipe uses an ice bath to cool the custard. Although that is the most ideal approach, if you prefer, you can skip the ice bath and just cool the custard with a large whisk and a strong arm.

YIELD: 1 PINT

4 egg yolks

1 vanilla bean, split lengthwise and seeds scraped out

65g (⅓ cup) granulated sugar

50g (½ cup) light rye flour

330g (1½ cups) heavy cream

56g (¼ cup) unsalted butter, cut into ½-inch or smaller pieces and chilled

65g (¼ cup) buttermilk

1 Fill a large stainless-steel bowl halfway with ice. Place it in your kitchen sink and add cold water to cover.

2 In the bowl of a stand mixer fitted with the whisk attachment, whisk the egg yolks on medium speed. Add the vanilla seeds, then gradually add the sugar and continue to whisk on medium speed for 90 seconds, stopping to scrape down the bowl with a rubber spatula as needed. Increase the speed to medium-high and mix for another 3 minutes, until the mixture has lightened to a pale color and visibly thickened. (This is known as ribbon stage.)

3 With the mixer running on low speed, add the flour and mix until combined. Add the cream and mix until combined.

4 Pour the mixture into a medium saucepan and set it over medium heat. Cook, stirring with a spatula, until the mixture begins to thicken, then taste to see if the starchy flavor of the flour has been cooked out. Allow the mixture to bubble lightly and slowly, stirring and scraping the bottom of the pan with a spatula, for 1 minute more. Remove from the heat.

5 Pour the custard into a stainless-steel bowl and place it in the ice bath (see Note). Let cool to 140°F, whisking to help the custard cool. Remove from the ice bath and add the butter one piece at a time, whisking each addition until incorporated before adding the next. Whisk in buttermilk, then blend with an immersion blender until smooth or transfer to a standing blender and blend until smooth.

6 Use right away (see suggestions in the headnote), or store covered in the refrigerator for 4 to 5 days.

Soft Red Winter Wheat

WHOLE-WHEAT PASTRY FLOUR

Currant Coriander
Wholemeal Scones 209

Graham Biscuits 210

Cardamom Tea Cakes 211

Rough Puff with Pecan Frangipane
and Louisiana Blood Orange 212

HIGH-EXTRACTION PASTRY FLOUR

Green Quiche 215

Portuguese Biscuits 216

Citrus Olive Oil Cake with
Chocolate Ganache 219

High-Extraction Cake with
Cinnamon-Infused Coffee +
Maple-Coffee Icing 220

Banana Bread with Walnuts,
Cardamom, and Cacao Nibs 221

Naturally Leavened
Carrot Cake 223

Biscotti with Roasted
Almonds, Bittersweet
Chocolate, and Sea Salt 224

High-Extraction Sugar Cookie 227

Mississippi Market Galette 228

CAKE FLOUR (CREMA)

Apple Mascarpone Cake 231

Evergreen's Lemon
Pound Cake 232

Crema Piecrust 234

Whole-Wheat Pastry Flour

This 100 percent whole grain flour pairs well with warming spices such as cardamom, cinnamon, and ginger, with orange, and with currants and other dried fruits.

High-Extraction Pastry Flour

We call this our 85 pastry flour (or 85P), as it is an 85 extraction, with just 15 parts larger bran sifted out. This flour delivers tooth and flavor and is especially well suited for sturdy cakes and rustic cookies.

Cake Flour (Crema)

We call our cake flour Crema because it feels like cream in powdered form. Stone-ground and finely sifted, this silky flour produces a delicate crumb in baked goods and pairs well with flavors such as lemon, almond, and vanilla.

CURRANT CORIANDER WHOLEMEAL SCONES

CAROLINA GROUND ◆ ASHEVILLE, NORTH CAROLINA

I spent my junior year of college studying in London, and it was there that I first discovered currant scones made with wholemeal flour (which is what the British call whole-wheat flour). The addition of coriander underscores the flavor-forward whole-grain flour and pairs perfectly with the currants.

1 Preheat the oven to 425°F. Line a baking sheet with parchment paper.

2 In a large bowl, combine the flour, baking powder, coriander, and salt.

3 Using the large holes of a box grater, grate the frozen butter and then add it to the flour mixture. Toss to coat the butter with the flour, then rub the butter into the flour until the mixture resembles coarse sand. Add the currants and sugar and continue to rub in the butter. Add the milk, then, using a dough scraper, bring the dough together into a ball. You don't want to knead the dough, just incorporate until a cohesive ball forms.

4 Turn the dough out onto a floured surface. Let rest for 5 minutes, then roll it out to about 1-inch thick. Stamp out 2-inch rounds and place them on a baking sheet spaced 1½ inches apart. (At this point, you can freeze the unbaked scones for up to 1 month in an airtight container, separated with parchment paper.)

5 Bake for 15 to 18 minutes, until the edges begin to turn golden brown. Transfer the scones to a cooling rack and allow to cool for 7 to 10 minutes. Best eaten warm. Store in an airtight container at room temperature. (Eat within a day or two.)

YIELD: 6 TO 8 SCONES

225g (2 cups) whole-wheat pastry flour

1 tablespoon baking powder

1 teaspoon ground coriander

½ teaspoon sea salt

75g (¼ cup + 1 tablespoon) unsalted butter, frozen

75g (½ cup) currants

25g (⅛ cup) turbinado sugar

100g (½ cup) whole milk

GRAHAM BISCUITS

ANSON MILLS ◆ COLUMBIA, SOUTH CAROLINA

YIELD: 10 (2-INCH) BISCUITS

227g (2 cups) whole-wheat pastry flour

71g (½ cup) finely sifted stone-ground pastry flour

1½ teaspoons baking powder

1 teaspoon fine sea salt

85g (6 tablespoons) unsalted European-style butter, cut into 6 cubes and chilled

180g (¾ cup) whole milk, at room temperature

This recipe came to us from Glenn Roberts's Anson Mills, located in Columbia, South Carolina. Anson Mills produces lovely heritage flours from historically significant Southern-grown varieties. I met up with Ansley Roberts, Glenn's daughter, at Flat Rock Village Bakery for coffee and to talk flour, and she asked me if we had a biscuit recipe. We didn't, and this landed in my inbox not long after that. Anson Mills developed this biscuit recipe using their stone-ground Antebellum Style Rustic Coarse Graham Wheat Flour and their Colonial Style Fine Cloth-Bolted Pastry Flour, both milled from Red May wheat, a variety of wheat of Virginia origin. Red May is one of America's first farmer-selected production wheat varieties (along with White May also of Southern origin). Previous to any domestic varieties, immigrants from the Old World carried their wheat seeds with them to America.

These biscuits are best made with a soft red wheat (Red May or other variety) and are lovely served fresh out of the oven with plenty of sweet butter and honey or sorghum syrup.

1 Position oven racks in the lowest and upper-middle positions and preheat the oven to 450°F. Line a baking sheet with parchment paper.

2 Place both flours, the baking powder, and the salt in a food processor and pulse to combine. Scatter the butter pieces over the surface and process until the mixture forms a coarse meal, about ten 1-second pulses.

3 Transfer the mixture to a large bowl and, using a rubber spatula, lightly blend in 150 grams of the milk. If the dry ingredients are not uniformly moistened or are not holding together, add up to 2 tablespoons more milk, 1 tablespoon at a time. (The dough will be fairly wet.) Cover the bowl with plastic wrap and let the dough rest for 5 minutes.

4 Turn the dough out onto a lightly floured work surface and roll out to 1 inch thick. Dip a 2-inch biscuit cutter in flour, stamp out five biscuits (push straight down with your biscuit cutter and avoid twisting the cutter), and place them on the prepared baking sheet, making sure the sides are touching shoulder to shoulder. Gently gather the dough scraps into a rough ball, roll it lightly until smooth and 1 inch thick and cut the remaining biscuits. You should end up with nine or ten biscuits. (Any scraps left over can be baked freeform.)

5 Bake the biscuits on the lowest rack until they are nicely risen and deep golden brown on the bottoms, 6 to 8 minutes. Transfer the baking sheet to the upper-middle rack and bake until the tops are nicely browned, 6 to 8 minutes more. Remove the biscuits from the oven and serve them hot.

CARDAMOM TEA CAKES

JACKIE VITALE ◆ CAPTIVA ISLAND, FLORIDA

I was looking for another use for whole-grain pastry flour, so I reached out to Jackie Vitale, who sent me a recipe for Florida Green Tea Cakes with Cardamom and Rose Water. She had not made them with 100 percent whole grain, but felt the recipe was well suited for the application. Whole-grain pastry flour made from soft red wheat pairs especially well with cardamom. In adapting her recipe to use 100 percent whole-grain flour, I let go of the fragrant green tea and rose water to allow the flavors of the cardamom and red wheat to take center stage.

YIELD: 24 TEA CAKES

280g (2⅓ cups) whole-wheat pastry flour

2 teaspoons baking powder

¾ teaspoon fine sea salt

1 teaspoon ground cardamom, plus more for dusting

144g (¾ cup) granulated sugar

100g (½ cup) canola oil or other neutral oil

2 eggs

1 teaspoon pure vanilla extract

confectioners' sugar, for dusting

1   In a large bowl, combine the flour, baking powder, salt, and cardamom.

2   In a separate medium bowl, whisk together the granulated sugar, oil, eggs, and vanilla. Stir the wet ingredients into the flour mixture until just combined.

3   Line a baking sheet with parchment paper. Scoop 1-inch balls of the dough onto the prepared baking sheet, spacing them at least 2 inches apart. Refrigerate for at least 30 minutes and no more than 2 days.

4   Preheat the oven to 350°F.

5   Bake the tea cakes for 10 to 12 minutes. Remove from the oven and let the tea cakes cool on the pan for 5 minutes, then transfer to a cooling rack set over a sheet of parchment paper.

6   In a small bowl, combine 2 parts confectioners' sugar with 1 part cardamom. Using a fine-mesh sieve, dust the mixture over the tea cakes before serving. Once fully cooled, store in an airtight container at room temperature.

ROUGH PUFF WITH PECAN FRANGIPANE AND LOUISIANA BLOOD ORANGE

LEVEE BAKING CO. ◆ NEW ORLEANS, LOUISIANA

YIELD: 6 SMALL GALETTES OR 2 10-INCH GALETTES

ROUGH PUFF

225g (1¾ cups) whole-wheat pastry flour

225g (1¾ cups) high-extraction all-purpose flour (85AP)

1 tablespoon granulated sugar

1 teaspoon fine sea salt

340g (1½ cups) unsalted butter, cubed and chilled

1 tablespoon distilled white vinegar

225g (1 cup) ice water

FRANGIPANE

zest from 1 orange or lemon

104g (½ cup) granulated sugar

109g (1 cup) pecans, toasted

2 tablespoons high-extraction all-purpose flour (85AP)

½ teaspoon fine sea salt

2 eggs

113g (½ cup) unsalted butter, cubed and chilled

FILLING AND FINISHING

blood oranges (or satsuma orange are also lovely)

1 egg

a splash of milk

raw sugar, for sprinkling

Levee Baking Co. uses whatever is in season as the filling for this galette. "Any macerated fruit or roasted vegetable, even cheese and herbs will work," says owner Christina Balzebre. "The possibilities are limitless." When I visited Christina at Levee in New Orleans, satsuma oranges were in season, so she used those. And regarding the flour, sometimes Christina uses light rye in place of the whole-wheat pastry in this recipe, pairing flavor with flavor and texture with texture.

Notes: You can cut the dough into circles instead, if you like, but Christina prefers squares to limit scraps.

If you prefer, you can make two large galettes instead of six smaller ones. Increase the oranges to 6 to 8, leave a 2-inch border, and adjust the baking time to 40 to 50 minutes, or until the frangipane has puffed up and the pastry is golden brown.

1 Make the rough puff: Combine both flours, the sugar, and the salt in a bowl. Add the cold butter and toss the butter in the flour mixture, separating the cubes and coating them with flour. Break down the butter by pinching the cubes until the pieces are the size of large beans (don't break them down too much). If it is a warm day, chill the mixture in the freezer just to get it cold. Make a well in the center and add the vinegar, then add half the water. Using a flexible plastic dough scraper, begin to slowly incorporate the flour mixture into the liquid until a dough forms. Add more water as needed, adding just enough for the dough to come together. When you can press all the dough together to form a ball that doesn't crumbling apart, you have achieved the correct consistency. If you add too much water, add a bit more flour to compensate. Wrap the dough in plastic wrap and refrigerate for 1 to 2 hours, until thoroughly chilled.

2 Make the frangipane: In a small bowl, rub the zest into the sugar until fragrant.

3 In food processor, combine the pecans, citrus sugar, flour, and salt and pulse until the pecans are completely ground up. With the food processor running, add the eggs one at a time until a loose paste forms. Scrape down the bowl. Again with the food processor running, add the butter a cube at a time until completely emulsified. Scrape the mixture into a container. Cover and refrigerate for at least a couple of hours or up to overnight.

4 Once the dough feels thoroughly chilled, roll it out on a lightly floured work surface into a long rectangle, ½ inch thick. Fold over one side of the dough to the middle, then the other side on top, like a letter that will go into an envelope. Repeat this two more times, rolling out the dough and folding it. Wrap the dough in plastic wrap and chill the dough again.

CONTINUED

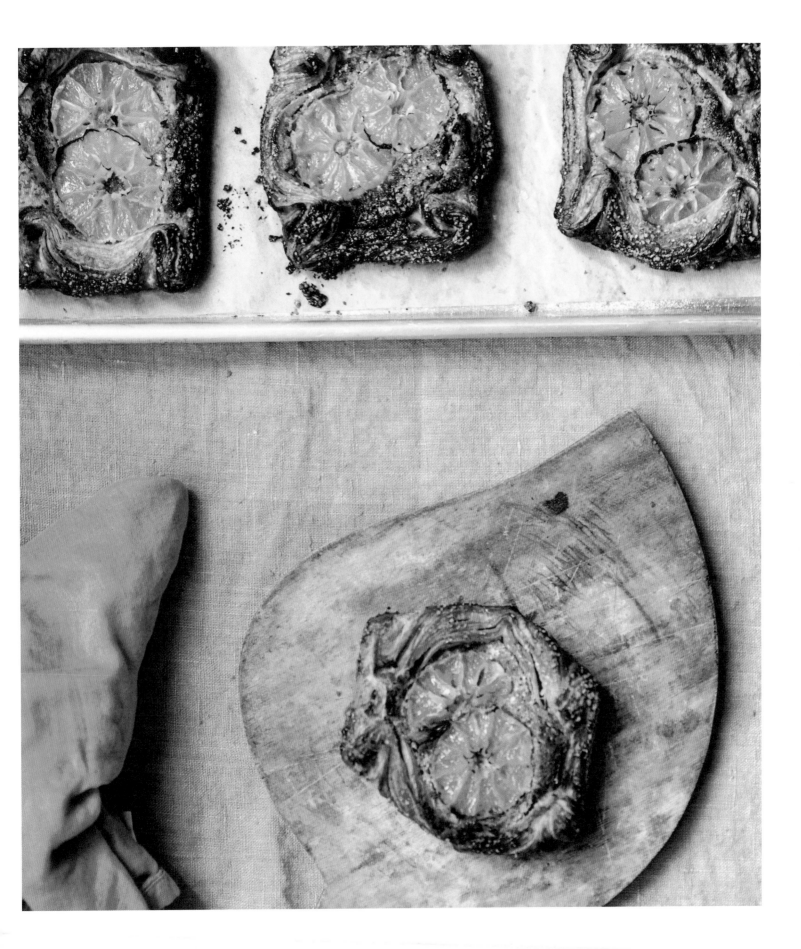

ROUGH PUFF WITH PECAN FRANGIPANE
AND LOUISIANA BLOOD ORANGE

CONTINUED

5   Preheat the oven to 425°F. Line a baking sheet with parchment paper

6   Prepare the fruit: Peel the citrus and then slice the flesh with a serrated knife into thin rounds, and deseed.

7   Whisk the egg and thin it with a splash of milk to make an egg wash.

8   Roll out the chilled dough into a long rectangle or square and cut it into six smaller squares (see Notes). Roll out each square to ⅛ to shy of ¼ inch thick. Spread a layer of the frangipane over the dough, leaving a 1-inch border. Place the fruit in the center and fold the sides of the pastry on top of and partially covering the fruit, making a little border wall. Brush the dough with the egg wash and sprinkle both dough and fruit with the raw sugar. Carefully place the galettes on a baking sheet.

9   Bake for 25 to 35 minutes, until the frangipane has puffed up and the pastry is golden brown. Remove the baking sheet from the oven and allow to rest on a cooling rack before carefully sliding the parchment paper and galettes onto a cooling rack. Cool for another 15 minutes before serving. Store covered in the refrigerator for 5 to 6 days.

GREEN QUICHE

JACKIE VITALE ◆ CAPTIVA ISLAND, FLORIDA

High-extraction pastry flour is an ideal choice for a rustic quiche application. Here it adds tooth and contributes to the layers of flavor, pairing beautifully with sharp cheese and bitter greens. I highly recommend baking this in a straight-sided pan for an elegant presentation.

1 Make the crust: In a large bowl, mix together the flour and salt. Add the cold butter and quickly incorporate it by gently smooshing the butter into the flour with your fingers, pinching all the butter cubes, until the mixture forms a shaggy mass with visible pieces of butter. Work fast so the butter doesn't warm up. Make a well in the center and add half the ice water. Quickly mix with your hands. Continue adding water a bit at a time as needed until the dough comes together, using just enough water that the dough doesn't crumble when you gather it into a ball. Gently flatten the dough into a disk, wrap it in plastic wrap, and refrigerate for at least 1 hour and up to 2 days, until thoroughly chilled.

2 On a lightly floured work surface (or between two sheets of parchment paper), roll out the chilled dough into a rectangle a bit bigger than a 9 x 13-inch baking pan. Flip the sheet of dough as you roll it out so it doesn't stick to the counter, but go easy on the flour. Patch any holes with dough from the edges. Carefully lift the sheet of dough and fit it into the pan. Take care to patch any holes or rips, especially at the corners. (Jackie likes a rustic look, so she keeps the edges pretty uneven and lightly presses a fork around the edge.) Stick the pan in the freezer and chill for at least 30 minutes and longer if necessary. (This can keep in the freezer for up to three months, wrapped in parchment, then tightly wrapped foil).

3 Preheat the oven to 350°F.

4 Remove the pan from freezer and line the dough with parchment, covering it completely. Fill the parchment with uncooked rice or beans, sugar, or pie weights. Bake for 45 minutes, or until the crust has taken on color. Set the pan on a cooling rack and carefully remove the parchment and weights. Let cool before adding filling. Keep the oven on.

5 Meanwhile, make the filling: In a large skillet, heat the olive oil over medium heat. Add the greens and lightly sauté them. You want them still good and bright colored, but tender.

6 In a large bowl, combine the eggs, half-and-half, garlic, salt, and pepper and mix with handheld mixer or whisk together by hand.

7 Sprinkle the cheese evenly over the bottom of the crust, then add the greens, then the herbs, and finally pour in the egg mixture.

8 Bake for 45 minutes, until the quiche is set but still wobbly. Transfer to a cooling rack and allow to cool for at least 20 minutes before serving. Once fully cooled, store covered, in the refrigerator for 3 to 4 days.

YIELD: 1 (9 X 13-INCH) QUICHE

CRUST

300g (2¾ cups) high-extraction (85P) pastry flour

1 teaspoon fine sea salt

190g (¾ cup + 1 tablespoon) cultured salted butter, cubed and chilled

125g (½ cup) ice water

FILLING

2 tablespoons olive oil

4 to 8 cups mix of hearty greens, such as kale, collards, arugula, asian greens

8 eggs

363g (1½ cups) half-and-half

1 teaspoon fermented or plain garlic, minced

1 teaspoon fine sea salt

½ teaspoon freshly ground black pepper

226g (2 cups) aged cheddar cheese, shredded

½ cup chopped fresh herbs, such as parsley, chives, dill, savory, and sage

PORTUGUESE BISCUITS

TROY DEREGO ◆ STARKVILLE, MISSISSIPPI

**YIELD: ABOUT
20 BISCUITS**

56g (¼ cup) unsalted
butter, melted

103g (½ cup)
granulated sugar

3 eggs

¾ teaspoon pure
vanilla extract

¾ teaspoon pure
almond extract

268g (2¼ cups) high-
extraction (85P) pastry flour

1¼ teaspoons
baking powder

¾ teaspoon fine sea salt

sesame and/or nigella
seeds, for sprinkling on top
(optional)

When Troy DeRego was running his DeRego's Breads, making artisan breads and whole-grain sourdough crackers using spent grains from a local brewery, he sent me a care package of all the different crackers he was making (his business later evolved into Grain Elevator). Among the amazing variety were these Portuguese biscuits, or biscoitos, a traditional cookie-like treat from the Azores. Troy shares, "They were popular at the Portuguese bakeries in New Bedford, Massachusetts, where my grandparents lived. My mother learned to make them and they became a staple in our house for holidays or to share with friends on camping trips. When I started my bread bakery in Starkville, Mississippi, I needed something sweet to lure customers to my market booth. Here in the South everyone was curious about this biscuit that looked like a doughnut and was hard like a cookie. One bite and they were hooked." High-extraction stone-ground pastry flour brings forward the tooth and mouthfeel.

1 In a large bowl, stir together the melted butter and the sugar to combine. In a separate bowl, whisk together two eggs and the vanilla, then add to the bowl with the butter mixture.

2 In a separate medium bowl, mix the flour, baking powder, and salt. Add the flour mixture to the butter mixture and stir to combine. (If using a stand mixer, set on the lowest speed and slowly add the flour mixture to incorporate it evenly.) The mixture should have a cookie dough consistency, not too sticky. Add a dusting of flour to adjust if needed. Turn the dough out of the bowl, wrap in plastic wrap, and refrigerate for 30 minutes.

3 Preheat the oven to 350°F. Line a baking sheet with parchment paper.

4 Divide the dough into 25-gram pieces. Roll each piece into a cylinder or rope with a diameter of about ½ inch. Taper the ends slightly. Bring the ends together to form a hoop. Touch the ends just enough to stick together, no need to smooth or shape. They will smooth over when baked. Place the biscuits 2 inches apart on the prepared baking sheet.

5 Whisk the remaining egg and thin it slightly with a bit of water to make an egg wash. Brush the egg wash over the biscuits. Sprinkle with sesame and/or nigella seeds (if using). Bake for 20 minutes, or until the biscuits are just starting to turn golden, rotating the pan every 10 minutes to ensure the biscuits bake evenly.

6 Transfer the biscuits to a cooling rack and let cool for 20 minutes. Once fully cooled, store in an airtight container for up to a week.

CITRUS OLIVE OIL CAKE WITH CHOCOLATE GANACHE

JACKIE VITALE ◆ CAPTIVA ISLAND, FLORIDA

This is one of two citrus olive oil cakes in this book. I chose to run both because each demonstrates a different direction within the same theme. This is a more rustic version, made with high-extraction pastry flour and freshly squeezed orange juice and topped with roasted citrus. Anisette's Orange Olive Oil Cake (page 247) is a more refined iteration, where cream replaces the orange juice and the flour choice—our Trinity Blend, a finely sifted blend of rye, soft wheat, and hard wheat flours—provides a more delicate crumb.

1 Roast the citrus: Position a rack in the center of the oven and preheat the oven to 425°F. Line a baking sheet with parchment paper.

2 Slice the citrus into thin rounds (you'll need 15 to 20 rounds to cover the top of the cake). Remove any seeds. Place the citrus rounds on the prepared baking sheet and sprinkle with sugar. Roast for 10 to 15 minutes, until the citrus begins to caramelize. Remove from the oven and set aside. Lower the oven temperature to 375°F.

3 Make the cake: Line the bottom and sides of a 9-inch-round cake pan with parchment paper cut to fit and lightly coat the parchment with olive oil.

4 In a large bowl, combine the flour, baking powder, salt, and baking soda.

5 In the bowl of a stand mixer fitted with the paddle attachment, combine the eggs, sugar, olive oil, orange zest, and orange juice and mix on low speed for 3 minutes. With the mixer running on low, add the flour mixture and mix until just incorporated.

6 Pour the batter into the prepared pan and bake on the center rack about 40 minutes, until the cake springs back when you touch the center lightly and a toothpick inserted into the middle comes out clean. Let the cake cool in the pan for 5 minutes, then carefully remove it from the pan. Gently peel away the parchment and transfer the cake to a cooling rack set over a sheet of parchment paper; let cool completely.

7 Make the ganache: Place the chocolate in a heatproof bowl. In a small saucepan, bring the cream to a gentle simmer. Pour the hot cream over the chocolate and stir until the chocolate has melted and the mixture is well combined.

8 To assemble: Pour the ganache over the cake, allowing it to dribble down the sides. Arrange the roasted citrus rounds on top. This is especially nice served while the ganache is still warm.

YIELD: 1 (9-INCH) ROUND CAKE

ROASTED CITRUS

2 to 3 medium oranges or 1 to 2 grapefruit

granulated sugar

CAKE

190g (1½ cups) high-extraction (85P) pastry flour

1 teaspoon baking powder

½ teaspoon fine sea salt

¼ teaspoon baking soda

2 eggs, large

198g (1 cup) granulated sugar

86g (½ cup) olive oil

2 teaspoons orange zest

⅔ cup orange juice (ideally freshly squeezed)

GANACHE

75g (3 ounces) good-quality dark chocolate (at least 60% cacao), chopped

115g (½ cup) heavy cream

HIGH-EXTRACTION CAKE WITH CINNAMON-INFUSED COFFEE + MAPLE-COFFEE ICING

CAROLINA GROUND ◆ ASHEVILLE, NORTH CAROLINA

YIELD: 1 (7-INCH)
ROUND CAKE

CINNAMON-INFUSED COFFEE

20g (¼ cup) ground coffee

½ teaspoon ground cinnamon

¼ teaspoon almond extract

½ teaspoon fine sea salt

340g (1½ cups) hot water

28g (2 tablespoons) whole milk

CAKE

103g (1 cup) high-extraction (85P) pastry flour

¾ teaspoon baking powder

¼ teaspoon baking soda

⅛ teaspoon sea salt

57g (¼ cup) unsalted butter

70g (⅓ cup) granulated sugar

1 egg, separated

MAPLE-COFFEE ICING

185g (¾ cup) confectioners' sugar

1 tablespoon maple syrup

This recipe was developed by Desiree Bridges, our summer intern from Johnson & Wales. Desiree's summer task was to do a study of our pastry flours, pairing flavors that accentuated the quality of each flour. The high-extraction pastry flour (85P) became our favorite flour that summer for its ability to amplify any recipe in which we put it to the task. Desiree reflects, "85P is a stronger-flavored flour that reminds me of honey-drenched roasted oats with an almost barely noticeable coffee aftertaste. This balance of sweet and robust creates a flour that is perfect for pairing with stronger flavors that you may want to use when baking, such as chocolate or cinnamon. 85P melds with these ingredients, creating a complex flavor profile. I wanted this recipe to enhance 85P's natural robust honey flavor."

1 Preheat the oven to 350°F. Line the bottom of a 7-inch springform pan with parchment paper cut to fit, then grease the parchment. Dust the pan and the parchment with flour, tapping out any excess.

2 Make the coffee: Add the cinnamon and almond extract to the coffee grounds and brew the coffee. Pour 28 grams of the coffee into a small bowl and stir in the milk. Set aside; reserve the remaining coffee for the icing.

3 Make the cake: Into a medium bowl, sift together the flour, baking powder, baking soda, and salt.

4 In the bowl of a stand mixer fitted with the paddle attachment, cream the butter and sugar on medium speed until fluffy, 4 to 5 minutes. Add the egg yolk and mix until fully incorporated. Stop and scrape down the bowl.

5 In two stages, alternate between adding the flour mixture and the coffee, mixing until just incorporated after each addition.

6 In a separate medium bowl, whip the egg white until it holds stiff peaks.

7 Remove the bowl from the stand mixer and, by hand, fold in the beaten egg white, then pour the batter into the prepared pan. Smooth the top with a spatula.

8 Bake until the cake springs back when you touch the center lightly and a toothpick inserted into the middle comes out clean, about 35 minutes. Remove from the oven and let cool on a cooling rack, then remove from the pan and transfer to a cake plate.

9 Make the icing: In a small bowl, whisk together the confectioners' sugar, maple syrup, and 2 tablespoons of the leftover coffee until the mixture has the consistency of a pourable icing. Add another tablespoon of coffee if necessary.

10 Spoon the icing onto the cake and smooth it out with a knife or the back of the spoon. Refrigerate the cake until the icing sets, about 30 minutes, then serve.

11 Can be stored in a covered container at room temperature for a couple days or up to a week in the refrigerator.

BANANA BREAD WITH WALNUTS, CARDAMOM, AND CACAO NIBS

FLAT ROCK VILLAGE BAKERY ◆ FLAT ROCK, NORTH CAROLINA

This is another solid recipe of Flat Rock's that predates the launch of Carolina Ground but became even better once they had the opportunity to switch to stone-ground high-extraction pastry flour. In testing this recipe for the book, my husband suggested I add cardamom (Scott launched Flat Rock, so I allowed him full license to chime in). I threw in the cacao nibs and bittersweet chocolate as well (with Scott's approval), as these deep flavors seemed like they would work, and they do.

1 Preheat the oven to 350°F. With a pastry brush dipped in olive oil, grease an 8 x 4-inch loaf pan. Line the pan with parchment paper cut to the length of the pan and wide enough to cover the two long sides, then grease the parchment as well. The narrow ends of the pan are left uncovered, so brush them with extra oil.

2 Line a baking sheet with parchment paper.

3 Roast the walnuts and prepare the topping: Spread the walnuts onto the prepared baking sheet and place in a preheated oven for 8 to 10 minutes, watching carefully so they don't burn. Remove from the oven and place the baking sheet on a cooling rack. Turn the oven down to 325°F.

4 Once the walnuts are cool, chop into ¼- to ½-inch pieces.

5 Place the cardamom seeds in a dry skillet (I prefer cast iron) and roast on the stovetop on low heat, stirring with a wooden spoon until it they begin to small fragrant and toasted. Transfer to a mortar and pestle and pound just enough to make a coarsely cracked consistency. Place in a medium bowl. Add the cacao nibs, chocolate chips (or pieces) and 25g (¼ cup) of the walnut pieces and stir to combine.

6 Make the cake: In a large bowl, mash the bananas until smooth. Add the sour cream, egg, oil, and vanilla. Mix until combined. In a separate medium bowl, combine the flour, sugar, baking soda, and salt. Fold the dry mixture into the wet mixture until just combined. Fold in the remaining walnuts.

7 Transfer the batter to the prepared loaf pan, sprinkle on the topping mixture, and place in the preheated oven. Bake until it begins to pull away from the pan and a toothpick inserted into the center comes out clean, 40 to 50 minutes.

8 Remove the pan from the oven and set it on a cooling rack. Let the banana bread cool in the pan for 10 to 15 minutes before removing it from the pan to cool completely or serve. Once fully cool, store in an airtight container in the refrigerator for up to 4 days.

YIELD: 1 (8 X 4-INCH) PAN LOAF

70g (¾ cup) walnuts

TOPPING

1 tablespoon cacao nibs

2 tablespoons dark chocolate (at least 70% cacao) chips or pieces

½ teaspoon whole cardamom seeds

CAKE

2½ ripe bananas

61g (¼ cup) sour cream

1 egg

54.5g (¼ cup) canola, safflower, or grapeseed oil

¾ teaspoon pure vanilla extract

125g (1 cup) high-extraction (85P) pastry flour

78g (⅓ cup) granulated sugar

½ teaspoon baking soda

¼ teaspoon fine sea salt

NATURALLY LEAVENED CARROT CAKE

HARRY PEEMOELLER • JOHNSON & WALES UNIVERSITY, CHARLOTTE, NORTH CAROLINA

Harry developed this recipe for On the Rise 3, Johnson & Wales University's third-annual International Symposium on Bread held at the university's Charlotte, North Carolina, campus. The point was to push the envelope, embrace various grains, and learn. Harry showed his class two versions of this cake. The initial version was without the 60 minutes of final fermentation in a warm location. Since the recipe contains baking soda, the final rise did not seem necessary, but the second version had the final rise and the difference between the two was pretty dramatic, with the second having risen into a much more open crumb. One of the gifts of baking is the lifelong process of learning—there's always more to discover.

Note: For this cake, because it is so moist, I have found taking the internal temperature to be a safer measure of doneness than a simple toothpick test.

YIELD: 1 (9-INCH) ROUND CAKE

LEAVEN (4 HOURS)

66g warm water (85°F)

33g starter

63g high-extraction pastry flour (85P)

FERMENTED CARROT CAKE BATTER

150g leaven

95g high-extraction pastry flour (85P)

135g granulated sugar

110g grapeseed oil

2 eggs

¾ teaspoon ground cinnamon

½ teaspoon fine sea salt

½ teaspoon baking soda

20g to 40g (as needed) milk or heavy cream

130g carrots, shredded

42g currants

BAKED CREAM CHEESE FROSTING

30g unsalted butter

160g granulated sugar

¼ teaspoon fine sea salt

¼ teaspoon lemon zest

500g cream cheese

1 egg

1 teaspoon pure vanilla extract

30g to 40g high-extraction pastry flour (85P)

1 Make the leaven: Measure the water into a small clear container with a lid, such as a pint mason jar, then add the starter. Using a spoon or your fingers, break apart the starter into the water. Add the flour and mix until fully incorporated. Cover and let stand at room temperature until fully developed (see the image on page 86).

2 Make the batter: In a medium bowl, add the leaven, flour, 35 grams of the sugar, the oil, and eggs and mix until the batter is smooth. Cover and let ferment at room temperature for 2½ hours to jump-start the fermentation, then refrigerate overnight. (Harry says he has left this batter in the fridge for 2 to 3 days with no problems.)

3 Line the bottom of a 9-inch springform pan with parchment paper cut to fit, then grease the parchment and the pan and dust with flour, tapping out any excess.

4 Add the remaining 100 grams sugar, the cinnamon, and salt to the batter and stir to combine.

5 In a small bowl, mix the baking soda with a little milk or cream for better distribution and then add it to the batter. Fold in the carrots and currants.

6 Pour the batter into the prepared pan. Cover and set aside in a warm spot to ferment for 1 hour.

7 Preheat the oven to 350°F.

8 Bake until the internal temperature of the cake reads 205°F, 35 to 45 minutes (see Note). Remove from the oven and let cool on a cooling rack in the pan. Leave oven on.

9 Meanwhile, make the frosting: In the bowl of a stand mixer fitted with the whisk attachment, cream the butter, sugar, salt, and lemon zest on medium-high speed until smooth. Add the cream cheese in increments and mix until smooth. Add the egg and vanilla. Add the flour.

10 Pipe or spread the frosting onto the cake and bake for an additional 10 minutes. Remove from the oven and let cool on cooling rack, then remove from the pan and transfer to a cake plate

11 Can be stored covered in the refrigerator for up to 4 days.

BISCOTTI WITH ROASTED ALMONDS, BITTERSWEET CHOCOLATE, AND SEA SALT

FLAT ROCK VILLAGE BAKERY ◆ FLAT ROCK, NORTH CAROLINA

YIELD: 25 BISCOTTI

210g (1½ cups) whole raw almonds

411g (2 cups) high-extraction (85P) pastry flour

266g (1⅓ cups) granulated sugar

1 teaspoon baking powder

¼ teaspoon fine sea salt

4 eggs

2 teaspoons pure vanilla extract

88g (3 ounces) bittersweet chocolate (60% to 70% cacao), chopped

TOPPING

1 egg yolk, whisked with a little water, for egg wash

2 teaspoons granulated sugar (optional)

½ teaspoon fine sea salt (optional)

Flat Rock Village Bakery produced this biscotti for years before Carolina Ground existed. It is a solid recipe that follows the traditional method with no added fat, so the biscotti store incredibly well in an airtight container and require dunking in coffee or tea to keep you from breaking a tooth. I loved these biscotti before the addition of Carolina Ground flour, but shifting from a roller-milled all-purpose flour to our stone-ground high-extraction pastry flour seemed to complete what this recipe was trying to realize: a rustic cookie of tooth and flavor. Simply perfect.

1 Preheat the oven to 350°F.

2 Spread the almonds in a single layer on a rimmed baking sheet and toast in the oven for 10 to 12 minutes, until golden. Set aside to cool; keep the oven on, but turn down to 325°F.

3 Line a baking sheet with parchment paper and brush the parchment with olive oil.

4 In a large bowl, combine the flour, sugar, baking powder, and salt.

5 In a separate medium bowl, whisk together the eggs and vanilla. Add the egg mixture to the flour mixture and mix until fully incorporated. This is a dry dough but it will come together. Stir in the toasted almonds and the chocolate.

6 Turn the dough out onto the prepared baking sheet and form it into a long rectangle about 1 inch thick. Brush the egg wash over the dough. If desired, combine the sugar and salt and sprinkle the mixture over the dough.

7 Bake for 10 minutes, then rotate the pan and bake for another 10 minutes, or until golden and firm. Remove from the oven and let cool for 10 to 20 minutes; lower the oven temperature to 275°F. Carefully slice the loaves crosswise into ½-inch-thick slices and set the biscotti cut-side down on the baking sheet. Bake for 25 to 30 minutes more until golden brown. Transfer to a cooling rack. Once fully cooled, the biscotti can be stored in an airtight container at room temperature for at least 2 weeks.

HIGH-EXTRACTION SUGAR COOKIE

JOE BOWIE ◆ COLUMBIA, SOUTH CAROLINA

Joe's choice to blend high-extraction pastry flour (85P) with high-extraction all-purpose flour (85AP)—which equates to two parts pastry flour to one part bread flour—results in a tender cookie with good structure and lots of flavor.

YIELD: ABOUT 48 COOKIES

232g (2 cups) high-extraction pastry flour (85P)

232g (2 cups) high-extraction all-purpose flour (85AP)

1 teaspoon baking powder

1 teaspoon fine sea salt

½ teaspoon baking soda

½ teaspoon nutmeg, ground

320g (1⅔ cups) granulated sugar

290g (1¼ cups) unsalted butter

orange zest from 1 orange

1 egg

1 egg yolk

7g (1½ teaspoons) pure vanilla extract

20g (1 tablespoon) honey

1 Preheat the oven to 350°F. Line two baking sheets with parchment paper.

2 Measure the flours, baking powder, salt, baking soda, and nutmeg into a medium bowl and whisk together. Set aside.

3 In the bowl of a stand mixer fitted with the paddle attachment, cream together the sugar, butter, and orange zest on medium-high speed until fluffy. Add the eggs and vanilla and mix until fully incorporated, then add the honey.

4 Add the dry ingredients to the butter mixture and mix to combine. Turn the dough out onto a sheet of plastic wrap, wrap it in the plastic, and refrigerate for at least 20 minutes or up to overnight to firm up the dough.

5 In a medium bowl, combine the cinnamon and sugar.

6 Using a 1-ounce scoop or a heaping tablespoon, scoop and roll the dough into 25-gram balls, then dredge them in the cinnamon-sugar to coat, and set them on the prepared baking sheets. Gently press down on each cookie with the palm of your hand to flatten them slightly.

7 Bake for 10 to 12 minutes, until the cookies take on only a bit of color on the edges and the bottom and are still quite soft (they will set up as they cool).

8 Remove the cookies from the oven. Feel free to sprinkle more cinnamon-sugar on them right out of the oven to ensure an even coating. Let the cookies cool completely on the cookie sheets and then transfer to an airtight container, where they can be stored at room temperature for 4 or 5 days.

CINNAMON SUGAR

200g (1 cup) granulated sugar

2 teaspoons ground cinnamon

MISSISSIPPI MARKET GALETTE

SUNFLOWER OVEN • JACKSON, MISSISSIPPI

YIELD: 8 OR 9 SMALL GALETTES

SOURDOUGH PIECRUST

250g (2 cups) high-extraction (85P) pastry flour

½ teaspoon fine sea salt

112g (½ cup) unsalted butter, frozen

1 cup sourdough culture, 100% hydration (see page 94)

ice water, as needed

FILLING IDEAS

sliced peaches with brown sugar and fresh basil

thinly sliced apples with pecan frangipane (see page 212)

goat cheese and blueberries

caramelized onions with roasted peppers and/or potatoes

roasted cubed kabocha squash and sautéed chard

1 egg, whisked with a dash of cream, milk, or water, for egg wash

From the balcony of Robert Raymond's apartment in Jackson, Mississippi, you can see the state farmers' market. There is a Cook Out fast-food restaurant between the apartment and the market, so close that you can hear the orders announced from the drive-through speakers, a strange juxtaposition when you experience the abundance of baked goods coming out of Robert's kitchen. Robert has turned his kitchen into a microbakery he's named Sunflower Oven. This is where he bakes the breads and pastries that he sells at the farmers' market across the road. This particular recipe highlights the locality and seasonality of what he is doing, trading bread with fellow farmer vendors and returning the next week with baked good inspired by their harvest.

Note: This recipe is a good place to use spent or extra sourdough culture, though it requires enough starter that you may need to make the starter. If you don't have any, weigh 136 grams water into a small clear container with a lid, such as a pint mason jar, then add 27 grams starter. Using a spoon or your fingers, break apart the starter into the water. Add 136 grams flour (this can be whole grain or sifted, wheat or rye) and mix until fully incorporated. Cover and let stand at room temperature for 6 to 8 hours, until fully developed (see image on page 86).

1 Make the piecrust: Combine the flour and salt and form the flour into a low mound on your work surface. Using the large holes of a box grater, grate the frozen butter and then scatter it over the top of the flour mixture. Sprinkle the butter with a little flour, then quickly roll the butter into the flour with a rolling pin. Pour the sourdough culture on top of this shaggy mixture and mix with a bench knife until a rough dough forms. Roll out and fold the dough over itself twice to further incorporate all the dry flour. If needed, splash on a little ice water, but sparingly. You should still be able to see some streaks of butter in the dough. Wrap the dough in plastic wrap and refrigerate for at least 1 hour or up to overnight.

2 Preheat the oven to 350°F. Line a baking sheet with parchment paper.

3 Roll out the chilled dough to between ⅛ to ¼ inch thick, then cut it into roughly 5-inch squares. Place the filling of your choice in the center of each square of dough, leaving a 1-inch border, then fold the edges of the dough in so the filling is partially covered, leaving the center exposed. Brush the dough with the egg wash and place the galettes on the prepared baking sheet.

4 Bake for 25 to 30 minutes, until the edges are nicely browned. Let cool on the pan for 10 minutes. Once fully cooled, store in an airtight container at room temperature for a day or in the refrigerator for 2 to 3 days.

APPLE MASCARPONE CAKE

ANISETTE ◆ RALEIGH, NORTH CAROLINA

Anisette makes various iterations of this cake depending on the season. Following their posts on Instagram is like watching the seasons change: in the springtime, Nicole posts images of strawberry fennel mascarpone cake; in the summertime, blueberry mascarpone cake; in the fall, red plum, and then pumpkin, and then ginger; in the winter, she uses citrus, posting an image of an orange mascarpone cake topped with roasted orange slices. Her choice of flour for this cake provides a plush cushion for the season's offerings.

1 Preheat the oven to 350°F. Grease an 8-inch-square cake pan with butter and line it with parchment paper cut to fit. Grease the parchment paper as well.

2 In a medium bowl, combine the flour, baking powder, cinnamon, and salt.

3 In the bowl of a stand mixer fitted with the paddle attachment, combine the sugar, eggs, mascarpone, rum, and vanilla and mix on low speed for 3 minutes. With the mixer on low speed, add the flour mixture and mix just until the dry ingredients are moistened. Stop and scrape down the sides and bottom of the bowl, then mix on low speed for 1 minute more, until smooth.

4 Pour 500 grams of the batter (a little more than half) into the prepared pan and use a spatula to create a smooth, even layer. Layer the apple slices evenly over the batter. Pour the remaining batter over the apple slices and smooth the top evenly.

5 Bake until the cake springs back when you touch the center lightly and a toothpick inserted into the middle comes out clean, 40 to 45 minutes. Let the cake cool in the pan for 10 to 15 minutes, then invert the cake onto a cooling rack and remove the parchment paper. Set the cake right-side up and let cool completely before serving.

6 Once fully cool, store in an airtight container in the refrigerator for 5 to 6 days.

YIELD: 1 (8-INCH) SQUARE CAKE

235g (2 cups) finely sifted stone-ground cake flour (Crema)

1½ teaspoons baking powder

1 teaspoon ground cinnamon

¼ teaspoon fine sea salt

260g (1¼ cups) granulated sugar

3 eggs, at room temperature

260g (1⅛ cups) mascarpone cheese, at room temperature

1 teaspoon dark rum

½ teaspoon pure vanilla extract

150g (1½ medium or 1½ cups loosely packed) apples, cored and sliced about ⅛ inch thick

EVERGREEN'S LEMON POUND CAKE

EVERGREEN BUTCHER + BAKER ◆ ATLANTA, GEORGIA

YIELD: 1 (13 X 4-INCH
PULLMAN) LOAF

280g (2⅔ cups) finely sifted
stone-ground cake flour
(Crema)

2 teaspoons baking powder

6 eggs, at room
temperature

400g (2 cups)
granulated sugar

lemon zest from 4 lemons

¾ teaspoon fine sea salt

160g (⅔ cup) heavy cream

180g (¾ cup + 1 tablespoon)
unsalted butter, melted
and cooled

GLAZE

250g (2 cups)
confectioners' sugar

60g (¼ cup) fresh
lemon juice

Evergreen Butcher + Baker, owned by husband and wife team, Emma and Sean Schacke (baker and butcher, respectively), is a butcher shop and bakery in East Atlanta that was just opening when I was in the depths of writing this book. They came to visit, talk flour, and learn about what we do. I asked them why they chose the name Evergreen, and standing in the mill room surrounded by one-ton totes of grain grown in the South and bags of flour piled high—evidence of the commitment we have made to our Southern growers—I was moved by their answer. They said they had no interest in trendy foods. They wanted to provide their community with staples made with the best ingredients sourced locally and regionally. To them, "evergreen" meant not changing with the trends, but remaining steadfast in what they do. When Emma offered this recipe, I knew we needed to include it, as it is a lovely example of a timeless classic elevated by the choice of flour. This cake is moist and rich, with a delicate crumb. Highly sifted cake flour is well paired with the flavors and mouthfeel of lemon and cream. Simple and elegant.

1 Preheat the oven to 325°F. Butter a 13 x 4-inch loaf pan and dust with flour, then tap out any excess.

2 Into a medium bowl, sift together the flour and baking powder.

3 In the bowl of a stand mixer fitted with the paddle attachment, combine the eggs, sugar, lemon zest, and salt and mix on medium speed for 1 minute. Alternately add the cream and the flour mixture, mixing until just combined after each addition and stopping to scrape down the sides of the bowl as needed. Stir in the melted butter. Pour the batter into the prepared pan.

4 Bake until the cake is pulling away from the pan and a toothpick inserted into the middle comes out clean, about 45 minutes.

5 Meanwhile, make the glaze: In a medium bowl, stir together the confectioners sugar and lemon juice.

6 Remove the pan from the oven and let the cake cool in the pan briefly, before removing it from the pan. While the cake is still warm, brush it with the glaze. Allow the glaze to set before serving.

7 Store in an airtight container at room temperature for a couple days or up to a week in the refrigerator.

CREMA PIECRUST

SMOKE SIGNALS ◆ POUND, VIRGINIA

YIELD: 1 (9-INCH)
CRUST FOR A SINGLE-
CRUST PIE

117g (½ cup) unsalted butter

180g (1¾ cups) finely sifted
stone-ground cake flour
(Crema)

2 teaspoons
granulated sugar

¾ teaspoon fine sea salt

54g (¼ cup) ice water

I used to bring Tara new crop pastry wheat to test for the mill. Piecrust was the testing medium. Is it flaky? Did it layer? I knew that Tara was well equipped to provide feedback, because Tara knows pie dough. Here's her recipe for a single crust using our Crema flour.

Note: The degree to which the crust gets baked depends on how long it will be baked again after it is filled. If you'll be using an unbaked filling, such as for a cream pie or an icebox pie, fully bake the crust to a rich golden brown, as it will not be going back into the oven again.

1 The day before making the crust, cut the butter into cubes and freeze it. Fifteen minutes prior to mixing the dough, transfer the butter to the refrigerator to thaw it to a workable state.

2 Into a large bowl, sift together the flour, sugar, and salt. Add the cubes of cold butter and use you fingers to coat them with the flour mixture. Turn the mixture out onto your work surface and cut in the butter with a bench knife for a few seconds. For a flaky crust, leave pea-size pieces of butter; for a mealy crust, cut the butter in further until the mixture resembles coarse sand. Form the mixture into a mound and make a well in the middle. Add the ice water and use the bench knife to combine it with the butter-flour mixture for a few seconds; use the bench knife to round up any water that escapes. Using the palm of your hand, smear the dough across the counter, then scrape it together with the bench knife and fold it onto itself. Smear, scrape, and fold again. Smear one last time, scraping and folding the dough fully together. There should still be visible portions of butter and no dry bits of flour. Shape the dough into a disk, wrap it in plastic wrap, and refrigerate for at least 30 minutes and up to 2 days.

3 Preheat the oven to 400°F.

4 Set the dough on a lightly floured work surface. Using a rolling pin, roll from the center out two times, applying light, even pressure. Give the dough a quarter turn and roll twice. Repeat the quarter turn and two rolls from the center until you have a 12-inch round of dough.

5 Place a 9-inch pie plate upside down in the center of the dough round and use a pastry wheel to trim the dough to 1 inch from the edge of the pie plate. Remove the pie plate. Starting from the side closest to you, gently roll the dough around the rolling pin, then unroll it over the pie plate and gently press it into the corners. Fold over the excess dough at the rim of the pie plate and crimp or flute as you desire. Using the tines of a fork, poke the bottom five or six times.

6 Line the dough with a 12-inch round of parchment paper and fill it with pie weights or dried beans (Tara uses dried black beans). Bake for 10 minutes. Remove the pie plate from the oven and remove the parchment and weights. Lower the oven temperature to 350°F and bake the crust for another 10 minutes (see Note).

7 Let the piecrust cool before filling it with the filling of your choice.

Tara's Pro Tips

- Use the best butter you can find. Anything at or over 80 percent butterfat is recommended; widely available brands include Plugrá and Kerrygold. If you use local, artisanal butters, be sure the butter and the ice water are well combined and the butter is not "weepy."

- Does your dough still need a bit more water? Try spraying it with water from a spray bottle rather than drizzling the water from a teaspoon or cup. It will evenly coat the dough, resulting in overall hydration.

- Even though we are using pastry wheat, it is still possible to work the dough too much. This will bring out the elastic quality of the gluten and cause your crust to shrink while baking. To avoid this, let the dough rest before rolling it out.

- Do not use excessive flour when rolling out the dough. The extra flour will toughen the crust and dry it out, creating a dough that cracks easily.

- When rolling out the dough, perform long, even sweeping motions with the rolling pin and keep the dough in constant motion, flipping to work one side after you've rolled for a minute on the other. Do not plow your rolling pin into the dough or roll it heavily in only one spot. The whole process should take under 5 minutes.

- Keep your work surface very cold. Rolling out the dough on chilled marble or a chilled baking sheet will keep the butter cold so it doesn't warm and break through the dough, causing the crust to fuse with the surface.

- If the crust balloons up after the parchment and pie weights have been removed, poke it a few times with a fork in the problem areas and put it back in the oven to finish baking. Next time, make sure the dough is pricked deeply enough and in several locations before adding the parchment and pie weights.

Blends and Outlier Grains

High-Extraction All-Purpose (85AP)

A 50/50 blend of pastry (soft) wheat and bread (hard) wheat sifted to a high-extraction flour (with 15 parts larger bran sifted out), this flour has broad applications. We make our all-purpose flour with a blend of red wheat and white wheat, and depending on the harvest, it is either a soft red pastry wheat and a hard white bread wheat, or the other way around. This flour is our attempt to wean people from the ubiquitous white all-purpose flour and encourage them to adopt a more flavorful and nutritious staple. You can make your own all-purpose flour by blending stone-ground bread flour and pastry flour in equal measure.

Trinity Blend

A blend of sifted soft wheat, hard wheat, and rye, this all-purpose flour of pastry application was a mistake in the mill room that has been a gift to bakers. Flavors such as orange, fig, honey, floral herbs, Earl Grey tea, and coffee pair well with this flour. In the mill room, we blend the three grains in the hopper, in equal measures by volume. You can make your own blend at home by mixing 1 cup sifted stone-ground pastry flour, 1 cup sifted stone-ground rye flour, and 1 cup sifted stone-ground bread flour.

Outliers: Spelt, Buckwheat, and Einkorn

Regionally adapted bread wheat varieties are the foundational grains for Carolina Ground. They serve the farmer with adequate yield, and the baker with a good price point. But built upon this foundation is the need for variety—both in the field and on our plate (or hearth). Outlier grains—the ancient and the very old—bring diversity to the regional grains movement—Einkorn, Emmer, and Spelt, Red May, Sonora, Red Fife, Turkey Red, Rouge de Bordeaux are all varieties that have been brought back into production throughout the United States. These older varieties have deep roots that enable them to sequester nutrients from the soil, making them especially well suited for the organic grower whose savings account is their soil. Buckwheat planted in rotation is good for the bees. And off the farm and into the bakery, no less important is the flavor of diversity.

SOURDOUGH DOUGHNUTS

SMOKE SIGNALS ◆ POUND, VIRGINIA

Tara Jensen says, "This dough is very flexible, but like all sourdoughs, time works in its favor. The doughnuts are best eaten fresh, so plan to make them right before you eat them or take them with you to a Fat Tuesday party. Depending on the flour you use, the dough will be looser or stiffer. You are looking for a soft, supple dough like a baguette. Adjust as necessary."

Note: To make filled doughnuts, allow doughnuts to cool completely on cooling rack and then using a pastry bag with a side nozzle, pipe into the cooled doughnuts. North Carolina Rye Custard (page 205) would make a great filling.

1 Make the leaven: Measure the water into a small clear container with a lid, such as a ½ pint mason jar, then add the starter. Dissolve the starter into the water. Add the flour and mix until fully incorporated. (Tara suggests doing this in the morning, between 8 and 9 a.m.) Cover the container and let stand in a warm location to ferment over the course of the day, until fully developed (see image on page 107).

2 Make the dough: Melt the butter 10 minutes prior to mixing the dough and let cool. Warm the milk 5 minutes prior to mixing the dough.

3 Pour the warm milk into a large bowl and add the melted butter and vanilla. Add the leaven, breaking it up with your fingers. Beat in the eggs.

4 In a separate bowl, whisk together the flour, sugar, salt, nutmeg, cinnamon, and cardamom. Fold the dry ingredients into the wet ingredients. Stir in the citrus zest (if using).

5 Turn the dough out onto a lightly floured work surface and knead for 3 to 5 minutes, until it is smooth and glossy. Lightly spray a large bowl with oil and transfer the dough to the bowl. Cover with a clean, dry kitchen towel or a lid. Set the dough aside in a warm spot until doubled in size, 4 to 5 hours at around 70°F, giving the dough a stretch and fold (see page 105) midway through.

Make sure the dough stays moist and warm. After rising, refrigerate the dough overnight or for up to 48 hours.

6 Bring the dough to room temperature and line a baking sheet with parchment paper. Roll out the dough to 1 inch thick. Using the rim of a drinking glass, cut out rounds of dough, then use a shot glass to cut holes in the center of each round. Transfer the doughnuts to a baking sheet, cover, and let proof at room temperature for 2 to 3 hours, until they feel pillowlike and soft to the touch.

7 Line a baking sheet or basket with torn brown paper and set it nearby. Fill a large, heavy-bottomed pan (such as a 4-quart Dutch oven) with at least 2 inches of oil and heat the oil over medium-high heat to 350°F). Test the oil by periodically tossing in doughnut hole bits. If they brown up quickly and bubble, the oil is ready. If they turn black and the oil is smoking, the oil is too hot. Working in batches, add the doughnuts to the hot oil and fry for 1 to 2 minutes on each side. Using a slotted spoon, transfer the doughnuts to the brown paper to drain.

8 If desired, fill a brown paper bag with confectioners' sugar or cinnamon sugar, add a few doughnuts (still hot and moist from frying) at a time, seal the bag, and toss to nicely coat.

YIELD: ABOUT A DOZEN DOUGHNUTS AND DOUGHNUT HOLES

LEAVEN

61g water

12g starter

61g high-extraction all-purpose flour (85AP)

DOUGH

134g unsalted butter

134g whole milk

8g pure vanilla extract

134g leaven

3 eggs, medium

383g high-extraction all-purpose flour (85AP)

38g granulated sugar

8g fine sea salt

¼ teaspoon nutmeg

¼ teaspoon ground cinnamon

¼ teaspoon ground cardamom

citrus zest from 1 orange or lemon (optional)

peanut oil, for frying

confectioners' sugar, for dusting (optional)

cinnamon sugar, for dusting (optional)

CHOCOLATE FRANGIPANE PLUM TART

YIELD: 1 (12-INCH) TART

TART SHELL

300g (2⅓ cups) high-extraction all-purpose flour (85AP)

1 teaspoon fine sea salt

1 teaspoon granulated sugar

226g (1 cup) unsalted butter, chilled

118g (½ cup) ice water

CHOCOLATE FRANGIPANE FILLING

113g (½ cup) unsalted butter, at room temperature

104g (½ cup) granulated sugar

96g (1 cup) almond flour

3 eggs, at room temperature

1 tablespoon flour (Meg uses our Crema pastry flour)

1 teaspoon pure vanilla extract

2 tablespoons unsweetened cocoa powder

½ cup dark chocolate (at least 60% cacao), chopped

6 or more plums, pitted and sliced into ½-inch wedges

local honey, for drizzling

With lovely layers of flavor and texture, this tart is the ideal desert when plums are ripe, though it also works well with frozen plums or even plum preserves. Or try changing the fruit altogether—I've made this with mixed berries and replaced the chocolate with vanilla bean seeds scraped into the frangipane.

Note: This recipe can be baked as two or three smaller (5-inch) tarts instead of one large tart. Line the unfilled tart shells with parchment paper or aluminum foil and pie weights or dried beans as directed, then bake for 15 to 20 minutes; carefully remove the parchment or foil and weights and bake for just 5 minutes more.

1 Make the tart shell: Combine the flour, salt, and sugar in a food processor and pulse until mixed. Add the cold butter and pulse 10 times, until the butter is broken down into small, crumbly pieces (it's better to undermix than overmix). Add the ice water and pulse a few more times, until the dough starts to come together. Turn the dough out onto a lightly floured work surface and form it into a disk. Wrap the dough in plastic wrap and refrigerate for 1 hour.

2 Set the dough on a lightly floured work surface. Using a rolling pin, roll from the center out two times, applying light, even pressure. Give the dough a quarter turn and roll twice. Repeat the quarter turn and two rolls from the center until you have a ¼-inch-thick round of dough. (See page 235 for Tara Jensen's tips on rolling out dough.)

3 Starting from the side of the dough closest to you, gently roll the dough around the rolling pin, then unroll it over a 12-inch tart pan and gently press it into the corners. Using the rolling pin, roll over the top of the pan to trim away the excess dough. Using the tines of a fork, poke the bottom five or six times. Line the dough with a piece of parchment paper or aluminum foil and fill it with dried beans or pie weights. Refrigerate for at least 15 minutes and up to 2 days.

4 Preheat the oven to 375°F.

5 Bake the tart shell for 35 minutes, then remove the parchment or foil and weights and bake for 10 to 20 minutes more, until the crust begins to color. Remove the crust from the oven; keep the oven on.

6 Meanwhile, make the filling: In a food processor, combine the butter and sugar and process until creamed. Alternately add the almond flour and the eggs, processing until each addition is fully incorporated before adding the next. Add the flour, vanilla, and cocoa powder and process until everything is incorporated. Fold in the chopped chocolate by hand, reserving a little for assembly.

7 Pour the filling into the tart shell. Arrange the plum slices over the filling and press them down lightly. Sprinkle the reserved chocolate over the tart.

8 Bake for 25 minutes, or until the filling has risen and feels set around the edges. Remove from the oven and transfer to a cooling rack. While still warm, drizzle the top with a good local honey for a nice gloss and a little extra sweetness. Once cooled, store covered in the refrigerator for up to 4 days.

HARDY KIWI AND GINGER GALETTE

MEG'S BREAD ◆ COOKEVILLE, TENNESSEE

I happened upon hardy kiwis, green-skinned fruits about the size of an olive, at a farmers' market in Hendersonville. It was the first time I'd ever seen them, although I had heard years before that there was a variety of kiwi vine that grew well in the South. Later that day, Meg posted an image of this galette on Instagram, with the little hardy kiwis artfully composed, halved, with their cut sides up. This recipe can be made with store-bought brown-skinned kiwis (the kind with fuzzy brown skins), but in case you do come across the small green variety, you'll know what to do with them.

Note: This recipe can be baked as six small galettes instead of one large one. Adjust baking time to 25 to 30 minutes, until pastry is golden brown.

YIELD: 1 LARGE GALETTE

3½ cups hardy kiwis, halved, or standard kiwifruits, peeled and sliced

1 tablespoon granulated sugar, plus more for sprinkling

2 teaspoons ground ginger

dough for 1 tart shell (see page 240)

1 egg, whisked, for egg wash

local honey, for drizzling

1 In a medium bowl, toss the kiwis with the sugar and ginger. The sugar will start to break down the kiwis a little bit.

2 Preheat the oven to 375°F. Line a baking sheet with parchment paper.

3 Roll out the chilled dough as directed on page 240 until you have a roughly 12-inch round, or until it is roughly ⅛ inch thick, then transfer it to the prepared baking sheet. Brush the dough with the egg wash, then top it with the kiwi mixture, leaving a 2-inch border. Fold the dough up over the fruit, leaving the center exposed. Brush the dough with egg wash and sprinkle with sugar.

4 Bake for 45 to 50 minutes until pastry is golden brown. Remove from the oven and drizzle the top with a good local honey, and serve. Store covered in the refrigerator for up to 4 days.

SWEET POTATO GALETTE

MEG'S BREAD ◆ COOKEVILLE, TENNESSEE

YIELD: 1 LARGE
GALETTE

GALETTE

1 pound (about 1)
sweet potato

1 tablespoon unsalted
butter, melted

100g (½ cup) light
brown sugar

2 tablespoons sorghum
syrup, plus more for
drizzling

1 teaspoon pure
vanilla extract

¼ teaspoon ground nutmeg

pinch of fine sea salt

dough for 1 tart shell
(see page 240), chilled
for at least 15 minutes

CRUMBLE TOPPING

68g (⅔ cup) rolled oats

65g (⅓ cup) light
brown sugar

50g (⅓ cup) high-extraction
all-purpose flour (85AP)

½ cup pecans,
finely chopped

1 tablespoon fresh
rosemary, finely chopped

½ teaspoon fine sea salt

4 tablespoons unsalted
butter, cut into pieces

1 egg, whisked, for egg wash

This is such a beautiful interpretation of a sweet potato pie. The sweet potatoes are sliced thin, like a gratin, tossed in sorghum molasses, topped with a crumble of oats, rosemary, and pecan, and then encased in a crust made of stone-ground high-extraction all-purpose flour.

Note: This recipe can be baked as six small galettes instead of one large one. Adjust baking time to 25 to 30 minutes, until pastry is golden brown.

1 Make the galette: Peel the sweet potato and use a mandolin to slice it as thinly as possible. Place the sweet potato slices in a large bowl and add the melted butter. Toss gently to lightly coat. Add the brown sugar, sorghum syrup, vanilla, nutmeg, and salt. Stir until fully incorporated and let sit for 10 to 15 minutes, until liquid pools at the bottom of the bowl.

2 Line a baking sheet with parchment paper. Roll out the chilled dough as directed on page 240 until you have a roughly 12-inch round or until it is roughly ⅛ inch thick, then transfer it to the prepared sheet. Using a slotted spoon, top the dough with the sweet potato mixture, leaving a 2-inch border; reserve the liquid remaining in the bowl. Fold the dough up over the filling, leaving the center exposed. Refrigerate for 1 hour.

3 Meanwhile, make the crumble: In a medium bowl, combine the oats, brown sugar, flour, pecans, rosemary, and salt. Add the butter and rub it into the dry ingredients until it forms small lumps, but do not overwork it.

4 Preheat the oven to 400°F.

5 Brush the dough with the egg wash and pour the reserved liquid from the sweet potato mixture over the filling at the center of the galette. Sprinkle the crumble evenly over the exposed filling.

6 Bake for 45 to 50 minutes until golden brown. Remove from the oven and drizzle with sorghum syrup, then serve. Store covered in the refrigerator for up to 4 days.

ORANGE OLIVE OIL CAKE

ANISETTE ◆ RALEIGH, NORTH CAROLINA

Olive oil and citrus zest combine well with flavor-forward flours. The choice of Trinity Blend flour provides a tender crumb, and the rye within the blend imparts a coffee undertone, pairing well with the coffee mascarpone cream filling. This cake is also lovely on its own with just a sprinkling of confectioners' sugar and perhaps a dollop of whipped cream.

Note: Nicole typically bakes this cake in an 8-inch-round cake pan with 3-inch-high sides; I've used an 8-inch-square pan with success, without any needed adjustments in baking time.

1 Make the cake: Preheat the oven to 350°F. Grease a 8-inch-round cake pan with butter and line it with parchment paper cut to fit.

2 Into a medium bowl, sift the flour, baking powder, and salt.

3 In the bowl of a stand mixer fitted with the paddle attachment, combine the sugar, eggs, olive oil, and orange zest and mix on medium-low speed for 3 minutes. With the mixer on low speed, slowly add the flour mixture and mix just until the dry ingredients are moistened. Stop and scrape down the sides and bottom of the bowl, then mix on medium-low speed for 1 minute, until smooth.

4 With the mixer on low speed, add the cream and mix for 30 seconds. Scrape down the s bowl, then mix on medium-low speed for 30 seconds. Pour the batter into the prepared pan and smooth the top with a spatula.

5 Bake until the cake springs back when you touch the center lightly and a toothpick inserted into the middle comes out clean, about 40 to 45 minutes.

6 Let the cake cool in the pan for at least 10 minutes, then invert the pan to remove the cake and transfer it to a cooling rack to cool completely.

7 Meanwhile, make the filling: In the bowl of a stand mixer fitted with the whisk attachment, combine the cream, mascarpone, confectioners' sugar, and instant coffee and whip on high speed until the cream holds stiff peaks.

8 Split the cooled cake horizontally and fill it with the coffee cream. Store covered in the refrigerator for up to 4 days.

YIELD: 1 (8-INCH) ROUND CAKE

CAKE

190g (1¾ cups) Trinity Blend flour (or your own blend; see page 238)

2 teaspoons baking powder

¼ teaspoon fine sea salt

230g (1¼ cups) granulated sugar

3 eggs, large, at room temperature

140g (1 cup) olive oil

orange zest from 1 orange

110g (½ cup) heavy cream, at room temperature

COFFEE MASCARPONE CREAM FILLING

120g (½ cup + 1 tablespoon) heavy cream, cold

120g (½ cup) mascarpone cheese, cold

3 tablespoons confectioners' sugar

1 teaspoon instant coffee granules

GUAVA CRUMBLE BARS

JOE BOWIE ◆ COLUMBIA, SOUTH CAROLINA

YIELD: 16 BARS

170g (1¾ cups) rolled oats

175g (1⅔ cups) Trinity Blend flour (or your own blend; see page 238)

200g (1 cup) light brown sugar

¾ teaspoon fine sea salt

½ teaspoon baking soda

170g (¾ cup) unsalted butter, melted and cooled slightly

1 (14.5-ounce) block guava paste

Like all the recipes Joe provided us with, this one is simple, smart, and easily accessible for the novice baker. Joe's choice of Trinity Blend flour paired with oats provides deep flavor sandwiching the guava filling, which has a bright, tart sweetness. My dear friend Cathy Cleary initially tested this recipe and said, "When I think of my husband's perfect breakfast food, this is what comes to mind." Cathy was unable to find guava paste in West Asheville, where she lives, so she whipped up some plum preserves (because this is what Cathy does) to use in place of the guava filling. I'm from Miami, where guava paste is readily available, but because we had a hard time finding it here, we've also included Cathy's recipe for plum preserves (see below).

1 Preheat the oven to 350°F. Butter a 9-inch-square pan and line it with parchment paper, leaving a few inches overhanging the sides. Butter the parchment as well.

2 In a large bowl, combine the oats, flour, brown sugar, salt, and baking soda. Give the mixture a stir. Add the melted butter and mix until well incorporated.

3 Press half the crumble mixture into an even layer over the bottom of the prepared pan.

4 Slice the block of guava paste into ¼-inch-thick slices and layer them in a single layer over the crumble layer, leaving about a ¼-inch border around the guava paste slices. Evenly distribute the remaining crumble on top of the guava layer. (There's no need to press down the crumble layer onto the guava.)

5 Bake for 25 to 30 minutes, until the crumble on top is golden brown and a tiny bit puffed.

6 Remove from the oven and set the pan on a cooling rack. Let cool completely, then remove from the pan using the overhanging parchment and transfer to a cutting board. (It should come out easily; if not, run a knife or offset spatula around the edges and then try again.) Cut into sixteen pieces. Once fully cool, store in an airtight container in the refrigerator for up to a week.

Cathy's Plum Preserves

Cook down about 4 cups pitted plums with about ¾ cup sugar and 1 teaspoon vanilla extract. The mixture should have the consistency of a "set" jam—one that is *not* pourable.

EARL GREY TRINITY CAKE WITH LEMON GLAZE AND THYME

CAROLINA GROUND ◆ ASHEVILLE, NORTH CAROLINA

This is another recipe developed by Desiree Bridges, our summer intern from Johnson & Wales. Part of her focus was to pair our flavor-forward pastry flours with flavors that accentuate the flour. Desiree describes the flavor of this flour: "The Trinity flour has an undercurrent of citrus notes to it. By using the Earl Grey tea, which is flavored with oil from the bergamot orange, we are shining a light on this more subtle flavor. Because Earl Grey tea can sometimes have a tannic aftertaste, I have made a glaze using lemon juice, zest, and lemon thyme to cleanse the palate. The end result is a very light cake that has many layers of flavors, all built around the flour used to make it. Enjoy!"

Note: The glaze recipe is quite flexible. Lemon balm can be substituted for lemon thyme, or it can be taken out altogether. Another option is opening up an Earl Grey teabag and sprinkling some of the tea leaves onto the glaze.

YIELD: 1 (7-INCH) ROUND CAKE

CAKE

57g (¼ cup) whole milk

1 tea bag Earl Grey tea

103g (1 cup) Trinity Blend flour (or your own blend; see page 238)

¾ teaspoon baking powder

¼ teaspoon baking soda

⅛ teaspoon fine sea salt

57g (4 tablespoons) unsalted butter

113g (½ cup + 2 tablespoons) granulated sugar

1 egg, separated

1 teaspoon pure vanilla extract

LEMON THYME GLAZE

1 lemon, large

170g (1½ cups) confectioners' sugar

1 tablespoon lemon thyme leaves, for sprinkling (see Note)

1 Make the cake: Preheat the oven to 350°F. Line a 7-inch-round cake pan with parchment paper cut to fit. Butter the bottom and sides, then dust with flour, tapping out any excess.

2 Pour the milk into a small saucepan and add the tea bag. Heat gently on low heat. Once hot to the touch, remove the saucepan from the heat and steep for 5 minutes, or until the milk tea has reached the desired strength. Remove and discard the tea bag.

3 Into a medium bowl, sift together the flour, baking powder, baking soda, and salt.

4 In the bowl of a stand mixer fitted with the paddle attachment, cream the butter and sugar on medium speed until fluffy, 5 to 8 minutes. Add the egg yolk and the vanilla and mix until fully incorporated. Stop and scrape down the sides of the bowl. With mixer on low speed, in two stages, alternately add the flour mixture and the milk tea, mixing until each addition is just incorporated before adding the next.

5 In a large bowl, whip the egg white until it holds stiff peaks. Fold the egg white into the batter by hand, then pour the batter into the prepared pan and smooth the top with a spatula.

6 Bake until the cake springs back when you touch the center lightly and a toothpick inserted into the middle comes out clean, about 35 minutes. Transfer to a cooling rack.

7 Meanwhile, make the glaze: Zest the lemon and transfer half the zest to a large bowl; set aside the remaining zest. Juice the lemon into the large bowl with the zest. Add the confectioners' sugar and mix until the sugar has dissolved completely.

8 Pour the glaze over the cake, using a knife to smooth the top if needed. Sprinkle the top with the reserved lemon zest and the lemon thyme. Chill until the glaze has set before serving. Store covered in the refrigerator for up to 4 days.

TRINITY TART WITH HERB-INFUSED PASTRY CREAM

OSONO BREAD ◆ ATLANTA, GEORGIA

YIELD: 1 (10-INCH) TART

TRINITY TART SHELL

135g (½ cup + 2 tablespoons) unsalted European-style butter, chilled

90g (½ cup) granulated sugar

1 egg

270g (2½ cups) Trinity Blend flour (or your own blend; see page 238)

½ teaspoon sea salt

HERB-INFUSED PASTRY CREAM

450g (2 cups) whole milk

handful of fresh herbs, edible flowers, or dried tea leaves, such as basil, marigold, chamomile—there are endless possibilities; see suggested flavor combinations (page 254)

1 vanilla bean, split lengthwise and seeds scraped out

6 egg yolks

150g (¾ cup) granulated sugar

2 tablespoons cornstarch

½ teaspoon fine sea salt

50g (3½ tablespoons) unsalted butter

2 to 3 cups fruit of your choice

edible flowers, such as pansies or bachelor's buttons, for garnish

From Betsy Gonzalez: "This is my go-to recipe for vanilla bean pastry cream—it's not too sweet and has a light but custardy texture to it. I love the idea of pairing the Trinity tart shell with herb-infused pastry cream and fresh fruit picked from the garden or from local farmers. Keep everything super cold when possible. Measure your flour in a small bowl and place it in the fridge or freezer until ready to use. Keep your eggs cold until ready to use as well."

Note: This recipe can be baked as four smaller, individual tarts instead of one large one. After rolling out the dough, cut it into four and use each to line a 4-inch tart pan. Bake the tart shells for 12 to 18 minutes, until golden brown, then let cool and fill as directed.

1 Make the tart crust: In the bowl of a stand mixer fitted with the paddle attachment, cream the butter and sugar on medium speed until just combined; do not beat until fluffy. Add the egg and mix until just combined. Stop and scrape down the sides of the bowl. Remove the bowl from the mixer, and by hand fold in the flour and salt until no dry bits remain, being careful not to overmix. Turn the dough out, form it into a rectangle, wrap it in plastic wrap, and refrigerate for at least 30 minutes, or until fully chilled.

2 On a lightly floured surface, roll out the chilled dough into a roughly ⅛-inch-thick round. Starting from the side of the dough closest to you, gently roll the dough around the rolling pin, then unroll it over a 10-inch tart pan and gently press it into the corners. Using the rolling pin, roll over the top of the pan to trim away the excess dough. Dock the bottom of the dough with a fork, then freeze the tart shell until chilled, about 30 minutes.

3 Preheat the oven to 375°F.

4 Bake for 20 to 25 minutes, until golden brown. Let cool completely before filling.

5 Meanwhile, make the pastry cream: In a small saucepan, combine the milk and herbs or flowers. Bring to a simmer over low heat and cook for 15 minutes, then remove from the heat and set aside to steep for 45 minutes. Strain the milk through a fine-mesh sieve, discarding the solids. (The infused milk can be stored in an airtight container in the refrigerator for up to 1 day.)

6 Place the milk in a heavy-bottomed medium pot and add the vanilla bean pod and seeds. Bring to a gentle boil over medium-high heat, then remove from the heat and set aside to allow the vanilla to infuse the milk.

CONTINUED

TRINITY TART WITH HERB-INFUSED PASTRY CREAM

CONTINUED

7   In the bowl of a stand mixer fitted with the whisk attachment, combine the egg yolks, sugar, cornstarch, and salt and whip on high speed for 2 minutes, until light and fluffy. Reduce the mixer speed to low. Remove the vanilla pod from the pot of milk and, with the mixer running, slowly drizzle the hot milk into the mixer bowl. When all the milk has been added, stop and scrape the down the sides of the bowl; set aside the pot you used to heat the milk. Whip on low speed for 30 seconds, until the mixture is evenly combined.

8   Strain the pastry cream through a fine-mesh strainer into the reserved pot. Heat over medium heat, whisking and stirring continuously (but not aggressively) to prevent it from burning on the bottom of the pot, until the pastry cream starts to lightly bubble, then cook, whisking and scraping, for 30 seconds. Immediately pour the hot pastry cream into a clean bowl. Using an immersion blender (or a whisk), pulse or whisk in the butter. Set the pastry cream aside to cool at room temp, or cover with plastic wrap pressed directly against the surface to prevent a skin from forming and refrigerate until cooled.

9   Spoon the cooled pastry cream into the tart shell, filling it three-quarters full. Gently arrange the fruit on top of the pastry cream. Decorate with edible flowers. Eat straight away or store covered in the refrigerator for up to 2 days. Best served chilled.

Flavor Combinations

Blueberry and basil

Stone fruit and chamomile

Strawberries and lemon thyme

Plums and rosemary

Berries and elderflowers

edible flowers, such as pansies or bachelor's buttons, for garnish

FIGGY NEWMANS

ALBEMARLE BAKING COMPANY ◆ CHARLOTTESVILLE, VIRGINIA

I love that a flour can inspire a recipe. Gerry Newman had been using our flour in his breads for years before he considered cold-stone-milled flour in a pastry application. But our Trinity Blend inspired some recipe development, and these little babies—rich little packages filled with fig—were born. Be warned: There are a number of steps to follow, but these Figgy Newmans are delicious and worth it.

Note: When my good friend Cathy Cleary tested this recipe, she cut the cookies into 1-inch slices, as she felt 2 inches was a lot of cookie.

1 In a medium bowl, combine the flour, baking powder, and salt.

2 In the bowl of a stand mixer fitted with the paddle attachment, cream the butter and sugar on medium-high speed until light in color, 5 to 10 minutes. Adjust to low speed and add the egg yolks, cream, and vanilla, then increase speed and mix until creamy and fluffy, then stop and scrape down the bowl.

3 With the mixer on low speed, add the flour mixture and mix until the ingredients are fully incorporated and a dough has formed. (This dough is very rich, so there is little danger of overmixing.) Turn the dough out, wrap it in plastic wrap, and refrigerate until thoroughly chilled.

4 Meanwhile, make the filling: In a medium saucepan, bring the water to a boil over medium-high heat. Add the figs and the sugar, cover, and reduce the heat to maintain a low simmer. Cook until most of the water has been absorbed, then remove from the heat. Allow to cool for 10 to 15 minutes and then transfer the mixture to a food processor, add the lemon zest and juice, and process to a smooth paste.

5 Cut two pieces of parchment paper the size of a baking sheet. Place the dough on one piece and lay the second piece on top. Roll out the dough between the two sheets of parchment to a 15 x 8-inch rectangle. Remove the top piece of parchment and cut the dough in half lengthwise to make two 4-inch-wide strips. Pipe (or spread) the filling lengthwise along the center of one strip of dough, then fold the long sides of the dough in so they meet in the center and enclose the filling, gently pinching the edges together to seal. Repeat to fill the second strip of dough. Refrigerate the logs of dough for 30 minutes.

6 Preheat the oven to 325°F. Line a baking sheet with parchment paper.

7 Turn the filled logs of dough seam-side down and cut them crosswise into 2-inch-wide cookies. Transfer the cookies to the prepared baking sheet. Lightly whisk the egg whites to make an egg wash and brush it over the cookies.

8 Bake for 25 to 30 minutes, or until nicely browned and then transfer to a cooling rack. Allow to cool for 20 to 30 minutes before serving. Once fully cooled, store in an airtight container at room temperature.

YIELD: 10 COOKIES (OR 20 IF CUT SMALLER)

302g (2¾ cups) Trinity Blend flour (or your own blend; see page 238)

5g (1 tablespoon) baking powder

½ teaspoon fine sea salt

150g (⅔ cup) unsalted butter, at room temperature

120g (⅔ cup) granulated sugar

3 eggs, separated, at room temperature

50g (¼ cup) heavy cream, at room temperature

1 teaspoon pure vanilla extract

FIG FILLING

90g (⅓ cup + 1 tablespoon) water

150g (1 cup) dried figs, quartered

35g (3 tablespoons) granulated sugar

1½ teaspoons lemon zest

1 tablespoon fresh lemon juice

SWEDISH GINGERSNAPS

WALNUT SCHOOLHOUSE ◆ WALNUT, NORTH CAROLINA

This is simple recipe that produces an extraordinary cookie. The texture is the perfect balance of crisp along the edges but chewy in the center. Trinity Blend flour pairs beautifully with the sorghum syrup and ground ginger.

1 Line a baking sheet with parchment paper.

2 Beat the butter, sugar, and sorghum syrup together until smooth.

3 Mix together the flour, ginger, salt, and baking soda and add into the butter mixture. Beat again until just combined.

4 Roll dough into a log about 1 inch thick by 1 wide, cut in half, and place the two on either end of a baking sheet. These will spread considerably while baking, so make sure to give them a good amount of distance.

5 Preheat the oven to 345°F and place the baking sheet in a refrigerator while the oven is preheating.

6 Bake the logs for about 15 minutes or until the edges are a golden brown and the center is a bit paler.

7 Remove from the oven and place the baking sheet on a cooling rack. Let cool partially; while still warm to the touch, cut into long strips, and transfer to cooling rack. They should be crisp on the outside and slightly chewy in the center.

8 Once fully cooled, store at room temperature in an airtight container for a week.

YIELD: ABOUT 20 SHORTBREADS

113g (1 stick) unsalted butter

70g (⅓ cup) granulated sugar

70g (¼ cup) sorghum syrup

160g (1½ cups) Trinity Blend flour (or your own blend; see page 238)

1 teaspoon ground ginger

½ teaspoon fine sea salt

¼ teaspoon baking soda

CARROT CAKE

THE LITTLE TART BAKESHOP • ATLANTA, GEORGIA

YIELD: 1 (10-INCH)
BUNDT CAKE

226g (2 cups) Trinity Blend
flour (or your own blend;
see page 238)

2½ teaspoons ground
cinnamon

1 teaspoon baking powder

1 teaspoon fine sea salt

½ teaspoon baking soda

270g (1⅓ cups)
granulated sugar

207g (1 cup) safflower oil
or sunflower oil

3 eggs

260g (2 cups)
grated carrots

50g (½ cup)
pecans, toasted

68g (½ cup) dried
cherries, chopped

**FROMAGE BLANC
FROSTING**

140g (⅔ cup) fromage
blanc, at room temperature

50g (½ cup)
confectioners' sugar

70g (¼ cup) water

When Sarah O'Brien first tested this recipe using our flour, she tried it with rye and she tried it with a blend of our whole-wheat pastry flour and a good-quality roller-milled all-purpose (AP) flour. She landed on the latter. And then we started producing our Trinity Blend, and it achieved what she had been aiming for in her own in-house testing, as the Trinity Blend contains all the components of Sarah's in-house blend—rye, soft wheat, and hard wheat—but with the added benefit of amplified flavor. This is a quick and easy cake to make, and delicious.

Note: As written, this recipe makes one large Bundt cake, but the batter can be used to make eight mini Bundt cakes instead. Just divide the batter evenly among 8 mini Bundt pans and reduce the baking time to 24 minutes.

1 Preheat the oven to 350°F. Butter a 10-inch Bundt pan and dust it with flour, tapping out any excess.

2 Into a medium bowl, sift together the flour, cinnamon, baking powder, salt, and baking soda,.

3 In a separate large bowl, whisk together the sugar, oil, and eggs. Stir in the carrots. Add the dry ingredients and fold them in with a spatula, then fold in the pecans and cherries. Pour the batter into the prepared pan.

4 Bake for 50 minutes, or until a toothpick inserted into the center comes out clean. Let cool in the pan for 5 to 10 minutes before unmolding, then turn the cake out of the pan and set it on a cooling rack.

5 Meanwhile, make the frosting: Put the fromage blanc in a medium bowl and whisk to loosen it. Add the confectioners' sugar and whisk to combine. Add the water a bit at a time, whisking until incorporated.

6 Frost the cooled cake and serve. Store covered in the refrigerator for up to 5 days.

SALTED PEANUT BUTTER COOKIES WITH CACAO NIBS

THE LITTLE TART BAKESHOP • ATLANTA, GEORGIA

I love that Sarah O'Brien chose spelt for this cookie. Spelt's nuttiness and tender crumb further accentuate the creamy peanut butter. The cacao nibs act as the staccato, pronounced though without drowning out the other flavors. It is a perfect balance of flavor, texture, and mouthfeel.

YIELD: 45 COOKIES

275g (1¼ cups) unsalted European-style butter, cut into tablespoon-size cubes

200g (1 cup) light brown sugar

170g (¾ cup + 2 tablespoons) granulated sugar

226.5g (2 cups) whole-spelt flour

1 tablespoon fine sea salt

1 teaspoon baking soda

2 eggs, at room temperature

400g (1½ cups) creamy peanut butter

1¾ teaspoons pure vanilla extract

150g (1¼ cups) cacao nibs

1 In the bowl of a stand mixer fitted with the paddle attachment, combine the butter and both sugars and beat on low speed for about 20 minutes, until fluffy, stopping to scrape down the sides of the bowl several times during mixing.

2 Meanwhile, into a medium bowl, sift together the flour, salt, and baking soda.

3 Add the eggs to the butter mixture, beating until well incorporated and scraping down the sides occasionally. Add the peanut butter and vanilla and mix thoroughly. (Be sure to scrape the bottom of the bowl thoroughly at this step.)

4 Add the flour mixture and mix until almost incorporated. Scrape down sides. Add the cacao nibs and pulse just until they are incorporated. Transfer the dough to an airtight container and refrigerate for at least 3 hours, or ideally overnight.

5 Line a baking sheet with parchment paper. Using a 1-ounce scoop or a heaping tablespoon, scoop the dough onto the prepared baking sheet. Cover with plastic wrap and place in the freezer for at least 2 hours.

6 Preheat the oven to 325°F.

7 Uncover the pan and bake the cookies directly from the freezer for 7 minutes, then rotate the pan and bake for another 7 minutes, or until the edges are lightly browned and the centers are set but still soft. Transfer to a cooling rack.

8 Once fully cooled, these can be stored in an airtight container at room temperature for at least a week, though they will not last that long.

SPELT SCONES WITH CARDAMOM, CHOCOLATE, AND CITRUS

LEVEE BAKING CO. ◆ NEW ORLEANS, LOUISIANA

YIELD: 8 SCONES

300g (2⅔ cups) whole-spelt flour

300g (2½ cups) high-extraction all-purpose (85AP) or white wheat flour

40g (¼ cup) raw sugar, plus more for sprinkling

1 tablespoon fine sea salt

1 tablespoon ground cardamom

1 teaspoon baking powder

12g candied citrus or candied citrus zest

225g (1 cup) unsalted butter, cubed and chilled

114g (¾ cup) dark chocolate, at least 60% cacao, chopped

2 cups buttermilk, yogurt, or crème fraîche

egg, whisked with a dash of cream, milk, or water, for egg wash

This is a solid scone recipe that could really be made with any flour and flavor combination with success. But seriously—made with whole spelt, cardamom, citrus, and dark chocolate, there is no reason to veer from the path.

1   Preheat the oven to 400°F. Line a baking sheet with parchment paper.

2   In a medium bowl, whisk together both flours, the sugar, cardamom, baking powder, salt, and candied citrus to combine. Add the cold butter and use your fingers to incorporate it into the flour mixture until the butter is broken down into pea-size pieces. If it is a warm day, chill the mixture for 30 minutes before continuing.

3   Stir in the chocolate. Make a well in the center of the mixture and add 1½ cups of the buttermilk. Mix with a spoon (or flexible dough scraper) until the dough comes together, adding more liquid as needed. You don't want to knead the dough, just incorporate until a cohesive ball forms.

4   Turn the dough out onto a floured surface. Let rest for 5 minutes, then pat it out into a roughly 1-inch-thick round. Cut the round into eight equal triangles and place them on the prepared baking sheet. (At this point, you can freeze the unbaked scones for up to 1 month in an airtight container, separated with parchment paper.) Brush each scone with the egg wash and sprinkle a generous amount of raw sugar on top.

5   Bake the scones until craggy on top, biscuit-like, and light golden brown, about 30 minutes, rotating the pan halfway through the baking time. Transfer to a cooling rack. Let cool 5 minutes before serving. Once fully cooled, store in an airtight container at room temperature and eat within a day or two.

TWICE-BAKED SPELT SHORTBREAD

JOE BOWIE • COLUMBIA, SOUTH CAROLINA

Spelt flour lends a nuttiness to these crisp shortbreads. Joe suggests baking these in an 8-inch fluted tart pan, but any pan with a removeable bottom should work well. They can also be baked in a 10-inch pie pan and cut into 12 wedge-shaped cookies.

YIELD: ABOUT
12 COOKIES

165g (¾ cup) unsalted butter, melted and kept warm

80g (⅓ cup) granulated sugar

1½ teaspoon pure vanilla extract

½ teaspoon fine sea salt

98g (½ cup + ⅓ cup) whole-spelt flour

98g (½ cup + ⅓ cup) sifted spelt flour

¾ teaspoon ground cinnamon

sugar of your choice (such as turbinado or cinnamon sugar), for sprinkling

1 Butter an 8-inch fluted tart pan with a removeable bottom.

2 In a large bowl, combine the melted butter, sugar, vanilla, and salt. Add both flours and the cinnamon and mix until just incorporated—the dough will be claylike. Transfer the dough to the prepared tart pan and pat it into an even layer over the bottom. Let the dough rest for at least 2 hours or up to overnight. (There is no need to refrigerate this dough.)

3 Position a rack in the bottom third of the oven and preheat the oven to 300°F. Line a baking sheet with parchment paper.

4 Bake the shortbread for 45 minutes, then remove from the oven; leave the oven on. Sprinkle the shortbread with sugar and cool for 10 minutes.

5 Carefully remove the shortbread from the pan, keeping it on the pan's removeable bottom. Using a thin, sharp knife, cut the shortbread into fingers, wedges, or squares. With a spatula, place the shortbread pieces slightly apart on the prepared baking sheet.

6 Bake the shortbread for another 15 minutes, until golden brown. Remove from the oven and again sprinkle with your choice of sugar. Transfer the shortbread to a cooling rack to cool completely. The shortbread will keep in an airtight container at room temperature for several weeks.

SPELT BISCOTTI

ALBEMARLE BAKING COMPANY ◆ CHARLOTTESVILLE, VIRGINIA

YIELD: 12 TO
15 BISCOTTI

314g (2¾ cups) whole-spelt flour

2 teaspoons baking powder

½ teaspoon fine sea salt

2 eggs

188g (¾ cup) granulated sugar

orange zest from 2 oranges

126g (½ cup + 1 tablespoon) unsalted butter, melted

1 teaspoon pure almond extract

1 teaspoon pure vanilla extract

126g (1 cup) blanched whole almonds

63g (½ cup) dried cherries, unsweetened

These biscotti are crisp and crunchy without being too hard. The choice of whole-spelt flour adds a nuttiness that is further accentuated with almond extract. The addition of butter to this dough produces a biscotti that one can bite into without dunking in coffee first.

1   Preheat the oven to 350°F. Line a baking sheet with parchment paper.

2   Into a medium bowl, sift together the flour, baking powder, and salt.

3   In the bowl of a stand mixer fitted with the paddle attachment, beat the eggs, sugar, and orange zest on medium-high speed until light and thick, about 3 minutes. Beat in the melted butter, almond extract, and vanilla. Stop and scrape down the sides of the bowl. With the mixer on low speed, add the flour mixture and mix until just combined; do not overmix. Fold in the almonds and cherries by hand.

4   Turn the dough out onto a flour-dusted work surface and shape it into a log about 7 inches wide and ½ inch thick. Place it on the prepared baking sheet.

5   Bake for 25 to 30 minutes. Remove from the oven and transfer the log to a cooling rack. Let cool completely. Lower the oven temperature to 300°F.

6   Carefully transfer the log to a cutting board and use a serrated knife to cut it crosswise into ½-inch-thick slices (Gerry says "roughly thumb-width slices"). Arrange the slices on the prepared baking sheet, cut-side up. Bake for 15 minutes, then flip the slices and bake for 10 to 15 minutes more, until crisp and golden. Transfer to a cooling rack to cool. These will crisp up as they cool. Once fully cooled, store in an airtight container at room temperature for at least a couple of weeks.

BUCKWHEAT SHORTBREAD COOKIES

FARM AND SPARROW ◆ MARS HILL, NORTH CAROLINA

**YIELD: ABOUT
24 COOKIES**

114g (¾ cup +
2 tablespoons) stone-
ground buckwheat flour

187g (1½ cups) high-
extraction all-purpose
flour (85AP)

169g (¾ cup) unsalted
butter, at room
temperature

104g (½ cup)
granulated sugar

1 teaspoon pure
vanilla extract

¼ teaspoon fine sea salt

1 tablespoon cacao nibs

When Dave Bauer was still baking, I used to go see him at the Saturday North Asheville Farmers' Market. I would always get a loaf of his incredible seeded rye bread and one of these cookies. They are not too sweet, but rich and earthy, with a sandy texture, which does not sound as appetizing as it should. I think these cookies have achieved perfection, and I am thrilled that he shared this recipe with me so I can share it with you.

1 In a medium bowl, combine the buckwheat flour and all-purpose flour.

2 In a food processor, combine the butter, sugar, vanilla, and salt and process until smooth. Add the flour mixture and process until a consistent batter is formed. Scrape the batter into a large bowl and fold in the cacao nibs. This is a dry dough but it will come together. Have faith, and squeeze it into a cohesive form. Refrigerate for 20 minutes, or until the dough feels cold.

3 Knead the dough in the bowl until it feels pliable and cohesive, then turn it out onto a flour-dusted work surface and roll it into a log 1½ to 2 inches in diameter. Wrap the log in a piece of parchment paper and freeze for about 15 minutes, until dough is close to frozen.

4 Preheat the oven to 350°F. Line a baking sheet with parchment paper.

5 Using a chef's knife, slice the log crosswise into disks approximately ¼ inch thick and place them on a baking sheet.

6 Bake for 15 to 20 minutes, until the edges start to turn a golden brown.

7 Transfer to a cooling rack. Let cool. Eat. Once fully cooled, store in an airtight container at room temperature for about 1 week, if you don't finish them all before then.

APPALACHIAN ANADAMA BREAD

WALNUT SCHOOLHOUSE ◆ WALNUT, NORTH CAROLINA

Brennan Johnson developed this bread as an Appalachian take on a classic bread from the American Northeast. Grits and sorghum syrup are used in place of the traditional cornmeal and molasses. He approaches this bread in the style of a Danish rye, which means a large portion of the dough is a cracked grain, in this case, the corn serves as that component.

Notes: The grits will increase in volume, so soak them in a large bowl with water to cover by about 3 inches. If you're using stone-ground grits, soak them in hot water. If using fine-ground grits that are not stone-ground, soak in cold water. Soak overnight.

The leaven is added after the autolyze, along with the salt and the grits, so begin the dough about 2 hours before your leaven is fully developed.

1 Make the leaven: Measure the water into a small clear container with a lid, such as a ½-pint mason jar, then add the starter. Using a spoon or your fingers, break apart the starter into the water. Add the flour and mix until fully incorporated. Cover the container and let stand at room temperature for 8 to 10 hours, until fully developed (see page 107).

2 Make the dough: Two hours before the leaven is developed, measure the water into a large bowl, then stir in the buttermilk and sorghum syrup. Add both flours and mix until fully incorporated. Let the dough rest for at least 30 minutes and up to 2 hours.

3 Squeeze out excess water in the grits and then add the grits to the dough, along with the leaven and the salt. Fold the dough over onto itself until the ingredients are fully integrated. Place the dough in a container (with a lid) large enough to allow the dough to expand, but not too large, so that as it expands, tension is created by constriction.

4 Bulk ferment the dough: Let the dough ferment at room temperature for 2 hours, stretching and folding the dough every 30 minutes (according to Step 3 on page 105). After the final fold, cover the dough with a kitchen towel and let rise, undisturbed, for another 1 to 2 hours.

5 Final rise: With a pastry brush dipped in olive oil or melted butter (or a combination of both), thoroughly grease a 13 x 4-inch Pullman loaf pan. Scoop the dough into the prepared pan, cover, and refrigerate for at least 8 hours or up to overnight.

6 Preheat the oven to 475°F.

7 Bake for 50 to 70 minutes, until the bread is deeply caramelized and the internal temperature reads 205°F. Transfer to a cooling rack and allow to cool completely before slicing.

YIELD: 1 (13 X 4-INCH PULLMAN) LOAF

LEAVEN

45g water

9g starter

45g whole-wheat bread flour

DOUGH

300g water

200g buttermilk

30g sorghum syrup

570g stone-ground Einkorn flour

30g stone-ground corn flour

600g grits, soaked (see Note) and drained

90g leaven

17g fine sea salt

Baker's Percentage Index

WHEAT

FLEMISH DESEM

LEAVEN

flour	100
water	90
starter	25

DOUGH

flour	100
water	95
leaven	20
sea salt	2.25

WALNUT DESEM

LEAVEN

flour	100
water	95
starter	25

DOUGH

flour	100
water	100
leaven	20
sea salt	2.25
walnuts	26

PIEDMONT LOAF

LEAVEN

flour	100
water	100
starter	25

DOUGH

flour, wwb	70
flour, 75b	30
water	85
leaven	20
sea salt	2

WHOLE-WHEAT FLAX BREAD

LEAVEN

flour	100
water	66
starter	8

FLAX SOAKER

flax	100
water	146

DOUGH

flour, wwb	70
flour, 75b	30
water	61
leaven	16
flax soaker	46
sunflower seeds	9
sea salt	2.35

NC SOURDOUGH + NC MICHE

LEAVEN

flour	100
water	100
starter	20

DOUGH

flour	100
water	72
leaven	48
sea salt	3.25

HIPPY DESEM

LEAVEN

flour	100
water	70
starter	35

DOUGH

flour, 85b	80
flour, wwb	20
water	70
leaven	16
honey	5
sea salt	2.2
pumpkin seeds	8
sunflower seeds	8
flax seeds	3
sesame seeds	3
poppy seeds	3

CIABATTA SANDWICH ROLLS

BIGA

flour	100
water	67
yeast	0.6

DOUGH

flour, 85b	90
flour, wwb	10
water	83
yeast	2.8
biga	44
sea salt	2.1

HEMP CRISP BREADS

LEAVEN

flour	100
water	100
starter	20

DOUGH

flour, 85b	80
flour, wwb	20
water	50
hemp hearts	13
sea salt	2.5

HIGH-EXTRACTION FOCACCIA

LEAVEN

flour	100
water	100
starter	20

DOUGH

flour	100
water	90
olive oil	5
leaven	20
sea salt	2.5

PORRIDGE BREAD

LEAVEN

flour	100
water	100
starter	17

DOUGH

flour, 75b	80
flour, wwb	20
water	80
leaven	20
porridge	75
soaker	25
sunflower seeds	12.5
sea salt	2.5

PIEDMONT MICHE

RYE LEAVEN

flour	100
water	95
starter	4

WHEAT LEAVEN

flour	100
water	66
starter	8

DOUGH

flour, wwb	60
flour, 75b	40
water	67
leaven rye	91
leaven wheat	300
salt	6

MICHE BABY

RYE LEAVEN

flour	100
water	100
starter	25

WHEAT LEAVEN

flour	100
water	100
starter	25

DOUGH

flour, 75b	80
flour, whole rye	10
flour, whole spelt	10
water	85
leaven rye	14
leaven wheat	14
sea salt	2

RUSTIC PEASANT BREAD

LEAVEN

cracked rye	100
water	100
starter	20

DOUGH

flour	100
scald	71
water	80
leaven	20
sea salt	2.25

SOUTHEAST SOURDOUGH

LEAVEN

flour	100
water	100
starter	20

DOUGH

flour, 75b	75
flour, white wheat	20
flour, whole rye	5
water	85
leaven	12
sea salt	2.5

ALL STONE-GROUND PIZZA DOUGH

LEAVEN

flour, white wheat	100
water	100
starter	20

DOUGH

flour, 75b	95
flour, white wheat	5
water	66
leaven	17
sea salt	3

GREGARIO'S CG PIZZA DOUGH

LEAVEN

flour, Khorasan / Kamut	100
water	100
leaven	20

DOUGH

flour, 75b	70
flour, sifted spelt	19
flour, Khorasan / Kamut	11
water	75
leaven	7
sea salt	2.25

RYE

DANISH RYE

LEAVEN

flour	100
water	150
leaven	75

DOUGH

flour	100
water	50
leaven	100
sorghum	5
salt	5

DARK RYE W/CARAWAY, FENNEL + CARDAMOM

LEAVEN

flour	100
water	95
starter	8

DOUGH

flour, whole rye	43
flour, 75b	57
water	75
leaven	82
sea salt	2.9
bread spice	.5

100% SOURDOUGH COFFEE CAN RYE

LEAVEN

flour	100
water	100
starter	25

DOUGH

flour, wrye	25
flour, lrye	75
water	75
leaven	60
malt	5
sea salt	2.1
caraway	1.1
anise	.6
fennel	.6

SEEDED RYE

LEAVEN

flour	100
water	100
starter	20

SOAKER

rye chops	100
pumpkin seeds	20
sunflower seeds	40
sesame seeds	40
nut milk	80
coffee	40
sorghum syrup	10

DOUGH

flour, wwb	50
flour, rye	25
flour, 75b	25
water	106
leaven	65
soaker	165
sea salt	3

RUGBRØD

LEAVEN

flour, rye	100
water	100
starter	25

SOAKER

cracked rye	100
water	158

DOUGH

flour, wwb	73
flour, rye	27
water	88
leaven	58
soaker	211
buttermilk	30
sunflower seeds	17
pumpkin seeds	17
flax seeds	39
sesame seeds	19
sea salt	3.3

VOLKORNBROT W/FEN + SESAME

LEAVEN

flour	100
water	95
starter	10

SOAKER

rye meal	100
water	135
sesame seeds	46.5
fenugreek	15.5
sea salt	6.5

DOUGH

flour	100
water	54
soaker	349
leaven	230

SEEDED RYE W/KVASS

LEAVEN

flour	100
water	100
starter	20

PRE-FERMENT

flour	100
water	60
leaven	32
soaker	172
salt	6

DOUGH

flour	100
water/kvass/beer	156
cracked rye	204`
preferment	1036

RUSSIAN SCALDED RYE

LEAVEN#1

flour	100
water	200
starter	10

LEAVEN#2

flour	100
leaven#1	186

DOUGH

flour	100
water	86
scald	205
leaven	205
sea salt	5

WHOLE RYE

LEAVEN

flour	100
water	100
starter	5

DOUGH

flour	100
water	78
rye sprouts	25
leaven	150
soaker	20
sea salt	2.5

NORDIC RYE W/ BEER+SORGHUM

LEAVEN#1

flour	100
water	100
starter	50

LEAVEN#2

flour	100
water	100
leaven#1	

SOAKER#1

old bread	100
water	100

PORRIDGE

rye berries	100
dark beer	208

DOUGH

flour	100
dark	
beer	70
leaven	179
porridge	79
sorghum	8
soaker#1	28
soaker#2	129
sea salt	5

SPROUTED +SEEDED RYE

LEAVEN

flour	100
water	100
starter	20

DOUGH

flour	100
water	101
buttermilk	35
beer	12
honey	5
leaven	49
sea salt	2.5
rye sprouts	35
buckwheat sprouts	25
sunflower seeds	10
pumpkin seeds	10
flax seeds	4
sesame seeds	4

BLENDS AND OUTLIER GRAINS

SOURDOUGH DOUGHNUTS

LEAVEN

flour	100
water	100
starter	20

DOUGH

flour	100
milk	35
butter	35
leaven	35
sugar	10
salt	2
vanilla	2

APPALACHIAN ANADAMA BREAD

LEAVEN

flour	100
water	100
starter	20

DOUGH

flour, Einkorn	95
flour, corn	5
grits, soaked	100
water	66
buttermilk	33
leaven	15
sorghum	5
sea salt	2.8

Resources

Mills and Online Stores

THE SOUTH
ANSON MILLS
Columbia, South Carolina
ansonmills.com

BELLEGARDE BAKERY
New Orleans, Louisiana
bellegardebakery.com

CAROLINA GROUND
Asheville, North Carolina
carolinaground.com

FARM AND SPARROW
Mars Hill, North Carolina
farmandsparrow.com

MUDDY POND SORGHUM MILL
Monterey, Tennessee
muddypondsorghum.com
For sorghum

POIRIER'S CANE SYRUP
Youngville, Louisiana
realcanesyrup.com
For cane syrup

RED TAIL GRAINS
Elfland, North Carolina
redtailgrains.com

STEEN'S SYRUP
Abbeville, Louisiana
steenssyrup.com

THE MIDWEST
JANIE'S MILL
Ashkum, Illinois
jainiesmill.com

MEADOWLARK FLOUR
Lancaster, Wisconsin
meadowlarkorganics.com

SHAGBARK SEED & MILL
Athens, Ohio
shagbarkmill.com

THE NORTHEAST
FARMER GROUND FLOUR
Trumansburg, New York
farmergroundflour.com

GROUNDUP GRAIN
Hadley, Massachusetts
groundupgrain.com

MAINE GRAINS
Skowhegan, Maine
mainegrains.com

THE SOUTHWEST
BARTON SPRINGS MILL
Dripping Springs, Texas
bartonspringsmill.com

HAYDEN FLOUR MILLS
Queen Creek, Arizona
haydenflourmills.com

THE WEST
CAIRNSPRING MILLS
Burlington, Washington
cairnspring.com

CAMAS COUNTRY MILL
Eugene, Oregon
camascountrymill.com

GRIST & TOLL
Pasadena, California
gristandtoll.com

HILLSIDE GRAIN
Bellevue, Idaho
hillsidegrain.com

OUTSIDE THE UNITED STATES
E5BAKEHOUSE
London, UK
e5bakehouse.com

FLOURIST
Vancouver, Canada
flourist.com

GILCHESTERS ORGANICS
Northumberland, UK
gilchesters.com

WOODSTOCK FLOUR
New South Wales, Australia
woodstockflour.com.au

Other Resources

ASHEVILLE BREAD FESTIVAL
ashevillebreadfestival.com

BREAD BAKERS GUILD OF AMERICA
bbga.org
A resource for information and workshops

BREADTOPIA
breadtopia.com
A source of information including bread-making tutorials, plus an online store for baking wares such as baskets and couche

CHALLENGER BREADWARE
Challengerbreadware.com
Producer of the Challenger Bread Pan, a well designed bread cloche or combo cooker. This website is also a resource for bread knowledge, books, bannetons, bench knives, lames, etc.

KING ARTHUR FLOUR
kingarthurflour.com
Offers a great selection of kitchen tools including the indispensable "orange scraper," sold on their website as a "Heavy Duty Dough Scraper"

LE CREUSET
lecreuset.com
Producer of enamel-lined Dutch ovens

MOCKMILL
mockmill.us
Maker of nifty little countertop stone mills for home milling

RACK MASTER
rackmaster.co.uk
A source for beautifully crafted bread pans, focaccia pans, and dough knives

WECK
weckjars.com
Producers of airtight glass jars ideal for storing and extending natural leavening

Further Reading

The New Bread Basket: How a New Crop of Grain Growers, Plant Breeders, Millers, Maltsers, Bakers, Brewers, and Local Food Activists Are Redefining Our Daily Loaf by Amy Halloran (Chelsea Green, 2015)

Bread, Wine, Chocolate: The Slow Loss of Foods We Love by Simran Sethi (Harper Collins, 2015)

The Third Plate: Field Notes on the Future of Food by Dan Barber (Penguin, 2014)

For More In-depth Baking Knowledge:

A Passion for Bread: Lessons from a Master Baker by Lionel Vatinet (Little Brown & Co, 2013)

Artisan Sourdough: Wholesome Recipes, Organic Grains by Casper Andre' Lugg and Martin Ivar Fjeld (Harper Design, 2017)

Bread: A Baker's Book of Techniques and Recipes, 2nd ed. by Jeffrey Hamelman, (Wiley, 2014)

Flour, Water, Salt, Yeast: The Fundamentals of Artisan Bread and Pizza by Ken Forkish (Ten Speed Press, 2012)

Home Baked: Nordic Recipes and Techniques for Organic Bread and Pastry by Hanne Risgaard (Chelsea Green, 2009)

Sourdough: Recipes for Rustic Fermented Breads, Sweets, Savories, and More by Sarah Owens (Roost Books, 2015)

The Sourdough School: The Ground-Break Guide to Making Gut-Friendly Bread by Vanessa Kimbell (Kyle Books, 2018)

Tartine Book No 3: Modern, Ancient, Classic, Whole by Chad Robertson (Chronicle, 2013)

The Rye Baker by Stanley Ginsberg (W. W. Norton & Co., 2016)

Acknowledgments

To begin, I'd like to thank my literary agent, Laura Nolan, who recognized the worth of this story and ensured that my voice could be heard. To my professors at Goucher's MFA Program—Jacob Levenson, Leslie Rubinowski, Laura Wexler and Diana Hume George, as well as Patsy Simms—who pushed me to dig deep, show not tell, cut, cut, cut, and DMSU (don't make s**t up). To the stellar team of women at Ten Speed Press, whom I've had the honor to work with—Dervla Kelly, Emma Rudolph, Lizzie Allen, and Ivy McFadden. Thank you for your amazing feedback, edits, and design.

To the farmers—thank you for taking the chance on this little mill. To the bakers—thank you for bringing our flour into your bakeries and for the resulting baked goods you bring to your communities; and for those of you represented in this book, thank you for your time and inspiring recipes. To Rinne Allen, for your stunning photography. Such a treat to get to travel around the South with you. And yes, you did warn me about this whole book writing endeavor and yes, you were completely on point. To Cathy Cleary and Lydia Stamm for the many, many bake tests and feedback. To my team at Carolina Ground: Scott Starling, Lydia Stamm, Lindsey Giglio, and Dante Campanaro, who kept the stones turning while I was distracted by the writing of this book. Thank you to Sharon Burns-Leader, Dr. Erin McKenney, Amy Halloran, Thor Oechsner, Glenn Roberts, Melissa Martin, Graison Gill, Mark Fowler, Tass Jansen, Roger Jansen, Dr. David Marshall, and Dr. Stephen Jones, all of whom contributed in some way to this book. And my foundation: my family. I won the lottery with my mom and dad, forever believing in us girls. To my sister, Liz, for always cheering me on. To my daughter Hannah, for reminding me to continuously broaden my perspective. To Emma, Siena, and Tim, thank you for your love and acceptance, even through the writing of this book. And to my husband and best friend, Scott Unfried. Forever grateful for your patience, your love, and your editing skills.

Index

Published in the United States by Ten Speed Press,
an imprint of Random House, a division of Penguin
Random House LLC, New York.
www.tenspeed.com

Ten Speed Press and the Ten Speed Press colophon
are registered trademarks of Penguin Random
House LLC.

**To the memory of my loving
father, Richard Lapidus, and
my mentor, Alan Scott.**

Library of Congress Cataloging-in-Publication Data
Names: Lapidus, Jennifer, 1969- author.
Title: Southern ground : a revolution in baking with
stone-milled flour /
by Jennifer Lapidus.
Description: First edition. | New York : Ten Speed
Press, an imprint of the
Crown Publishing Group, a division of Penguin
Random House LLC, 2021.
Identifiers: LCCN 2020015335 (print) | LCCN
2020015336 (ebook) |
Subjects: LCSH: Cooking, American–Southern style. |
Baking. | Bread. |
LCGFT: Cookbooks.
Classification: LCC TX715.2.S68 L373 2021 (print) |
LCC TX715.2.S68
(ebook) | DDC 641.5973--dc23
LC record available at https://lccn.loc.
gov/2020015335
LC ebook record available at https://lccn.loc.
gov/2020015336

Hardcover ISBN: 9781984857484
eBook ISBN: 9781984857491

Printed in China

Editor: Dervla Kelly
Production editor: Emma Rudolph
Designer: Lizzie Allen
Art Director: Emma Campion
Production designers: Mari Gill and Faith Hague
Production manager: Dan Myers
Prepress color manager: Neil Spitkovsky
Food stylist: Rinne Allen
Prop stylist: Rinne Allen
Copyeditor: Ivy McFadden
Proofreader: Nancy Bailey
Indexer: Ken DellaPenta
Publicist: Kristin Casemore
Marketer: Allison Renzulli

10 9 8 7 6 5 4 3 2 1

First Edition

"The inspired and delicious recipes in Jennifer Lapidus's *Southern Ground* make the case that fresh flour—which is to say freshly milled flour—is the foundation of Southern cuisine. Which makes this more than a cookbook—it's a blueprint for the future of American baking, powered by a dedicated community of millers, farmers, and bakers."

—**DAN BARBER**, executive chef and co-owner of Blue Hill at Stone Barns

"*Southern Ground* is a collection of smart, deeply flavorful recipes that also tell the fascinating story of what we have given up in the name of extractive food production and how we can get it back. Jennifer Lapidus will change the way you look at the power of food and farming."

—**ANDREA REUSING,** chef and owner of Lantern, author, *Cooking in the Moment: A Year of Seasonal Recipes*

JENNIFER LAPIDUS is the founder and principal of Carolina Ground flour mill in Asheville, North Carolina. She launched Natural Bridge Bakery in 1994, where she milled her flours in-house and baked her naturally leavened breads in a wood-fired brick oven. Her bakery was the first of its kind in western North Carolina and was featured in *Peter Reinhart's Whole Grain Breads*. Jennifer has appeared on *The Splendid Table* podcast and in the *New York Times*, *Wall Street Journal*, *Bon Appétit*, *Food & Wine*, *Saveur*, *Taste of the South*, and numerous other local publications. Jennifer sits on the board of Carolina Farm Stewardship Association and is co-organizer of the Asheville Bread Festival.